United States
Military Assistance

PRAEGER SPECIAL STUDIES IN
INTERNATIONAL POLITICS AND PUBLIC AFFAIRS

United States Military Assistance

A STUDY OF POLICIES AND PRACTICES

Harold A. Hovey

FREDERICK A. PRAEGER, Publishers
New York • Washington • London

The purpose of the Praeger Special Studies is to make specialized research monographs in international economics and politics available to the academic, business, and government communities. For further information, write to the Special Projects Division, Frederick A. Praeger, Publishers, 111 Fourth Avenue, New York, N.Y. 10003.

FREDERICK A. PRAEGER, *Publishers*
111 Fourth Avenue, New York 3, N.Y., U.S.A.
77-79 Charlotte Street, London W.1, England

Published in the United States of America in 1965
by Frederick A. Praeger, Inc., Publishers

Library of Congress Catalog Card Number: 65-23123

Printed in the United States of America

FOREWORD

We have no eternal allies - nor perpetual friends. We
do have interests, both eternal and perpetual. And
those it is our duty to follow.

Lord Palmerston
Prime Minister of England 1855-1865

The Military Assistance Program, since its inception, has
been predominantly in the self-interest of our country--enlightened
self-interest, we would hope, but self-interest nonetheless. In
the basic legislation authorizing this program, the Congress has
proclaimed its intention to promote:

...the peace of the world and the foreign policy,
security, and general welfare of the United States
by fostering an improved climate of political independence and individual liberty, improving the
ability of friendly countries and international
organizations to deter or, if necessary, defeat
Communist or Communist-supported aggression,
facilitating arrangements for individual and
collective security, assisting friendly countries
to maintain internal security, and creating an
environment of security and stability in the
developing friendly countries essential to their
more rapid social, economic, and political progress.

The tasks are clear--and note the emphasis on the word
security; it is used four times and in four different connotations,
but all four are interrelated and all four stem from American self-
interest.

What then is Military Assistance?

It is not economic aid, or development loans or agricultural
assistance, or technical grants, or food for peace or the Peace
Corps. It is not money given to foreign governments. It is not a
contribution to the United States gold outflow.

v

It is a program which provides military equipment and weapons and training to those allied and friendly nations which share our view as to the threat of international communism.

It is a program which funds purchases from American industry for shipment overseas to the military forces of those countries which have the will and the manpower but not the means to defend themselves.

It is a program which brings to our country some 10 to 15,000 foreign military students annually, exposing such students not only to American military knowledge but also to the American way of life.

It is an arm of United States foreign policy. It is an extension of United States defense posture and at bargain basement rates.

It is predominantly in our own national self-interest.

A great country cannot avoid either the responsibilities or the risks of greatness. In the world of today the United States bears the mantle of leadership. It must carry burdens which other great powers have carried in other days. To do less would not be in keeping with its legacy from its own past.

Mr. Hovey has performed a most useful service in compiling within the covers of this book an up-to-date presentation of the facts and figures of military assistance, together with the conclusions he has deduced therefrom. His work shows painstaking research and a high order of scholarship. It fills a gap in the knowledge of most Americans. I recommend it to all who would learn the truth about Military Assistance--a program which will remain of extreme importance to our country as long as the threat of Communism exists to the Free World.

Robert J. Wood
General, U. S. Army

PREFACE

Since 1950 the United States has invested over $30 billion to provide military equipment and training to over seventy different countries. Under the auspices of this program more foreign students have been brought to the United States for training than under all other government programs combined. These facts would suggest the existence of considerable study of this program and the availability in a variety of readily available sources of facts about the program and the policy disputes surrounding it. No such literature exists. Most of the publicly available information is in the form of arguments for and against foreign aid of which military assistance is considered a part. Factual information about the program is particularly difficult to acquire as most of it is tucked away in Congressional hearings and obscure government publications.

Some of the impact of military aid can be discerned from writings of journalists and scholars on relations between the United States and various foreign governments. However, such books by their very nature cannot consider military aid as a worldwide program.

The primary purpose of this book is to provide a factual description and an analysis of the present United States military aid program. It is my hope that this book will prove useful to the interested citizen as well as scholars in international relations by giving them a general impression of the military aid program and guidelines as to where to look for further information. The book is also an attempt to make military aid intelligible for officials of both United States and foreign governments who give and receive it. My hope is that by putting most basic information about the program in one place the time of the public and policymaking officials of the government can be saved for the more valuable task of using the program for the purposes for which it can be best used and, no less important, eschewing it for purposes for which it is not suited.

This book is the product of outside research illuminated by the insights I gained working in the Office of the Director of Military Assistance in the Pentagon. Although the writing of this book has been eased by my years of association with the military assistance program, this is not an "inside" book. All the material used in this book is available to any person in published sources. By the time of publication I had left the government for private employment and, therefore, was under no obligation to speak the Administration's voice.

Drafts of various chapters have been read by a number of helpful military and civilian personnel familiar with the subject. Many of these men would prefer not to be mentioned; there seems to be little value in singling out others. General Robert J. Wood, in addition to providing a foreword, has improved my thinking by catching most of my major errors for several years. His review of this book in draft was no exception. Despite the help of these men, there remain many conclusions with which they do not agree. I alone must assume responsibility for all conclusions.

Five years ago this book could not have been written because almost all significant information about military aid was considered "classified." Although too much about this program remains classified today, significant improvement has been made in large part because of the leadership and staff of the Office of Security Review in the Pentagon, particularly Mr. Roger Delaney and Commander Robert Monahan, U. S. Navy.

CONTENTS

United States
Military Assistance

CHAPTER 1

MILITARY ASSISTANCE: A BASIC POSTWAR POLICY

> For a short time the wartime alliance held together, but
> it was not long before quarrels took place and Athens
> and Sparta, each with her own allies, were at war with
> each other, while among the rest of the Hellenes, states
> that had their own differences now joined one or the other
> of the two sides.
>
> Thucydides - The Peloponnesian War

Thucydides wrote of the wars between Athens and Sparta. In the
conflicts between these two city states before the birth of Christ
there are many similarities to today's struggle between the free
world and communism. In each case the struggle was a protracted
one involving decades of conflict, occasional truces and détentes,
economic competition and extensive alliance structures. The competition between these two city states and their ideas and ideals was
carried out in the midst of a larger number of smaller city states,
most of which found it impossible to remain neutral.

Athens realized that it could not defend itself against Sparta
without allies. Therefore, it soon began by a combination of
friendly relations, propaganda and even military and economic
pressures to develop an alliance structure which would permit the
development of a powerful group of opponents to Spartan aggression. Meanwhile, the Spartans, feeling themselves threatened by
the Athenians, did likewise.

As part of this alliance structure both states coordinated military actions with their allies so that all of the armies of the city
states could do battle more or less as a unit. Undoubtedly in both
city states debates raged as to whether all this international (inter-
city state) entanglement really was necessary.

Over two thousand years later the United States was being settled by Englishmen while the French government attempted to as-
sert its own rights to the newly founded rich country. For assistance in their efforts, the French turned to the Indians. To the
French the Indians represented an inexpensive method to develop
sufficient military strength to prevent British control of the country.

Because the Indians wanted to prevent control of their country by any white man, they were happy to accept training and encouragement wherever they could get it.

Later, numerous Americans who had been military leaders in the wars against the Indians led the revolt of the United States against the British. The Americans were only a small number of widely separated colonists facing one of the greatest powers in the world. To have any chance of success they required outside support in the form of military material and advice. Again the French entered the picture, this time with a military advisory group headed by Lafayette. This French assistance helped the United States to force the British government to grant independence. Since the Revolutionary War, various European nations have used military aid to advance their national interests. [1]

As early as 1888 the United States had adopted the device of sending United States officers as military advisors to other countries. In that year three officers were dispatched as the first United States military advisory group to Korea. [2]

When faced with the greatest military challenge in its history, the Second World War, the United States had already become a strong nation with economic capabilities second to none. As it became increasingly clear that it would be impossible to avoid becoming embroiled in the war, the United States began to provide assistance to the nations which were to be its partners in the war against Germany and Japan. First, destroyers were provided to the United Kingdom; later, a Lend Lease Program was developed that by the end of the war had cost the United States over $45 billion.

ASSISTANCE TO GREECE AND TURKEY[3]

In February, 1947 the hard-pressed British government announced that it could no longer give economic and military assistance to Greece and Turkey. Greece at the time was in the midst of a guerrilla war against communists supported by the Soviet satellites bordering Greece. In Turkey, there was no active guerrilla fighting but the possibility that the Russians might forcibly seize the Dardenelles was ever present.

Recognizing that the nation's defense depended on stopping communism well before it reached United States shores, on March 12, 1947, President Truman delivered a message to the Congress recommending that the United States act. After explaining the situation in each of these countries the President stated the policy which, in one form or another, has guided much of American aid programs since that time.

I believe that it must be the foreign policy of the United States to support free people who are resisting attempted subjugation by armed minorities or by outside pressures. The free peoples of the world look to us for support in maintaining their freedom. If we falter in our leadership, we may endanger the peace of the world, and we shall surely endanger the welfare of our own nation.

This so-called "Truman Doctrine" did not win rapid unanimous support. Over two months passed before the Congress enacted legislation which the President had requested. Critics pointed out that the United States was interfering in the internal affairs of other nations, that reactionary governments were being supported, that the United States was being asked to emulate British imperialism, that the action was anti-Soviet and, finally, that the proposals were too costly.

The act finally passed by the Congress did not make an explicit division between military and economic assistance. It has been suggested that the apparent emphasis on economic assistance was due in part to an attempt to avoid the appearance of directly confronting the Soviet Union.

Greece in June and Turkey in July signed agreements containing the conditions established by the United States Congress as a basis for receiving assistance under the new law, and American assistance began to flow. An initial appropriation of $400 million in 1947 and a second appropriation of $225 million were made. Of this total of $625 million, $345.3 million was used for military assistance in Greece and $152.5 million was used for military assistance to Turkey. The remainder was used for economic assistance.[4]

In Greece the United States military mission worked with the British military mission. Because a substantial part of existing Greek military equipment was of British origin, some $70 million of the Greek aid was spent in the United Kingdom for repair and replacement. By June 30, 1949 the United States military mission in Greece (Joint United States Military Advisory and Planning Group in Greece) had expanded to 527 persons. American advisors were used down to the battalion level, although they were not part of the chain of command. The chief of the United States military group sat as a non-voting member of the Greek Supreme National Defense Council.

In Turkey, because the Turkish forces were not attempting to fight an active war, as was the case in Greece, American assistance took the form of a balanced attempt to build up the Army, Navy and Air Force as well as to improve logistic facilities. Roads were built and arsenals improved. By the middle of 1949 the United States military mission included 410 persons.

AID TO CHINA

After the end of the Second World War the Chinese Communists, building from the base areas developed in the fighting against Japan, began to expand throughout China. American policy toward China during this period remained ambiguous until it was too late to prevent the Chinese Communist advances by military and economic assistance alone.

Shortly after the end of the fighting of World War II, President Truman assured the government of China that the United States would help modernize and strengthen Chinese armed forces "of moderate size." Part of this commitment was fulfilled by continuation of lend lease operations in support of 39 divisions and 8 1/3 air force groups. Much of the assistance was used to transport, in United States military aircraft or vessels, Chinese Nationalists to important areas which had been occupied by the Japanese. The total cost of the continued lend lease has been estimated to be $769 million. [5]

When lend lease expired on June 30, 1946 the United States continued military assistance to China under a variety of legal authorizations and expedients. Naval assistance was furnished under a special law[6] passed in 1946 which authorized the dispatch of a non-combatant naval mission, various types of technical assistance and the transfer of naval vessels. Ultimately some 131 vessels with an acquisition cost of $141.3 million were transferred under this program.

Although no special law was passed authorizing the action, the President in February of 1946 authorized the Secretaries of War and Navy to establish a military advisory group in China. These were established without a special agreement with the government of China. In addition to this assistance the China Aid Act of 1948 resulted in a total of about $123 million of additional military aid to China.

PHILIPPINES

Another of the early postwar military assistance programs was developed with the Philippines. This assistance was related both to the continued American use of the extensive base structure built up in the Philippines during World War II and the need to assist the legitimate Philippine government in suppressing the Huk guerrilla activities.

This assistance was furnished under the Philippines Military Assistance Act of 1946, [7] which authorized the training of Philippine personnel, the establishment of a military mission and transfer and rehabilitation of military equipment. To achieve the purposes of the Act, the President was authorized to use up to $19.75 million from the regular Department of Defense (then National Military Establishment) appropriation. In the agreement concerning this assistance, [8] the Philippines explicitly agreed to give the United States the use of 23 different bases in the Philippines. In addition to more normal undertakings, the Philippine government undertook to procure its military equipment from the United States, or from other sources, only with the agreement of the United States.

KOREA

The United States continued to keep a military mission in Korea even after regular American forces were withdrawn. This group continued the training of Korean forces which had been handled previously by the American occupation forces. Korean forces were left with various United States-owned equipment, including 60,000 Japanese rifles and ammunition, various supplies with an acquisition cost of $56 million said to be sufficient to equip 50,000 troops and some small naval craft. [9]

IRAN

The United States in 1947 agreed to a credit of $25 million for
the purchase of surplus military items by Iran. Though not all of
this credit was used, by 1949 Iran did purchase, for $5.2 million,
material with an acquisition cost of $26.5 million.[10] Acting under
an agreement negotiated in 1943, the United States continued after
the war to maintain a small military mission charged with the function of advising the Iranian gendarmerie. Prior to 1948 this mission
had substantial control over the operations of this force, but after
1948 it lapsed into an advisory role. Another small mission was
maintained in Iran to advise the army under an agreement established
in 1947. These United States advisors acted strictly in an advisory
role.

LATIN AMERICA

The United States in the early postwar period continued its military cooperation with a variety of Latin American nations, continuing a practice which had originated long before World War II.

MUTUAL DEFENSE ASSISTANCE PROGRAM

During 1948 and 1949 the nations of Europe were proceeding in
the development of European military cooperation. These efforts at
joint planning and organization ultimately evolved into the North
Atlantic Treaty Organization (NATO). On July 25, 1949 President
Truman signed the instrument of ratification of the Atlantic Treaty.
On the same day the President presented to the Congress a program
of military assistance to Europe. This proposal, with substantial
amendment, eventually became the Mutual Defense Assistance Act
of 1949. That Act in turn became the basis for all subsequent military assistance legislation. The Mutual Defense Assistance Act
brought together in one bill and under one policy the various United
States military aid efforts and inaugurated military aid to Europe.
The original authorization under this bill was $1,314 million.[11]
As deliveries from this program were just beginning, the communists attacked in Korea.

This attack resolved all lingering doubts about the communists'
intention to use force where they could get away with it, and kindled

a United States resolve to meet force with force. Within a few
months after the Korean attack the Administration had received
authorization to commit an additional $5.2 billion for military aid.
Most of these funds could not be spent immediately because the first
priority for the limited United States capability to produce war
materials was naturally given to Korea. The basic outline of the
program presented to Congress was that the United States would provide directly, or indirectly by assisting European defense production,
most of the equipment for the new armies being raised in Europe in
addition to its other military aid commitments.

THE KOREAN WAR

When the North Koreans attacked South Korea in June of 1950 the
United States was ill prepared to fight a ground war in the Far East.
The major United States deployment in the Far East was the occupation
garrison in Japan. Military transport capabilities were limited as
was the reservoir of trained manpower already in our forces. There
was no ally in the Far East which the United States could rely upon
for assistance. Japan had no military capability. Chiang Kai-shek
had just been driven off the China mainland and Southeast Asia was
embroiled in conflicts of its own.

United Nations forces in Korea fought under the command of a
United States officer who also served as the United States commander. All of these forces relied upon the logistical services of
the United States. Neither the costs of contributions of support to
the South Korean forces nor those associated with the logistic support of other United Nations forces were charged to something called
a foreign aid or military assistance program. Instead the costs
were considered as part of the costs of feeding, supplying, transporting and arming our own forces. This approach was adopted
because of the obvious difficulties of using separate funding methods
and logistic systems for United States and United Nations forces
fighting side by side in Korea.

Meanwhile the assistance to Greece and Turkey continued as
these nations joined NATO. Certain other countries, such as Spain,
also became grant aid recipients. While United Nations forces were
heavily engaged in Korea, communists were undermining the French
position in Vietnam. Especially as the situation began to worsen,
the United States became extensively involved. Although a decision

was made to withhold direct United States deployments to Indochina,
the United States did deliver much of its military assistance to
France in the form of deliveries to French forces stationed in Indochina and provided almost a billion dollars worth of assistance to
Indochina itself. This assistance was terminated at the fall of Dien
Bien Phu in 1954. Much of the equipment provided to the French
was moved by them with their forces to Algeria. Some was destroyed
on the spot and some no doubt found its way into the hands of the
communists in North Vietnam.

The end of the Korean War permitted the United States to use
the productive capabilities built up to fight that war to supply the
military equipment needed in Europe to build up forces in the general
direction of then existing force goals. In the Far East the responsibility for the continued provision of equipment and training to Korean
forces was turned over to the military assistance program, with
close field relationships between the United States commander in
Korea and the Military Assistance Advisory Group. Some assistance was provided to the Japanese self-defense forces and the
Philippines continued to request and receive American aid. The
United States had taken a sufficiently expansive view of the Russian
threat to attempt to lead the nations of Latin America into the Rio
Pact of 1947 and had begun the rudiments of Western Hemisphere
defense planning against a common aggressor. United States military missions functioned throughout Latin America.

In the Middle East the British and French governments, who relied upon the area as the essentially sole source of petroleum, organized with United States encouragement a Baghdad Pact composed
of Iran, Pakistan and Iraq in addition to the European powers. The
defense posture of the Middle East was badly shaken when one of the
key powers in this pact, Iraq, underwent a coup and turned away
from the Western powers. Headquarters of the organization were
moved from Baghdad to Tehran, and it was renamed the Central
Treaty Organization (CENTO). The United States did not join the
pact but continued to send observers and to assist all of the member
nations with military equipment and training.

Meanwhile, despite American military assistance, the British
government was finding it impossible to continue to support its far-
flung interests. British forces in Hong Kong were opposite a vastly
superior Chinese Communist force. Chinese Communist intentions
were enigmatic. British garrisons were maintained in Singapore

and in Malaya. Administration of British colonies in Africa was requiring some force and additional efforts might well prove to be necessary. The Middle East situation continued to be uncertain and
British interests in the Suez Canal and British oil sources might
well need protection. In this context the government of Britain informed the United States that it would no longer be able to continue
to support the government of Jordan in the style to which it had been
accustomed. The United States picked up this responsibility and
began programs of both economic and military assistance to both
Jordan and Lebanon.

Thus, by 1957 the United States had assumed the role of protec-
tor of the free world. United States military assistance was being
poured into Europe at the rate of almost one billion dollars per
year. The United States had deployed the equivalent of five divisions
in Europe under the NATO organization and the United States intention to abide by the NATO treaty obligation to treat aggression
against any treaty members as aggression against itself was reasonably clear. Military bases or facilities had been established in
Spain and North Africa (Morocco, Tunisia, Libya and Ethiopia) and
United States economic and military assistance went with the bases.

In the Middle East the Eisenhower Doctrine indicated that the
United States was prepared to stand as a guarantor of peace. United
States funds were carrying the costs of the Palestine refugees in an
effort to minimize the pressures for renewed hostilities which could
be caused if the refugees were starving or discontented. Military
assistance was being provided in large quantities to Jordan, Lebanon,
Iran and Pakistan, and United States troops had been deployed to
Lebanon at the request of that government.

In the Far East United States policy and aid programs were built
around maintaining the viability of the governments of the Republics
of Korea and China and rearming Japan. In Latin America military
cooperation against a common external enemy was the keynote of
United States policy. Only in Africa had the United States continued
to let other Western nations assume primary responsibility, as at that
time most African states were still European colonies. By fiscal
year 1957,[12] United States assistance was being delivered to 42 different countries.

In the years since 1957 the basic policies underlying the United
States military assistance program have changed little although

changing circumstances have produced changing applications of that policy, and resource limitations have not been without effect. The basic policy that the United States would stand ready to help any nation protect itself against communist aggression--internal or external--remained the cornerstone of United States military assistance policy.

Since 1957 it has been possible to curtail sharply grant aid programs in Europe as a result of Europe's astounding economic recovery. The emergence of independent African states has produced minor military assistance programs in many African countries, and programs in others are probable as time passes and these countries desire to maintain connections with the West while loosening ties to their former colonial rulers. The Chinese Communist attack on India convinced the Indian government that military strength was the only sure basis for dealing with the communists. United States assistance was provided as part of the basic policy of assisting any free world nation needing and wanting help. Communist pressures also induced requests for substantial assistance from Vietnam and Laos which have been met by additional programs there. As significant as these programs are, they represent only elaborations and extension of policies conceived during the Korean War and fully developed by 1957.

PRESENT SCOPE AND NATURE OF THE PROGRAM

The Military Assistance Program presented to the Congress for fiscal year 1965 amounted to a total of $1,215,000,000. Of this amount $1,055 million was requested in new obligational authority and the remainder was expected to become available from recoupments and reappropriations from prior year appropriations.[13] Secretary of Defense McNamara advised the Senate Appropriations Committee that this $1,215 million was to be spent as follows:[14]

	Amount ($ million)	Percent of Total
FORWARD DEFENSE PROGRAMS (11 countries) Greece Turkey Laos	861.6	71

	Amount ($ million)	Percent of Total
FORWARD DEFENSE PROGRAMS (continued)		
Vietnam		
Korea		
Republic of China		
Philippines		
Thailand		
Pakistan		
India		
Iran		
ALLIANCE FOR PROGRESS SECURITY PROGRAMS (Latin America)	69.1	6
MILITARY BASE PROGRAMS (4 countries)	27.9	2
FREE WORLD ORIENTATION PROGRAMS	18.7	2
GRANT AID PHASE OUT PROGRAMS	61.5	5
UNITED STATES FORCE SUPPORT AND MAP ADMINISTRATION	(176.3)	14
NATO Infrastructure	60.0	
International Military Headquarters	15.9	
Credit Assistance	50.0	
Program Administration	23.5	
Regional Costs (Miscellaneous)	26.9	
TOTAL	1215.0	100

This distribution represents a fairly consistent pattern in military assistance programs. In the fiscal year 1966 program presented to Congress in the spring of 1965, the only significant change in percentage distribution was a 2% decrease in 'phase out" programs and 1% increases in "forward defense" and "base rights."

Programs for fiscal year 1965 were offered for 53 countries of which 40 programs included military materiel and 13 were confined solely to training. As can be seen above from the fact that 70% of the total program was to go to the "forward defense" programs, the distribution of funds among country programs is sharply skewed with a few very large programs and a large number of smaller ones.

Eleven countries were programmed for a total of $862 million. Costs not associated with country programs amounted to $176 million (NATO infrastructure, credit assistance and administrative costs). Thus, 42 countries were scheduled to receive the remaining $177 million in the fiscal year 1965 program presented. Of those 42 countries, 17 were to receive grants worth less than one million; 12 were to receive from $1 to $3 million worth of equipment and training and 13, grants from $3 to $20 million.

The program presented in fiscal year 1965 provided primarily for training and military materiel; the remainder was for special programs, such as NATO infrastructure, for administration and for construction and services. It should be noted that under the military aid program foreign governments do not receive money--only military goods and services.

Hearings on the fiscal year 1965 program indicate the types of equipment which are provided by the program. For the forward defense countries, discussion by members of Congress centered on items like F-5 aircraft, howitzers, Cessna liaison and observation aircraft, trucks and jeeps, ships such as destroyers and patrol craft, small arms and ammunition. By contrast the Alliance for Progress security programs concentrated upon equipment for civic action, such as road building equipment, medical equipment and transport aircraft, as well as maintenance supplies for Latin American navies and small arms and vehicles for maintaining internal security. The same emphasis reappears in the Africa programs. The Administration programs presented for those countries where military aid is being phased out (Denmark, Norway and Japan) concentrated on sophisticated military hardware, such as air defense equipment in Japan and F-5 aircraft in Norway.

As mentioned above, military assistance does not include the granting of money to foreign governments. As a result, not all the costs of maintaining a foreign army are a part of this program. Normally, the recipient country pays the costs of paying and housing its forces as well as for their food and allowances even in those countries where the United States is most deeply committed to its military assistance program. In some cases, such as Korea, much of the resources used for this purpose comes through United States economic aid programs.

"Military assistance" as used in this book and by the government is much less broad than the two words "military" and "assistance" might imply. It does not include the assistance to foreign
governments which occurs when the United States deploys its own
forces in support of an ally. It does not include the assistance which
the United States promises in undertaking certain treaty obligations.
Instead, it is confined to the program for the grants and sales of
military equipment and training to foreign governments. [15]

CONCLUSION

United States military assistance programs are part of a fundamental postwar United States policy of assisting free world governments to defend themselves against communism. The program has
now expanded to the point that over 50 different countries are receiving assistance each year. Most of the funds go to a few key
countries directly threatened by communist aggression. The assistance provided takes the form of grants and sales of military equipment, services, and training, but never money.

NOTES

1.. This discussion of foreign aid in world history is intended
only to remind the reader that present policies and problems are
not new. For a complete treatment of foreign aid since the Greeks
see Chapter 2 of George Liska's The New Statecraft: Foreign Aid
in American Foreign Policy (Chicago: University of Chicago Press,
1960).

2. Robert K. Sawyer, Military Advisors in Korea: KMAG in
Peace and War (Washington: U.S. Government Printing Office for the
Office of the Chief of Military History, Department of the Army,
1962), p. 4.

3. The material on military assistance through 1949 is largely
drawn from W. A. Brown and R. Opie, American Foreign Assistance (Washington: The Brookings Institution, 1953).

4. More elaborate statistics and extensive discussion of the
progress of these programs can be found in the periodic reports to
the Congress on this program. U.S. Department of State, Assistance to Greece and Turkey, Quarterly Reports to the Congress,
No. 1-8 (Washington: U.S. Government Printing Office, September 30,
1947 - June 30, 1949).

5. The decisions to give and withhold aid to China were only a part of one of the most vehemently argued incidents of United States foreign policy. For details see Herbert Feis, The China Tangle (Princeton: Princeton University Press, 1953); Owen Lattimore, The Situation in Asia (Boston: Little, Brown and Company, 1949); Harrison Forman, Blunder in Asia (New York: Didier Publishers, 1950) as well as Congressional hearings on the far eastern situation which occurred during and after the China Civil War.

6. 60 Stat 539.

7. 60 Stat 315.

8. Agreement between the Government of the United States of America and the Government of the Republic of the Philippines on Military Assistance to the Philippines, March 14, 1947. TIAS 1775.

9. Sawyer, op. cit., p. 96.

10. Brown and Opie, op. cit., p. 444.

11. Statistical information, unless otherwise indicated, is from Department of Defense reports, some of which are reprinted in the Appendix. See the Appendix for a discussion of how to find factual information on United States military assistance.

12. The United States fiscal year begins on July 1 of the preceding year. Thus, fiscal 1957 began on July 1, 1956, and ended on June 30, 1957. Because most government statistics are kept on this basis, fiscal years will be used frequently in this volume.

13. Technical terms like "new obligational authority" and "recoupments" are explained in the Glossary.

14. U.S., Congress, Senate, Committee on Appropriations, Hearings, on H.R. 11812, Foreign Assistance and Related Agencies Appropriations for 1965, 88th Cong., 2d Sess., 1964, p. 241. In recent years hearings on military aid have been held in four different Congressional committees each year. For convenience abbreviated citations to these hearings are used showing only the committee and the calendar year in which the hearings were held (as distinguished from the fiscal year for which appropriations are being considered). HFAC is used for the House Foreign Affairs Committee; HAC for the House Appropriations Committee; SFRC for the Senate Foreign Relations Committee and SAC for the Senate Appropriations Committee. Thus, the above citation would appear as "SAC, CY 1964, p. 241."

Footnotes have not been used for information readily available in a variety of forms. See the description in the Appendix on how to find such information.

15. The estimates of the cost of military aid used in this book exclude the pay of U.S. military personnel working on military aid problems who are paid by the Army, Navy and Air Force.

2

MILITARY ASSISTANCE
IN THE FAR EAST

With few exceptions the story of postwar United States military aid to countries in the Far East is a story of the United States' attempts to prevent the spread of Chinese Communism.[1]

During the Second World War both Chiang Kai-shek and Mao Tse-tung had been building their armies with one eye on the enemy and one eye on each other. The end of the war meant peace to most of the world but in China it meant resumption of the civil war which had been interrupted only long enough to repulse a common enemy. Shortly after the war the United States began to realize that all of Asia could be lost by success of the communists in China. Some United States military equipment was provided to Chiang, but the United States did not commit much of its wealth or forces to Chiang's cause.

The assistance to China was provided under the authority of the Lend Lease Program and successor programs. It did not mark the beginning of what is now considered the military assistance program. Much of the equipment provided to Chiang's armies for use against the Japanese or Chinese Communists eventually found its way into Chinese Communist hands. Indeed, some of it was used by the Chinese in the Korean War.

In 1949 Chiang Kai-shek took his forces from the mainland of China to Taiwan, a reasonably large fertile island some 70 miles from the mainland which at various times had been occupied by both Japan and China. He managed to take with him considerable quantities of American equipment previously furnished to his forces. While Chiang was establishing a government on Taiwan and occupying the Pescadores and the offshore islands, Mao was beginning the development of the governmental apparatus which would permit the communists to establish a strong central government in China.

With the Chinese Communists building their strength on the mainland, prospects for Chiang's continued tenure on Taiwan did not look good. The United States did not wish to become involved and indicated this publicly. On January 5, 1950, President Truman stated that the United States had no intention of interfering militarily in the situation and that the United States would not provide military aid or advice to the Chinese forces on Formosa.

The attack in Korea quickly resulted in a reversal of United
States policy. In late June of 1950 the President ordered the Seventh
Fleet to prevent any attack on Formosa. The policy of assisting the
Nationalist Chinese in the defense of Taiwan has persisted to the present day. Deliveries of assistance to the Republic of Korea forces
began immediately after the communists attacked. Not until 1956
was this expense borne by the military assistance program rather
than by the appropriations of the Army, Navy and Air Force. Assistance programs to Japan, Thailand and Cambodia were initiated as
the Chinese Communists became more and more threatening. As
previously mentioned, the United States supported the French effort
in Indochina with military equipment and supplies, though not with
United States forces. When the Geneva Accords began to appear
inadequate to protect against subversion in South Vietnam and Laos
the United States also came to the aid of these nations. There is
also a small military sales program in Burma. Credit sales under
the military aid program have recently been made to Australia and
New Zealand.

THE MILITARY PROBLEM

China, with a population of 700 million, is the largest single
country in the world. At times in its history China has been the
most militarily and culturally advanced nation of the world. There
can be little doubt that communist doctrine coincides with the
aspirations of the leaders of China to a return to the world status
which China formerly occupied.[2] In fact, Mao Tse-tung once stated:

> In defeating China in war, the imperialist powers have
> taken away many Chinese dependent states and a part
> of her territories; Japan took Korea, Taiwan and the
> Ryukyu Islands, the Pescadores Islands, Port Arthur;
> England seized Burma, Shutan, Nepal and Hong Kong;
> France occupied Amman; and even an insignificant
> country like Portugal...took Macao.[3]

The thought that China may be working toward reasserting its control
over countries like Korea and Burma has not been lost on the leaders
of these countries.

Chinese Communist doctrine postulates that the free world
powers will not give up their position peacefully. Thus, China under

the communists has become a tightly organized authoritarian state geared to efficiency in production which can produce power in war. Indications of the role accorded to military power in international politics in the Far East can easily be found in statements of Chinese Communist leaders. For example, Mao is reported to have stated:

> It is impossible to hope that imperialists and the Chinese reactionaries can be persuaded to be good-hearted and repent. The only way is to organize strength and to fight them, as for example, our people's liberation war, our agrarian revolution, our exposing of imperialism, "provoking" them, defeating them and punishing their criminal acts, and "only allowing them to behave properly and not allowing them to talk and act wildly." Only then is there hope of dealing with foreign imperialist countries on conditions of equality and mutual benefit. [4]

Confronted with a potential enemy which is committed to the use of force as an instrument of expanding communism, the free nations of the Far East have themselves been forced to arm, and the United States has been asked to assist them and has done so. Some measure of the threat is indicated by the fact that present Chinese Communist forces have been estimated to consist of over 2 1/2 million men. [5]

Against this ponderous force no single nation in the Far East can hope to fight unassisted. For that reason alone, Korea, Nationalist China and even Japan have been forced by the sheer logic of their position to seek alliance with the United States. The United States in turn has provided economic and military assistance to those countries willing to stand up to Communist China.

THE REPUBLIC OF CHINA

At the present time the government of the Republic of China on Taiwan is committed to: (1) the defense of Taiwan and the Pescadores, (2) the defense of the offshore islands, primarily Quemoy and Amoy, two small islands within shelling distance of the Chinese mainland, (3) a return to the mainland to replace the communist government presently in control there. The United States is committed by treaty[6] to assist the Republic of China in achieving the first of these objectives.

In its attitude toward the defense of the offshore islands the
United States has not been wholly consistent. On occasion the
United States has characterized the extensive commitment to the
offshore islands as "foolish" and Christian Herter as Under Secretary of State once called the nationalist commitment to these islands "pathological."[7] On the other hand, the United States provides
military assistance to practically all of the Republic of China forces,
a substantial number of which are on these islands,[8] and various
American statements, particularly those of John Foster Dulles,
have seemed to imply a commitment to assist in the defense of the
islands.

The United States has not publicly committed itself to providing
assistance to Chiang Kai-shek in regaining the mainland by force.
However, United States officials have occasionally pointed out the
contribution which the threat of a return to the mainland makes by
tying down Chinese Communist troops in a position to defend against
such an attack, and occasionally mention a "rollback" of communist
power in the Far East.[9] Then Secretary of Defense Thomas Gates
said in 1960 that:

> The forces on Formosa represent free world forces
> available to help the United States forces if called
> upon in the general Asian area.[10]

American military aid has permitted the Republic of China to
maintain a force of almost 600,000 men organized into 21 infantry
divisions, 2 armored divisions and special units,[11] most of which
are primarily composed of Chinese nationals who retreated to Taiwan
with Chiang Kai-shek. Younger native Taiwanese are also beginning
to find places in the Army, so that by 1960 they formed 35% of the
Republic of China forces.[12]

United States assistance has centered primarily upon the equipment which is necessary for the single clearly agreed upon mission
for Chinese Nationalist forces, the defense of Taiwan and the Pescadores.

The sheer magnitude of the present Republic of China forces is
indicated by the fact that the armed forces represent about 5% of the
population. In the United States the present active duty forces are
less than 2% of the population. The burden of supporting this large
a military establishment is obviously substantial, both for United

States military assistance and for the Republic of China economy.
Through fiscal year 1965 the United States had programmed $2.3
billion in military assistance and over $1.4 billion of economic as-
sistance to the Republic of China. Because of the size of the force
being maintained and the magnitude of the United States' investment
previously made for equipment and materiel, the United States military aid programs in recent years have been primarily devoted to
maintenance of existing equipment, rather than to modernization or
improvement by replacing equipment furnished in earlier years.
Secretary of Defense McNamara has stated that nearly two-thirds
of the value of the fiscal 1965 request for the Republic of China was
required to maintain these forces.[13]

The costs to the United States of the Taiwan military establishment
and the retardation of economic development, which inevitably results from a large diversion of human and financial resources to
military purposes, have caused numerous observers to suggest that
the forces in the Republic of China should be reduced. For example,
Senator McGee, after inspecting the defenses of Taiwan and the offshore islands, suggested that:

> The burden of maintaining nearly 600,000 troops on
> Taiwan seemed disproportionate to the needs of the
> area.[14]

Those who support United States assistance to maintain a force of
this size point out the danger of reducing any anti-communist forces
so long as the Chinese Communists represent a threat in Southeast
Asia.

The United States has provided fighter aircraft, including the
highly sophisticated F-104's. Military assistance training has helped
Chiang Kai-shek to develop a first-rate air force, which distinguished
itself with an eight-to-one kill ratio over the Chinese Communists
in 1958 during the Taiwan Straits crisis. As one Defense Department
witness put it during hearings in 1964:

> ...control of the air is crucial in any communist military
> effort against Taiwan.[15]

In 1964, F-86 aircraft, the type used in the 1958 crisis, still constituted the bulk of the fighter force.[16]

The withdrawal of Soviet technical assistance from China in 1960 undoubtedly had some effect on Chinese Communist air capabilities, as air forces require substantial technical sophistication for manufacturing new planes and maintaining them. For this reason it has been argued that further assistance to the Republic of China air forces is unnecessary.[17] Nationalist China already has NIKE missiles and F-86D aircraft for all weather air defense[18] and F-5 aircraft are being introduced but at a slower rate than the Defense Department desires.[19]

The capability of Chiang's forces to defend Taiwan and the Pescadores, not to mention the offshore islands, against Chinese Communist attack is in large part dependent upon the capability to interdict landings by a combination of air power and sea power. Air power is discussed above. In the case of sea power, United States military assistance has not been so complete. In 1960, the Chinese Navy had become a collection of 140 ships of various types up to destroyer size.[20] As stated by a Defense representative:

> Because most of the Republic of China naval ships are 20 years old or more and have had hard usage, qualitative improvement is badly needed if they are to meet mission requirements of providing for the coastal and harbor defenses and patrol of the Taiwan Strait.[21]

Although Communist China's navy is not particularly impressive, in any attempt to invade Taiwan by sea the communists could utilize the innumerable junks available on the mainland. Although junks are not sophisticated weapons of war, their sheer numbers could place a significant burden on naval defense forces.

JAPAN

The devastating effects of the Second World War upon Japan convinced large numbers of Japanese that their country's future could best be assured by avoiding rearmament. This view coincided with that of American occupation authorities. The result was that the constitution of Japan includes a provision aimed at preventing the rearmament of Japan.

The provision, combined with the ideological opposition of the Japanese socialists to rearmament, has made it extremely difficult

for both United States and Japanese leaders who see rearmament of
Japan essential to prevent communist hegemony in the Far East.
The course of Japanese rearmament has been a stormy one in
Japanese politics.

The United States military assistance deliveries to support
Japan's rearmament began in 1954. From that time through the end
of fiscal year 1965 the United States has programmed $866 million
of military assistance to Japan. The Defense Department planned to
expend $37.6 million for aid to Japan in fiscal 1965 and an equal
amount after July 1, 1965. [22] The United States assistance, especially in the late 1950's and early 1960's, was confined to more complex
military items which Japan did not have the capability to manufacture
without extensive retooling. Examples are fire control and elec-
tronics gear for naval vessels.

Much of this assistance was provided by the United States under
"cost-sharing programs." These programs involve agreements
that the receiving country will purchase certain items and that the
United States will give away certain related items. The theory
underlying these agreements is that minimum expenditures of
United States military aid funds encourage recipients to make large
efforts.

The present Japanese military posture is significant, but by no
means large in terms of that maintained by other free nations in
Asia. The "Self Defense Forces" have an estimated strength of about
200,000 men, including an air force of some 1,300 planes and the
beginnings of a modern navy. [23]

As a result of the economic development of Japan, the United
States is initiating no new programs for the granting of military
equipment to Japan. [24] A limited military training program is being
continued in connection with the United States military sales program.

However, under earlier commitments the Executive Branch was,
as late as fiscal year 1965, requesting funds for an air defense ground
environment system and anti-submarine warfare assistance. The air
defense system is to be cost-shared so that the United States pays
only 25% of the cost. Most of the equipment will be procured in the
United States. [25]

KOREA

During the Korean War the United States and Korean logistic systems were combined and the Korean and other United Nations forces received equipment and supplies purchased from the regular Department of Defense budget. For some time after the cease-fire in Korea while, it will be remembered, there seemed a substantial possibility of resumption of hostilities, the United States continued to share its military equipment with the Koreans without the initiation of a formal military assistance program.

In 1955, a decision was made to release to the Republic of Korea the responsibility for its own logistic system, and the United States again began to consider grants of equipment to the Koreans as "military assistance," to be paid for from foreign aid appropriations rather than out of the funds available for the United States Army, Navy and Air Force. The Executive Branch admitted in 1960 that:

> The ROK was not prepared in 1955 to establish immediately an effective logistic system, nor did they pursue the task aggressively. Therefore, it can be said that an error was made in deciding to release logistic responsibility without insuring that the ROK possessed the necessary capability. [26]

This situation was severely aggravated by the fact that the United States left large quantities of supplies and equipment in Korea, both when it left the country following the Second World War and again at the end of the Korean War. The formidable task of merely developing a reasonable inventory of what was in Korea was not completed until 1960. [27]

These difficulties were compounded by Korea's economic backwardness. Despite the training provided during the Korean War, the Koreans were attempting to progress in a few short years from a relatively simple people with little technical sophistication to a society that could manage military equipment and inventories with the sophistication of the United States. In addition, the Korean civilian economy was sufficiently behind the military technology introduced into the country so that in many cases the military supply system contained better food, clothing and tools than were available in the civilian system. In many cases the military supply system was the only place in Korea from which repair parts and tires for vehicles could be found. The result of the inadequate military

logistics system and civilian demands for military goods was a rather
large loss of military supplies diverted to the civilian economy by the
Korean government itself and supplies pilfered by Koreans. This
situation was not brought under anything approaching control until
1960. [28]

Supply difficulties of the type that occurred in Korea in the late
1950's tend to be self-propagating. For example, if the inventory
or requisitioning system is inadequate, there will be a tendency to
ask the United States to furnish needed equipment which records
indicate is not on hand. Because Military Assistance Advisory
Group advisors, like the country officials, have no way to determine
whether the item is already in stock somewhere in the country, they
must either furnish the requested assistance or watch equipment
become unusable for lack of parts.

The possibility of renewed communist aggression in Korea made
it impossible to withhold assistance until the supply system could be
straightened out. As a result, maintenance and supply problems continued, with accompanying shipments in excess of needs, inadequate
records and other logistic difficulties. Though the General Accounting Office was quick to point out these problems, and opponents of
the foreign aid program were quick to use the evidence thus provided,
in retrospect it would seem that no reasonable alternatives were
available to policymakers at that time. Defense Department witnesses,
in appearances before Congressional committees, have cited various
improvements being made in supply management. The military aid
program is continuing to provide training in logistics as well as a
continuing supply of parts and replacements for equipment and supplies furnished under earlier military aid programs.

United States military assistance programs for Korea, from the
time responsibility for supply was turned over to the Koreans to the
end of June, 1965, have amounted to $2.3 billion, including an esti-
mated $150 million in fiscal year 1965. [29] During the same period
United States economic assistance, not counting surplus agricultural
commodities, amounted to over $2.3 billion. In addition to its foreign
assistance efforts, the United States still maintains the equivalent of
two divisions with appropriate ground and air supporting units in
Korea.

Much of this economic aid and all of the military aid is connected with the continued maintenance in Korea of the present force

strength estimated to be about 600,000 men. Most of the forces are
in the army which has been called "well equipped and intensively
trained" by William P. Bundy, formerly an Assistant Secretary of
Defense responsible for the military aid program. [30]

Although the cost of maintaining this large force is considerably
less than it would be if the United States forces were to be used instead of Korean forces, it is nonetheless substantial. In 1963, for
example, in addition to United States military aid, the Koreans
spent $370 million for their defense effort, a large part of which
was made available indirectly through United States commodity import and surplus agricultural product programs. Because of these
costs and the fact that North Korea has an estimated strength of
only 350,000 in its army, [31] many observers have suggested that
Korean forces be reduced. Of course South Korea, though heavily
dependent upon United States support, is a sovereign nation and a
decision by the United States that Korean forces will be reduced does
not necessarily mean that those forces will be reduced. However,
the United States could limit its military and economic assistance
programs to the support of whatever level of forces the United
States considered necessary.

A report presented to the Senate by Senator McGee presents one
side of the argument:

It may even be possible, moreover, to effect substantive
economies in our military program in Korea. While this
may be more open to question than in the preceding case of
Taiwan, both the size of the forces and the amount of the
commitment in Korea, it would seem to us, should be
reassessed vis-a-vis the capabilities of the counter threats
on the other side. For example, is it realistic to try to
maintain in the field enough troops to counter an all-out
attack by Communist China through North Korea, or is it
more realistic to concentrate strictly on the North Korean
threat in the field in the knowledge that, should the Chinese
commit their troops again, it would require new and quite
even different policy decision by our own high command in
the context of the global security picture as a whole? We
do not pretend to our own conclusions on this question but
only urge a hard re-examination of the fundamental
postulates involved. [32]

As implied in Senator McGee's statement, so long as a threat of Chinese Communist involvement exists and is considered relevant, it is difficult to make the argument that the present Korean forces are oversized unless United States forces are to be made available to meet any deficiencies. Therefore, it seems unlikely that either United States forces in Korea or Korean forces will be reduced so long as the United States is involved in Vietnam and the Chinese continue to act aggressively.

In addition to the substantial army, Korea maintains a small navy composed primarily of vessels provided under the military aid program. The purpose of this force is primarily minelaying and sweeping, patrol, and coastal defense missions. As Admiral Felt, who managed both United States defense and military assistance programs in the Far East, put it, there is a division of labor between the United States Navy and the smaller local navies in the Far East:

All of free Asia is dependent on sea lines of communication. The 7th Fleet carries out its functions in international waters. Local defense in coastal waters is a responsibility, however, of each of the other nations concerned with the mutual security effort. [33]

United States assistance to the Republic of Korea Air Force has included a variety of older-type jet aircraft as well as the newer F-5 jet fighter. The Republic of Korea also has NIKE air defense missiles. Although the United States has provided significant quantities of aircraft to South Korea, this assistance has not matched that available to the communist forces of North Korea. Secretary of Defense McNamara told a Congressional committee that:

The North Korean jet air force is over 100 percent larger than the South Korean jet air force. [34]

In recent years, more as a result of fund shortages in the overall military assistance program than deliberate policy, military aid deliveries to Korea have dropped unevenly but sharply, as is shown in the following table:

Fiscal Year	Value of Military Assistance Supplies, Services and Equipment Delivered[35]
1956	$201.5 million
1957	258.8 million
1958	331.1 million
1959	190.5 million
1960	187.1 million
1961	192.2 million
1962	136.9 million
1963	160.4 million
1964	124.4 million
1965 (estimate)	198.3 million

This declining level of deliveries has created major problems in the defense of Korea because of the heavy expenditures associated with continued operation of Korean forces. Certain expenditures, such as those for training, ammunition, repair of equipment, parts and gasoline and lubricants, continue year after year and in order to maintain equipment already provided and forces already mustered, these costs must have first call on available military assistance resources. These "operating costs" were estimated to consume all but 20% of the Administration's fund request for fiscal year 1965. In the preceding fiscal year (1964) a total of $151.8 million was allocated to Korean programs; maintenance costs accounted for $117.3 million of this amount.

Naturally, this basic cost means that as the program decreases the effect is an equal, or nearly equal, reduction in provision of new weapons. The Defense Department inserted material in the Passman subcommittee hearings to attempt to show that the Congressional reduction in the Administration request in 1963 (fiscal year 1964) had damaged military posture. In the case of Korea this material indicated that:

(1) Aircraft were deleted from the program, thereby extending the period of modernization for the Korean Air Force.

(2) The program for the Korean Navy was "almost completely eliminated."

(3) "There is a need for additional coastal patrol and mine warfare vessels as well as modernization of existing vessels."

(4) The program for vehicle replacement was reduced.[36]

The United States maintains one of its largest military assistance advisory groups in Korea. This group of over 1,000 men administers United States military assistance to Korea and acts as advisor to the Korean Army, Navy and Air Force from the highest to the lowest level.

VIETNAM

United States involvement in Vietnam began when the United States provided military assistance to French forces in Vietnam until they were defeated at their military stronghold of Dien Bien Phu on May 7, 1954 by communist forces. In fiscal year 1953 the United States spent over $350 million and in 1954 over $400 million to provide military equipment and supplies for this unsuccessful French effort.

Following the military defeat, agreements were reached in Geneva in July of 1954 partitioning Vietnam into a Communist North and a non-Communist South.

The prospects for survival of South Vietnam were bleak. The country was faced with a substantial military threat from the communist forces in the North, almost a million refugees in a population of 14 million, economic chaos and pockets of communists within the newly formed country.

In the fall of 1954 the Vietnamese turned to the United States for assistance. President Eisenhower responded to this request with a letter to Vietnam's President Diem on October 25, 1954, offering United States assistance. As the President put it:

The purpose of this offer is to assist the Government of
Vietnam in developing and maintaining a strong viable
state, capable of resisting attempted subversion or
aggression through military means.[37]

The military portion of this program cost $167.3 million in fiscal year 1956 (July, 1955, to June, 1956) and an additional $110.5 million the following year. In subsequent years through fiscal year 1961 the program averaged about $50 million per year. During these years

the program was administered by a United States advisory group of
340 men which was soon enlarged by personnel assigned to recover
equipment given to the French for use in the earlier war.

From 1955 to 1961 the Vietnamese economy prospered in large
part as a result of the extensive United States economic assistance.
However, at the Third National Congress of the Lao Dong (communist) Party in Hanoi, North Vietnam in the fall of 1960, it was announced that the party's new task was "to liberate the south from the
atrocious rule of the U.S. imperialists and their henchmen."[38] An
all-out campaign of terrorism and subversion was launched to under-
mine and destroy the government of South Vietnam.

In 1961 the government of South Vietnam appealed to the United
States for additional help. The United States responded with increased economic and military aid as well as more military and
economic advisors. Deliveries of military equipment were increased to $144 million in United States fiscal year 1961. This
effort and accompanying economic assistance resulted in sufficient
improvement so that President Kennedy was able to say in early
1963 that "the spearpoint of aggression has been blunted in South
Vietnam." However, progress in Vietnam stumbled over a series
of Vietnamese domestic political problems which began in 1963.
President Diem eventually lost the confidence of many of his people
and in November of 1963 was deposed by a group of military officers.
Since that time power has changed hands frequently in Vietnam with
attendant deleterious effects on the military and economic efforts.[39]

The present United States military effort in Vietnam is a combination of military assistance and more direct support provided by
United States units assigned to Vietnam. In response to criticism
of United States operations in Vietnam by servicemen assigned there
whose comments were widely circulated by newspapers and magazines, Secretary McNamara detailed the exact advisory relationship
in Vietnam in testimony before a Congressional committee in July of
1964. This material is quoted in full below both because it is important in the Vietnamese instance and because similar problems of
the role of United States advisors and support units have arisen
before--for example in postwar China--and may well arise again.

You must understand the missions of our forces
there. We are there to provide training, logistical
support, and transport support.

We are not there to enter into combat apart from whatever combat may be associated with these three primary functions. The Army, in carrying out its role, provides transport support to Vietnamese combat forces. It moves them from their base, if you will, into combat in helicopters. The helicopter as it enters the combat zone is exposed to fire. To protect the helicopter from destruction, the Army uses not only transport helicopters, but armed helicopters.

The armed helicopters are authorized, when they are flying with the transport helicopters, to return ground fire. So, the Army engages in that type of activity but it is not for combat's sake per se but to provide the transport of the Vietnamese troops who carry on the combat.

The Air Force has a transport role, but it doesn't transport into combat. There is no requirement for it. Its transport is of cargo in formal logistical operations. It also has a combat training role. It trains the Vietnamese Air Force pilots, some in this country, some in Vietnam. It carries on what I would describe as on-the-job combat training.

The story of the United States role in Vietnam is in part the story of the evolution from the advisory relationship described by this statement to that of allies in a full-scale war.

The difficulty in distinguishing between an advisory role, a logistical support role and a combat role in Vietnam and similar situations is paralleled by the question of what programs should provide the necessary resources for an effort of this type, and how the effort should be organized.

With certain special exceptions, [40] the United States Army, Navy and Air Force have no legal authority to turn equipment or supplies over to other countries, except through the military assistance program. When such equipment and supplies are provided through military assistance the law requires that the military departments be reimbursed for its cost. [41] It follows that equipment and supplies for Vietnam which are intended for use by Vietnamese forces must be paid for out of the appropriations for military assistance.

On the other hand, military assistance appropriations are obviously not sufficient to provide for equipment used by United States forces operating in countries receiving military assistance. The equipment used for these forces, in Korea and Vietnam for example, is paid for out of the regular appropriations to the Army, Navy or Air Force. Pay and allowances of United States military personnel--whether working on military aid or not--are paid for out of regular defense appropriations, not military assistance funds.

The military assistance costs of the Vietnam effort were estimated to be $211.5 million in fiscal year 1963, $216.4 million in fiscal year 1964 and the President's budget for fiscal year 1965 included $205.8 million ($55 million of which was added by a special Presidential request submitted to the Congress on May 18, 1964). The costs of the Vietnam operation to the United States military departments in fiscal 1964 were estimated at various amounts, including a widely circulated estimate of $250 million per year. Although official figures have not been released, unofficial estimates indicate that the costs of Vietnam operations to the military assistance program will probably exceed $300 million in 1965 and the direct costs to the United States defense budget are undoubtedly higher than the military assistance costs.

While the legal distinction between the costs of military aid and the costs of regular United States forces seems relatively clear in theory, it unquestionably leads to some close questions in practice. For example, in the summer of 1964 the Department of Defense had under active consideration proposals for amalgamation of the military assistance office in Vietnam (the Military Assistance Advisory Group) with the staff of the Commander of the United States forces in Vietnam (COMUSMACV). This proposal was based on the assumption that there was duplication in the efforts of the two groups. Likewise, the costs of combined headquarters or jointly used airfields could validly be allocated either to the Vietnamese (military assistance) or to United States forces (defense budget).

The military assistance costs of over $200 million per year for three years running have caused a severe strain on the military assistance programs elsewhere, as the total appropriation for military assistance for those three years has been only $1,325 billion in fiscal 1963, $1 billion in fiscal 1964 and $1,055 billion in fiscal 1965.[42] The Vietnam effort has been given first priority in the use of all the resources of the entire United States military establishment--people,

money, equipment, etc. [43] As a result other military assistance has
had to be curtailed to make necessary funds available.

The funds expended by the Defense Department for Vietnam are
only a fraction of the total effort by the United States to help Vietnam
defend itself against the communists. By the summer of 1964 it was
widely recognized that military assistance and United States military
support alone could not "win" in Vietnam. As the Chairman of the
Joint Chiefs of Staff put it:

> The problem out there is not only a military problem.
> It is a political problem, it is an economic problem, and I
> believe even a social problem. ... The point is that the
> final touch out there is not going to be the achievement of
> "a military victory." I believe parallel to our achieve-
> ments in the military field there must be equal accomplish-
> ments in the political and economic field if you are going
> to obtain in the long term, a free South Vietnam able to
> pursue its own destiny. [44]

The Administration requested $207 million for economic assist-
ance for Vietnam in fiscal year 1965 alone, not including surplus
agricultural commodities.

LAOS

United States military assistance deliveries to Laos began in
fiscal year 1956 after the French defeat in Indochina. A comparatively small program was continued until 1960 when the United States
recognized the communist Pathet Lao threat to the continued independence of Laos. Military assistance deliveries were then stepped
up to a level of $33 million in fiscal year 1961 and $37 million in
fiscal year 1962.

The political situation in Laos from 1956 to the present is much
too complicated to be presented in detail in a book of this type. There
are three significant groups in Laos, each with its own military
forces. The Pathet Lao or communists have from time to time
participated in the Lao government and have consistently attempted
to expand the territory which they control in the country. The second
group, usually called the "neutralists," under their leader Kong Le
is more or less loyal to the government and clearly anti-communist.

This group receives military assistance from the United States.
The third group, called the "conservative forces," has consistently
received support in the form of military assistance from the
United States.

The reasons for providing economic and military assistance to
Laos have been stated by the State Department to be to contain the
Pathet Lao without the commitment of American troops and to forestall the development of a dangerous flanking threat to our crucial
involvement in the defense of South Vietnam, as well as our position
in Thailand. [45]

The materiel provided to Laos under the military aid program
has primarily been small unsophisticated weapons designed for use
by relatively untrained troops, such as communications equipment,
trucks, rifles and ammunition. In addition to the United States effort, the French maintain a military mission in Laos.

Estimates of the costs and precise content of United States military assistance given to Laos since fiscal year 1962 have not been
made available.

THAILAND

Thailand, a ringside observer of the communist attempts to take
over the former Indochina states (including Vietnam) after the end
of the Second World War, was quick to request and receive United
States military assistance as soon as it was available under the
Mutual Defense Assistance Program. The military assistance
agreement with Thailand was signed in October of 1950.

Before the United States programs began, the Thai forces had
been advised and assisted by the British. As Senator Chavez put it,
upon returning from an inspection trip:

When the U. S. military aid program in Thailand
began in 1950 the Royal Thai Army had military equipment on hand which was a varied collection from several
foreign armies. Support for this equipment was difficult
and in some cases impossible since the ammunition and
spare parts resupply for many items had ceased to exist

since the end of World War II. Although ammunition was
available, it was not sufficient to support training for very
long. [46]

From 1950 through fiscal 1964 the United States has delivered
equipment and services valued at over $460.1 million to Thailand, an
average of over $32 million per year. Deliveries were increased in
fiscal years 1962 through 1964 in light of the general communist
pressures in Southeast Asia. This assistance has enabled the Thai
Army to re-equip itself with American equipment, develop stan-
dardized United States tactics, build adequate military schooling and
housing facilities and build hospitals for military use. Over 360 aircraft had been furnished to Thai forces through 1960, including 40
jets.

While Vietnam and Laos have been torn by civil war, insurgency
and confusion, Thailand has remained a steadfast anti-communist
nation closely allied to the United States and fully cognizant of the
dangers of communist domination of Southeast Asia. Thailand is a
member of the Southeast Asia Treaty Organization and thus sits
with the United States in any SEATO military planning. When the
Pathet Lao with the support of the North Vietnamese were apparently
succeeding in overrunning most of Laos, Thailand requested and received a garrison of United States troops in the parts of Thailand
which abut the Mekong River. [47]

Recently the United States has been placing increasing emphasis
in military assistance upon civic action and counterinsurgency missions of the Thai forces. However, in 1964 the United States was
still helping "to maintain a Thai conventional capability sufficient to
withstand an initial external assault and to carry out the various missions envisaged in SEATO contingency plans."[48]

Deliveries of military equipment to Thailand have no doubt been
stepped up since fiscal 1964 in response to the Vietnam situation and
the announcement by the North Vietnamese of renewed interest in
subversion in Northeast Thailand. However, costs and other details
on the program in 1965 and 1966 have been kept classified.

In 1965 it is estimated that over 500 persons will serve in the
United States Advisory Group in Thailand.

CAMBODIA

Cambodia is part of Indochina which was formerly a possession of the French. In 1954 Cambodia became an independent country which has since that time attempted to carry a more or less neutral line in foreign affairs. Until 1963, however, Cambodia was accepting assistance, both military and economic, from the United States. In 1963, Prince Sihanouk decided that the American missions in Cambodia were threatening his existence and asked that they leave. They did.

Sihanouk's move was widely interpreted as a decision that Communist China, not the United States, held the key to the future of Southeast Asia and his decision so interpreted was a setback for United States policy there. Cambodia retains a large part of the $83 million worth of the military assistance which the United States has provided.

BURMA

Throughout its history Burma has stood either in alliance with or in fear of the ruling powers in China. The development of a strong centralized Chinese government under the communists has convinced this former British colony that it must not pursue a strongly pro-Western policy. The coolness of Burma toward the West was aggravated for many years by the continued presence of an armed camp of vanquished Chinese Nationalists in Northern Burma. Burma wished to see these forces removed from its territory but the military costs of forcible removal would have been great, as these forces had no place to retreat but to China, a retreat undoubtedly carrying with it a rapid death. Burma has aligned itself with the "non-aligned nations" and has consistently declared its neutralism whenever a forum was available. The Burmese have accepted assistance from both Russia and the United States.

Little detail has been released concerning the United States-Burma sales agreement but it appears that some United States military equipment has been provided to Burma under sales arrangements begun in 1958 and renewed in 1961. [49]

INDONESIA

Indonesia--a former Dutch colony--is an island group of some 7,000 inhabited islands which occupy a strategically important position in Southeast Asia. With the fifth largest population in the world and extensive natural resources, such as rubber and tin, and a geographic position astride many sea-lines of communications, both the United States and the Soviet Union have looked upon Indonesia alternatively as a potential ally or enemy of considerable importance. The political structure of Indonesia essentially consists of a large communist party, a large and powerful army and a powerful President who has developed a kind of chauvinistic leadership made possible because he led the original independence movement. Indonesia also has a large (even by Western standards) navy and air force.

Part of the reason for Indonesia's substantial military posture is the fact that both the United States and the Soviet Union have provided significant quantities of military aid. The American assistance provided to Indonesia is, however, only a token contribution as compared to the extensive Russian program which has been estimated at almost $1 billion. By contrast United States military assistance deliveries to Indonesia through the middle of 1964 were estimated to have been $66 million. The Russian assistance was originally in the form of credits to be repaid primarily in the form of goods and/or local currency, in some cases over 10 years with a 2 or 5 year grace period at 2% interest to be charged from the date of delivery. Another part of this credit was to be repaid in 5 years beginning in 1961 and 1962 at 2% interest. [50] United States assistance to Indonesia has been concentrated primarily on materiel for the Indonesian Army while Soviet assistance has included such items as submarines and surface ships. Both Soviet and United States military technicians have at one time or another been stationed for certain periods in Indonesia. Some 1,200 Indonesian officers have been trained under the United States military aid program, including the Army and Air Force Chief of Staff and about two-fifths of the Army staff. [51]

On the American domestic political scene Indonesia has provided a test case of assistance to a communist-leaning neutral nation. President Sukarno's socialist and pro-Russian statements have attracted widespread attention in the American Press. Indonesia's record of United Nations voting and diplomatic maneuvers is clearly not pro-United States even though the United States, at the expense of its relations with NATO allies, did not actively oppose Indonesia's claim to West New Guinea (West Irian). American congressmen have been understandably concerned, especially after Sukarno began a policy of confrontation against Malaysia which seemed to many to be little more than naked aggression. After considerable criticism of any assistance to Indonesia, the Congress in 1963 amended the Foreign Assistance Act to require a special determination by the President before assistance could be given to Indonesia.[52]   During 1964, Congressional criticism of the continued program to Indonesia was unabated although the Executive Branch announced that it had discontinued deliveries to Indonesia of all "materiel that relates to combat."[53] The Indonesians were by that time taking active aggressive military steps against Malaysia. However, a move to prohibit any assistance to Indonesia was defeated by Administration forces in the Congress.

THE PHILIPPINES

The United States has always enjoyed a special relationship to the Philippine Islands, stemming quite naturally from the fact that the Philippines were once a United States possession and that the United States was relatively quick to not only grant Philippine independence, but to make every effort to make the Philippines a successful nation. The United States still maintains on the Philippine Islands a substantial base structure, including a very large naval base at Subic Bay and one of the largest air bases in the Far East at Clark Field. The Philippines can legitimately be characterized as underdeveloped by statistical indicators such as per capita gross national product.[54] Economic aid through fiscal 1963, excluding surplus agricultural commodities, amounted to $276 million. Military assistance through fiscal 1964 was $315.6 million. The United States military mission in the Philippines (called JUSMAT) had a strength of about 100 men in 1964.

The Philippine Army is backed up by a constabulary which is one of the finest police-type organizations in the world. Philippine forces are battle-hardened from their struggles with the Huks and the Philippine people on the whole have gained from the Huk campaign a realization of the lengths to which communists will go to gain control of their country. In part, as a result of this, the Philippines have been fast to contribute their manpower in any East-West confrontation. For example, there was a Philippine contingent in Korea during the Korean War. One of the United States objectives in providing military aid to the Philippines is to "help develop forces deployable within the SEATO area for mutual defense tasks."[55]

United States aid has included ground force equipment such as transportation, small arms and ammunition and a wide variety of maintenance items. Assistance for the air force has included various air defense electronic equipment, F-86 aircraft, F-5 aircraft, and airfield construction.

One of the major problems in the military assistance program in the Philippines has been the development of an adequate logistics and maintenance capability in the Philippine forces. Since 1950 there have been several reports by the United States General Accounting Office criticizing Philippine maintenance practices.

CONCLUSION

The Far East presents an area in which the primary challenge to United States interests is posed in military terms. The United States response, logically enough, has also taken a military form. United States forces are deployed in Okinawa, in the Philippines, in Japan and in substantial force in Korea. United States military assistance to Far Eastern countries was some $600 million in fiscal year 1964 alone. The United States has some type of alliance and/or treaty relationship with Japan, Korea, Republic of China and Thailand. In addition, both Vietnam and Laos are so-called SEATO "protocol states," indicating that the SEATO nations would consider aggression against either of these two nations as endangering the peace and safety of SEATO members.

In many areas of the world United States military aid and military decision making follows diplomatic necessity. In the Far East, on the other hand, it may be said that the military tail wags the diplomatic dog. The necessity to assemble enough military force to resist Communist China has required a United States policy of close friendship with and substantial assistance to a conglomeration of nations like Japan, Korea, Republic of China and Thailand. This military necessity has also forced somewhat closer ties to Indonesia, Burma and Cambodia, not to mention somewhat greater involvement in Laos and Vietnam than might have been the

case were not the military pressures on the United States position
so great and were not the intentions of the communists to use military force wherever they could get away with it so obvious.

NOTES

1. However a report issued by Senators McGee, Church and
Moss in 1963 indicated that our policy in the Far East suffered from
a preoccupation with the Russian threat. U.S., Congress, Senate,
Committees on Appropriations, Foreign Relations, Interior and
Insular Affairs, Study Mission to Southeast Asia November-Decem-
ber 1962, Report of Senators Gale W. McGee, Frank Church, and
Frank E. Moss, 88th Cong., 1st Sess., 1963.

2. The suggestion that continuity of Chinese thought explains
much of the acceptance of communism in China and that communism
in China has followed much that already existed in Chinese thought
is explored in Mary C. Wright, "Modern China in Transition,"
The Annals, January, 1959.

3. Mao Tse-tung, The Chinese Revolution and the Chinese Com-
munist Party (November 15, 1939) quoted in Robert C. North, "The
Sino-Soviet Alliance," The China Quarterly, No. 1 (London: January-
March, 1960) p. 57.

4. George Paloczi-Horvath, Mao Tse-tung: Emperor of the
Blue Ants (London: Secker and Warburg, 1962) pp. 381-382. No
source is indicated nor are the quotation marks within the quotation
explained. Despite occasional faults in documentation and concluding chapters which are emotionally highly charged, this is undoubtedly the best biography of Mao.

5. A good discussion of Chinese Communist military strength
can be found in A. Doak Barnett, Communist China and Asia (New
York: Vintage Books, 1960).

6. Mutual Defense Treaty entered into force on March 3, 1955,
TIAS 3178.

7. See Barnett, op. cit., pp. 424-425 and material quoted
therein.

8. Ibid., p. 414. Barnett estimates one-third of the total
forces are on these islands.

9. Testimony of William P. Bundy, Assistant Secretary of
State (Far East), HFAC, CY 64, p. 170.

10. Testimony of Secretary of Defense Gates, HFAC, CY 60,
p. 78.

11. U.S., Congress, Senate, Committee on Appropriations,
Report on United States Military Operations and Mutual Security

Programs Overseas by Senator Dennis Chavez, 86th Cong. , 2d
Sess. , 1960, p. 46.

    12. Testimony of Secretary Gates, HFAC, CY 60, p. 138.

    13. HFAC, CY 64, p. 92.

    14. Report of Senator McGee, et al, op. cit. , p. 5.

    15. Testimony of then Deputy Assistant Secretary of Defense
Frank Sloan, HFAC, CY 64, p. 499.

    16. Testimony of Secretary of Defense McNamara, HAC, CY 64,
p. 321.

    17. U.S., Congress, Senate, Committee on Foreign Relations,
Report on Foreign Assistance Authorizations, Part II, individual
views of Senator Wayne Morse. One administration witness called
the Chinese Communist Air Force "large, but obsolescent."
Testimony of William P. Bundy, HFAC, CY 64, p. 170.

    18. HFAC, CY 64, p. 499.

    19. Testimony of General Robert Wood, HAC, CY 64, pp. 424-
425.

    20. Chavez Report, op. cit. , p. 46.

    21. Sloan testimony, loc. cit.

    22. Department of Defense, Military Assistance Facts,
February 15, 1965.

    23. Barnett, op. cit., p. 120.

    24. Statement by Secretary of Defense McNamara, SFRC, CY 64,
p. 514. This conclusion is required by Section 610 (m) of the Foreign
Assistance Act of 1963 which prohibits furnishing military assistance
to countries capable of bearing their own defense costs.

    25. Bundy testimony, op. cit., p. 177.

    26. HFAC, CY 60, p. 971.

    27. Ibid.

    28. Ibid. , pp. 521-522.

    29. Until the spring of 1965, the Defense Department provided
in its publication Military Assistance Facts estimates of the dollar
value of military assistance programs by country for the current
fiscal year. For reasons unknown to the author this set of facts
was dropped from the 1965 publication, making it difficult for the
public to derive exact program amounts even for past programs.
Estimates for fiscal year 1965 programs in this book are derived by
subtracting cumulative programs through fiscal 1964 shown in the
spring 1964 version of Military Assistance Facts from cumulative
programs through fiscal 1965 shown in the 1965 version of the
same publication. The resulting figures are actually the algebraic
sum of the fiscal 1965 program and increases and decreases in

programs of 1964 and earlier years. In most cases these figures will be within 10% of the actual fiscal 1965 program figure.

30. HFAC, CY 64, p. 170.

31. Barnett, op. cit., p. 119.

32. Report of Senator McGee, et al, op. cit.

33. Testimony of Admiral Felt, then Commander in Chief, Pacific, HFAC, CY 60, p. 537.

34. HFAC, CY 64, p. 102.

35. In reading this table and others throughout the book, it is important to remember the distinction between deliveries and "programs" which result in deliveries.

36. HAC, CY 64, p. 350.

37. This quotation as well as most of the other material in this section is taken from the Johnson Administration's first "White Paper" on Vietnam given in the form of a speech by the Secretary of Defense before the National Security Industrial Association, Washington, D. C., March 26, 1964, the text of which was printed in the New York Times the following day.

38. Ibid.

39. The situation after Diem's death has been explored extensively in the press, magazine articles, books and Congressional hearings.

40. See Chapter 4 on programs in Latin America and Chapter 11 on training.

41. Section 632 (d) of the Foreign Assistance Act of 1961, as amended.

42. To readers who shudder when they read the word "only" before figures given in millions and billions, the author must apologize but point out that by comparison with the entire Defense budget of over $50 billion per year, $1 billion is not as large a sum as it might seem.

43. See the statement of Secretary of Defense McNamara to the Senate Appropriations Committee (SAC, CY 64, p. 185) and similar statements in other hearings on Vietnam.

44. Testimony of General Wheeler, SAC, CY 64, p. 188.

45. Testimony of Assistant Secretary of State Bundy, SAC, CY 64, p. 289.

46. Chavez Report, op. cit., p. 96.

47. "President Sends Troops to Thailand," Department of State Bulletin, Vol. 45 (June 4, 1962), 904-906.

48. Testimony of Assistant Secretary of State Bundy, HFAC, CY 64, p. 174.

49. Ibid., p. 176.

50.   Testimony of Secretary of State Rusk, HAC, CY 64, p. 287.

51.   Bundy testimony, op. cit., p. 178.

52.   Section 620 (j).

53.   Wood testimony, op. cit., p. 419.

54.   The Philippine per capita GNP in 1964 was less than $150 compared with over $3,000 in the United States.

55.   Testimony of Secretary of Defense McNamara, HFAC, CY 64, p. 92.

3

In the Far East, as has been indicated, military assistance and military deployments form the cornerstone of United States policy. Politics tends to follow the dictates of military necessity once the basic United States political objective of resisting communist aggression is accepted. In the Middle East a contrasting situation prevails. United States policy in the Middle East is constrained by the basic political tension that prevails as a result of the establishment of Israel and Pan-Arabism.

The peace of the world would undoubtedly be endangered if war were to break out in the Middle East. Given the avowed intention of most of the Arab powers to return Palestine to Arab control, one of the major deterrents to war in the area is the continued strength of Israeli armed forces. Substantial United States programs of military assistance to the Arab Middle East would endanger this tenuous balance and for that reason, military aid has been sharply limited. Even if considerations of international politics should make assistance on a large scale to the Arab states desirable, United States domestic political constraints would undoubtedly prevent such a program.

While desire to preserve the balance of power in the Middle East and domestic political considerations effectively limit the United States involvement with the Arab states, other considerations have limited United States involvement with Israel. The Arab states are in geopolitical terms important. Taken together these states comprise some 1.4 million square miles, about a third of the size of the United States. Their combined population is over 50 million which is about 30% of that of the United States. One of them is centrally astride the Suez Canal and the others under critical air routes for commercial and military flights. The Arab states are voting members of the United Nations and control much of the world's oil resources. Communist penetration in the Arab states would permit the communists to have a gateway to all of Africa. For these reasons United States policy has by no means written off the Arab states. American action in ending the Anglo-French Israel action against Egypt is a fine example of the necessity for the United States to side with the Arab states on occasion.

The desire to avoid upsetting the balance of power in the Middle East forces the United States to limit any military assistance in the form of either grants or sales given to Israel. Grant assistance is also limited because, in comparison with most recipients of United States grant assistance, Israel and some of the Arab states are economically quite well off and do not require grant assistance.

All these factors serve to keep the United States involvement in the Middle East at a minimum. Only when particularly pro-Western states seem to be in trouble and request assistance or where United States bases are at stake has military equipment been provided. [1]

ISRAEL

The United States does not now give and has never given grant military aid to Israel. As part of an over-all military sales program United States equipment has been sold to Israel on credit although the total of these sales through fiscal year 1964 amounted to only $27.6 million. Much of that total is accounted for by the sale of HAWK air defense missiles. [2] The HAWK sale was a logical conclusion of the balance of power approach to Middle Eastern politics. It followed shortly after the Russians had concluded a military assistance agreement with the Egyptians which included the provision of advanced versions of the MIG fighter. The HAWK is strictly an air defense missile with infinitesimal offensive capabilities. [3]

ARAB STATES

For the reasons outlined above no United States military aid has been given to Egypt and military assistance to Syria has been limited to provision of occasional training. At the end of fiscal year 1964 the total of this assistance amounted to only $20,000. By contrast the constraints on United States policy by no means bind the Russians who have much to gain and little to lose by fomenting military conflict in the Middle East. It is, therefore, not surprising that much of the military aid which Russia has given has been provided to three Middle Eastern countries--United Arab Republic (Egypt), Syria and Iraq.

The United States for many years had a special interest in relations with Saudi Arabia. The Daharan airfield, one of the largest base complexes in the Middle East, was for many years one

of the most important United States installations in this area. The
desire for continued use of this facility dictated that military cooperation between the United States and Saudi Arabia be more close
than that with the United Arab Republic. This cooperation was
facilitated by a Saudi Arabian attitude toward Israel which seemed
somewhat more sensible than that enunciated by the United Arab
Republic. Through fiscal 1965 over $32 million of military aid
had been programmed for Saudi Arabia.

United States relationships with Afghanistan have never been
close. The United States policy of close military cooperation with
its SEATO ally Pakistan and the extensive military aid to Pakistan,
which periodically engages in border quarrels with Afghanistan,
have kept relations with Afghanistan cool. However, Afghanistan
has accepted some $150 million of United States economic assist-
ance. United States military assistance to Afghanistan has amounted
to a total of $3.3 million since the program began in 1958. Although
the figure sounds impressive, it actually covers only the training
of a few Afghan officers and men in the United States.[4]

The Afghans do not have United States military equipment. Despite this fact some Afghans have received training as pilots in
addition to technical and English language training.

Prior to the coup which overthrew the pro-Western government
of Iraq in the summer of 1958, the United States provided extensive
military assistance to Iraq which was one of the key members of
the Bagdad Pact. For example, in the last year before the coup,
military assistance deliveries amounted to $21.3 million, which
helped to maintain armed forces with a strength somewhat over
50,000.[5] After the coup the new Iraq government denounced
United States military assistance and the existing United States military mission was sent home. Since that time an occasional Iraq
officer has been invited to the United States for training. Those
costs are carried as charges to the military assistance program.
In the period since the coup the United States has never expended
more than $100,000 a year for this training.

When the British government determined that it could no longer
bear the substantial burden of continued support for the governments
of Jordan and Lebanon, the United States stepped into the breach.
Since that time United States economic assistance to both countries
has amounted to almost $400 million, and military assistance

programs to $45. 8 million through fiscal 1965, including $9. 2 million to Lebanon and $36. 6 million for Jordan.

The nature of United States military assistance has been controlled by the type of threat which the United States has considered to be the most important in the case of both countries. Because of the political instability in the Middle East there has always been a possibility of overthrow of these two governments by nomadic tribesmen, other Arab states and indigenous disaffected minorities. For that reason, internal security requirements have been the keynote of United States military assistance.

Military assistance to Jordan has provided a substantial part of the costs of equipping and maintaining Jordan's 35, 000 man force. In calendar year 1963 it was estimated that Jordan spent $65 million for defense, [6] including a United States military assistance contribution of less than $5 million. [7]

In the case of Lebanon, United States assistance has provided support for Lebanon's force of approximately 10, 000 men. Lebanon has turned down an apparent Soviet offer to re-equip its entire army. [8] After relatively large deliveries in the late 1950's military assistance to Lebanon was reduced to a program of $85, 000 in fiscal 1964.

CONCLUSION

Because of the comparative wealth of Middle Eastern countries and the numerous political considerations which inhibit extensive United States involvement, military assistance in the Middle East has been limited in both scope and objectives. Military aid programs in this area are extensions of United States political interests and are not designed to add to the strength of United States allies in the event of armed conflict with the Soviet Union.

NOTES

1. The analysis above implies, without explicitly stating, that the present United States policy in the Middle East is the only one which the United States could rationally pursue. While that analysis coincides with the views of the author and does make a useful tool

for study of United States military aid in the Middle East, it is by no means universally accepted in the United States. An interesting colloquy in which Congressman Farbstein attempts to get Assistant Secretary of State Talbot to take a position on the question of the circumstances under which the United States would provide military aid to Israel is found on pp. 254-255 of HFAC, CY 64.

2. Testimony of General Adams, HFAC, CY 64.

3. Characteristics of all missiles provided to foreign governments are listed in HAC, CY 60, p. 2370.

4. By quirks of financing it is customary to speak of military assistance programs, when in fact all that is involved is permitting foreign students to participate in selected United States military training installations maintained for the use of United States forces. Military assistance pricing policy and the costs of air transportation and per diem allowance paid to these trainees makes these actions appear to be full-scale military aid programs.

5. U.S., Congress, Senate, Special Committee to Study the Foreign Aid Program, Foreign Aid Program: Compilation of Studies and Surveys, 85th Cong., 1st Sess., 1957, p. 1250.

6. SAC, CY 64, p. 262.

7. Calendar year data by interpolation of fiscal year data in Military Assistance Facts, March 1, 1964, published by the Defense Department.

8. Senate Special Committee, op. cit., p. 1245.

CHAPTER **4** MILITARY ASSISTANCE
TO LATIN AMERICA

Military assistance to Latin America in the form of training and
other services began before the First World War. [1] Legislation
passed in the 1920's expanded the authority to conduct this assistance and some thirty-two United States military missions were sent
to Latin America from 1920 to 1938 to assist Latin American nations in building their military organizations. The Latin American
nations were exempted administratively from the restrictions of
1923 on the private sale of arms and were exempted from the arms
embargo in the Neutrality Act of 1936. [2]

European nations also furnished military missions to Latin
American nations before World War II. The German influence was
strong in South America, particularly in Argentina. French missions operated in Brazil and Peru and Italian missions in Ecuador
and Bolivia. The United States achieved a virtual monopoly of mission activity soon after World War II began when the European
nations became concerned with problems closer to home. However,
during the Second World War German and Italian missions continued
to be active in some countries and German arms were sent from the
Axis powers to some Latin American nations.

The United States in 1938 embarked upon a program of sup-
planting Axis influence in the military establishments of Latin
America. Army, Navy and Air Force missions were established
and professional instruction was offered at less than cost. Training
in military schools in the United States was expanded.

Under the Lend Lease Program during World War II the Congress
authorized furnishing the Latin American countries up to $400 million
of military goods. The objectives of this program were to assist in
developing forces for defense against possible external aggression,
to help prevent threats of internal subversion, to insure political cooperation and to obtain needed bases and facilities for United States
forces.

By January of 1942 at a conference in Rio de Janeiro all Latin
American republics had taken at least minimal steps toward military
cooperation with the United States. These nations agreed "to consider any act of aggression on the part of a non-American state
against any one of them as an act of aggression against all of them."
They established an Inter-American Defense Board to study and

recommand measures for the defense of the hemisphere. However,
many Latin American nations were not enthusiastic participants in
World War II and it is not surprising that this board accomplished
little. In addition to the Inter-American Defense Board, two bilateral boards were established--one with Brazil and one with
Mexico.

Near the conclusion of the Second World War the participating
nations decided to retain the structures established for defense cooperation among the nations of the Western Hemisphere in the postwar period. The representatives of these nations met at Chapul-
tepec, Mexico in February of 1945 to plan the course of future military cooperation. They decided that the Inter-American Defense
Board would be made a permanent organization. The nations declared that an attack on any American state by any state would be considered to be an attack against them all and that collective measures
would be taken to repel such aggression. This declaration was included formally in a treaty signed at Rio de Janeiro on September 2,
1947.[3]

In May of 1946 and again in 1947, President Truman presented
and Congress failed to pass proposals for inter-American military
cooperation by provision of military equipment. When the Administration proposed the legislation which eventually became the Mutual
Defense Assistance Act of 1949, Latin America was not included
as one of the grant aid recipients, although Latin American nations
were eligible for reimbursable assistance (actually military sales
with no "aid" involved) under that act.[4]

After the outbreak of the Korean War, President Truman recommended military participation by the Latin American nations
and joint planning against the communist threat. The assembled
republics in response to the President's request passed a resolution recommending that the Latin American nations undertake
military cooperation and

> increase those of their resources and strengthen
> those of their armed forces best adapted to the
> collective defense, and maintain those armed forces
> in such status that they can be promptly available
> for the defense of the continent.[5]

To assist the Latin American republics in this contemplated military buildup, provision for military aid to Latin America was made in the foreign aid legislation recommended to the Congress in 1951, which ultimately became the Mutual Security Act of 1951. The President's request included $40.0 million for military aid to Latin America, $38.15 million of which was approved by the Congress. Continued appropriations for military assistance to Latin America made since that time have permitted deliveries at the following levels to Latin America.

MILITARY ASSISTANCE DELIVERIES TO LATIN AMERICA[6]
($ millions)

Fiscal Year	Amount	Fiscal Year	Amount
1952	.2	1959	31.5
1953	11.2	1960	32.3
1954	34.5	1961	45.0
1955	31.8	1962	54.3
1956	23.5	1963	51.8
1957	27.1	1964	62.9
1958	45.6	1965	51.3

Under the Mutual Security Act of 1951 and successor legislation, foreign nations, before receiving grant military assistance, must agree to a variety of terms and conditions. Acceptance of these terms was made in the form of bilateral agreements which the Latin American governments signed with the United States. These agreements made explicit the underlying purpose of assistance, which was to help the recipient nation assist the United States in the defense of the hemisphere. The first agreement to be signed, that with Ecuador, is typical of the language employed:

Preamble:

> ... Conscious of their pledges under the Inter-
> American Treaty of Reciprocal Assistance and
> other international instruments to assist any Amer-
> ican state subjected to an armed attack and to act
> together for the common defense and for the
> maintenance of the peace and security of the
> Western Hemisphere;

Article 1

Such assistance shall be so designed as to promote
the defense and maintain the peace of the Western
Hemisphere and be in accordance with defense plans under
which both Governments will participate in missions
important to the defense and maintenance of the peace
of the Western Hemisphere.

Article 9

The Government of Ecuador... agrees to fulfill
the military obligations which it has assumed under
multilateral or bilateral agreements, or treaties to
which the United States is a party; to make, consistent with its political and economic stability, the
full contribution permitted by its manpower, resources, facilities, and general economic condition
to the development and maintenance of its own defensive
strength and the defensive strength of the free world;
and to take all reasonable measures which may be
needed to develop its defense capabilities. [7]

The other articles in the standard agreement dealt with such
matters as the diplomatic status of persons in the military mission,
prohibitions against diverting assistance, publicity, treatment of
classified information, etc.

Other Latin American nations made similar agreements in the
following order:

Country	Agreement Entered Into Force	Treaties and Other Inter-national Acts Series Number[8]
Ecuador	February 20, 1952	2560
Cuba	March 7, 1952	2467
Colombia	April 17, 1952	2496
Peru	April 26, 1952	2466
Chile	July 11, 1952	2703
Brazil	May 19, 1953	2776
Dominican Republic	June 10, 1953	2777
Uruguay	June 11, 1953	2778

Country	Agreement Entered Into Force	Treaties and Other International Acts Series Number
Nicaragua	April 23, 1954	2940
Honduras	May 20, 1954	2975
Guatemala	June 18, 1955	3283
Haiti	September 12, 1955	3386
Bolivia	April 22, 1958	5197

These agreements were all "executive agreements" and, therefore, did not require ratification by the Senate, as would have been the case had they been considered treaties.

Through fiscal year 1959 military assistance from the United States was given only to these thirteen nations which had signed the requisite bilateral agreement with the United States. However, under flexibility permitted by the Foreign Assistance Act passed in 1961 and under agreements recently negotiated, military assistance, training and/or materiel was delivered to nineteen Latin American nations in fiscal 1964, every significant nation in the hemisphere except Canada, Haiti and Cuba. Until 1960 most of this assistance was designed to improve the capability of Latin American nations to assist in the defense of the hemisphere from external attack.

THE EFFECT OF UNITED STATES MILITARY POLICIES BEFORE 1960[9]

For a variety of historical and sociological reasons the Latin American nations have always, with few exceptions, maintained large military forces which are extensively involved in Latin American politics. This fundamental fact was bound to induce American policymakers, even before the Second World War, to attempt to maintain close relations with Latin American military forces. However, this United States involvement was bound to "feed back" into the military policies and problems of the Latin American nations themselves.

Most of the larger Latin American countries have maintained military establishments along American lines with separate naval and ground forces and an air force which is combined with the army in some countries and separate in others. The

American military missions sent to Latin America before 1960 were
the representatives of the United States Army, Navy and Air Force.
Because at the time there was little unification of these departments
in the United States, there was normally little coordination and cooperation among their representatives in Latin American nations.
In fact, there was probably a tendency for Americans to transplant
their inter-service rivalries to Latin America. This situation was
aggravated by the fact that American military advisors were accepting emoluments from the forces they were advising under special
statutory authority passed in 1922.

While Latin American military forces have frequently argued
over how the budgetary pie should be distributed among them, there
is general Latin American military agreement that civilian governments have neglected the military forces in Latin America. It,
therefore, is not surprising that on occasion military authorities
combined to put civilian governments under considerable pressure
to increase military expenditures. It is doubtful that American
military advisors did very much to discourage this, especially in
those periods when United States policy called for increased Latin
American military efforts.

The drive for increased military expenditures for both equipment and military pay was undoubtedly behind many of the frequent
military coups in Latin America. In other cases, military intervention to remove a corrupt or inept civilian government may well
have had the support of a majority of the civilian population. In
any case, military coups are a widely accepted phenomenon in Latin
America. Some Latin American rulers, such as Peron in Argentina, attempted to secure themselves against military coups by following a divide-and-conquer approach to the military by pitting one
service against another or enlisted men against officers.

Thrust into this situation of rivalries among military services
and of frequent military-civilian hostilities, United States military
missions probably aggravated the problem instead of alleviating it.
United States naval advisors, United States army advisors and
United States air advisors brought to Latin America the same arguments concerning the respective values and interrelationships of
weapons systems which they had learned in the context of inter-
service rivalries in the United States. The result was that the
United States, instead of speaking with a single voice, tended to
become a party to all sides of the rivalries within each Latin
American country.

The United States advisors came to Latin American nations
armed with authority to provide some training and to give equipment.
In a technical sense much of this activity was not "military assistance" because the authorization for such activities was not to be
found in the then existing foreign aid (Mutual Security or Mutual Defense Assistance) legislation. Instead, the authority to establish
these service missions was found in the legislation pertaining to each
of the military departments and the training was provided under a
hodgepodge of statutes and administrative determinations.

Especially in the early 1950's, the training provided by United
States military departments outside of the controls of the Mutual
Security Act tended to exceed that under the Act. For example,
the Army military school in the Caribbean trained over 2,400 students through these programs, a larger number than were trained
at the same school with military assistance funds. [10]

Equipment, particularly naval vessels, was also provided to
these nations by special legislation. Although Argentina was not
eligible to receive grant aid materiel assistance under the military
aid program because it had failed to sign an agreement embodying
the conditions which Congress had established for aid recipients,
a variety of naval vessels, including two submarines, were provided under ship loan agreements negotiated with Argentina in 1951
and 1960. [11]

In addition to these programs, the military missions maintained
in Latin America were continued at a substantial level. At the end
of 1958 some 558 United States military personnel were serving in
missions in the area. Army missions were assigned to every Latin
American country except Argentina, the Dominican Republic (which
had a Military Assistance Advisory Group) and Haiti. Naval missions
were present in practically every Latin American nation with any
naval force--in all countries but Bolivia, Costa Rica, Dominican
Republic, El Salvador, Guatemala, Honduras, Nicaragua, Panama
and Paraguay. Air Force missions were present in all countries
but Costa Rica, the Dominican Republic and Panama. [12]

It is difficult to imagine that military assistance deliveries of
the level provided to Latin America in the 1950's, large quantities
of excess stocks given without cost, extensive military sales, over
500 United States military personnel, and United States statements
encouraging development of military potential for hemispheric

defense could have been without effect in encouraging the development of larger and larger military establishments in Latin America.

A NEW POLICY

This was an obviously unsatisfactory situation. In the 1960's, United States policymaking began to integrate more closely political and military policy in Latin America. This development occurred simultaneously with President Kennedy's re-analysis of Latin American policy and re-emphasis on progressive development in Latin America through the Alliance for Progress. A number of factors led to the discarding of many of the old policies.

Within the Pentagon the Draper Committee recommendations resulted in taking control of military assistance programming from the separate military departments and centralizing responsibility under a senior military official in the Office of the Secretary of Defense. A similar step was taken in the field when the United States commander of land, sea and air forces in the Caribbean was given control of military assistance programs in Latin America. These reforms necessarily resulted in greater coordination within the military missions in Latin America.

President Eisenhower, in the late years of his administration, undertook to emphasize the Ambassador's position of control over the representatives of various United States agencies in each country. To initiate this program he issued both an Executive Order[13] and a stiff memorandum to all government agencies stating the control which the Ambassador should exercise.[14]

After President Kennedy took office he quickly acted to reiterate and expand earlier guidance that the Ambassador was the United States chief diplomatic representative in each country, with authority over all United States agencies including military missions and Military Assistance Advisory Groups. As his letter put it:

> You are in charge of the entire United States Diplomatic Mission, and I shall expect you to supervise all of its operations. The Mission includes not only the personnel of the Department of State and the Foreign Service, but also the representatives of all other United States agencies which have programs of activities in (the country to which you are

accredited). I shall give you full support and backing in
carrying out your assignment. 15

Simultaneously with these organizational developments both
United States and Latin American military and civilian policymakers
were beginning to realize that they had misperceived the nature of
the communist threat. The policy of preparation for external defense of the hemisphere, typified by the Rio Pact and indicated by
the nature of United States assistance, was seen to involve preparation for a threat that did not exist. Russian public statements, such
as Khrushchev's statement to the Twenty-second Party Congress,
began to show that the communists were adopting a carefully conceived policy of fomenting "wars of national liberation"which would
not necessarily involve direct Russian military action. Castro
had succeeded in Cuba and his plans for the communization of Cuba
and the subversion of the hemisphere were becoming apparent.
Indigenous Latin American communist parties, taking heart from
the actions of Castro, became increasingly militant and active
communist insurgency developed in countries like Venezuela and
Colombia.

The result of this combination of factors was a change in United
States military assistance policy from one of encouraging external
defense to one of assisting in economic development and internal
security.

The swiftness of the shift, at least in announced policy, if not
the policy itself, is striking. In 1960 the then Assistant Secretary of
State for Inter-American Affairs indicated that the United States
interest in Latin American military establishments did not extend
beyond supporting units intended for hemispheric defense. He stated
to the House Appropriations Committee on May 9, 1960:

We have made clear to countries participating in the
grant program that U.S. military interests in the program
do not extend beyond those units which they have consented,
in agreements with the United States, to maintain for
regional defense under the Rio Treaty. 16

His Pentagon counterpart told the same committee, speaking about
the total grant aid request for Latin America:

Of this total, $47.8 million is programmed to assist
specified units of eligible grant aid countries in attaining
a capability to participate in hemisphere defense missions
important to the security of the United States. [17]

Only $1.3 million of the grant aid request was for purposes other
than hemispheric defense.

Less than two years later, the Defense witness advised the
House Foreign Affairs Committee that:

The role of the security forces in Latin America,
both police and military therefore, assumes paramount
importance. If the Alliance for Progress is to have its
chance, governments must have the effective force required
to cope with subversion, prevent terrorism, and deal with
outbreaks of violence before they reach unmanageable
proportions. They must be able to sustain themselves against
attacks by the international Communist organization and its
indigenous members. [18]

Vestiges of the old policy persist, however, mainly because the
actions taken by the United States in the 1950's implied a commitment
not to leave high and dry those who had consistently followed United
States policy of hemispheric defense during that period. For example,
under ship loan legislation the United States had provided to Latin
American nations a total of 20 destroyers and submarines, [19] as well
as minor vessels which did not require special legislation. Considerable expenditures in training, manning, dockage and shore support facilities had been undertaken by recipient nations to support
these vessels. These efforts had been consistently encouraged by
the United States.

For the United States to have simply announced one day that it
would no longer provide the specialized training, spare parts and
maintenance services required to keep these vessels in combat-
serviceable condition would have understandably produced adverse
reactions on the part of those who had faithfully followed the United
States leadership in developing those forces. In addition, sharp
reductions of United States support would have required the Latin
American navies to turn to their own political leaders for markedly
increased financial support. Most of the Latin nations were not in
a position to provide this support without slighting their own internal

security efforts or economic development, especially in light of the
fact that purchases of the types of equipment and training required
would have required use of scarce foreign exchange. United States
authorities were also reluctant to write off the large investment
which had been made to equip and train hemispheric defense forces.

A sharp curtailment of United States support for hemispheric
defense forces created at United States instigation could, therefore,
not only have caused adverse political reactions against the United
States, but could have triggered substantial domestic conflicts and
perhaps attempted coups against civilian authorities intent upon con-
serving government funds for economic and social programs.

This factor was combined with the fact that a change in announced
United States policy did not inevitably produce a change in the strategic situation or the perception of that military situation by officials
of both United States and Latin American governments. As late as
1960 the United States Joint Chiefs of Staff were quoted as having

concluded that there is a valid military requirement for
Latin American participation in measures important to
the defense of the Western Hemisphere and that it is
necessary for the United States to render military assistance to those countries with which the United States has
concluded bilateral military plans. [20]

In 1962 the United States military commander in the Caribbean
stressed the contribution of these Latin American navies to the
hemispheric defense tasks of mine warfare and anti-submarine
warfare. [21] In 1964 the Chairman of the Joint Chiefs of Staff stated
that "Support for the Latin American navies has been cut below the
danger point. "[22] It is hard to imagine that the principles which
had guided United States policy for decades could be or were dropped
overnight by all United States and Latin American officials.

The new approach to military assistance to Latin America and
the necessity to continue some of the programs which had flourished
under the old policies meant continued substantial military assistance
to Latin American navies. The justifications for these programs included "retain the competence which we have already developed"[23]
and maintain "internal security, "[24] in addition to military justifications phrased in terms of an external threat.

The military assistance program for fiscal year 1965 presented
to the Congress included 24% of the total for "Naval defense."[25]
However, the extent of the change in American military assistance
is indicated by the fact that, when queried about the value of Latin
American navies, General Taylor, then Chairman of the Joint Chiefs
of Staff, responded in terms of coastal patrol vessels, not major
vessels like destroyers.[26] General O'Meara, the Unified Commander
responsible for Latin American programs, also spoke in coastal
defense terms but included destroyers within it as essential for
"offshore all-weather surveillance."[27] The Secretary of Defense
stated that the military assistance program for the fiscal year 1965
does not provide a substantial contribution to Latin American
navies, and stressed that only small vessels were being given.[28]

Except for these naval defense programs, military assistance
to Latin America has been focused on internal security and civic
action. Of the fiscal year 1965 program presented to the Congress
for Latin America, Secretary McNamara estimated that 52% was for
internal security and 15% for civic action.[29]

Internal security is a term of art used to apply to training and
equipment provided to meet threats of internal aggression, subversion, insurgency and the like. In light of the attempts by Castro-
communist forces to export their revolution to other Latin American
countries, vigilance on the part of all these nations is clearly required.[30] A variety of events, such as the discovery of a communist arms cache in Venezuela, have brought home to Latin
American nations the immediacy of this threat.

Military assistance to meet this threat consists of equipment
to permit the army, acting in its police-like role, to quickly become
informed of possible dissidence and to move quickly against it.
Thus, the equipment requirements are for light communications
equipment, jeeps, trucks as well as light arms and ammunition. In
countries where the existing road structure is inadequate, internal
security requires the provision of helicopters, transport aircraft
and river patrol craft.

The claim that military assistance is one of the causes of militarism in Latin America has caused the Congress to require a
special determination by the President before internal security can
be used as a basis for programming assistance for Latin America.[31]
This requirement has probably slowed the implementation of the

Latin American military assistance program. For example, the
funds for fiscal 1964 programs for most Latin American countries
were not available until the fiscal year was three-fourths completed. [32] This provision is a holdover from the days when the
Executive Branch was selling military assistance to Congress on
the basis that it was required for defense against external attack.
Working on that theory the Congress limited assistance which did
not contribute to that defense. Now, though the general feeling as
to the nature of the problem in Latin America has changed in both
the United States and in Latin America, this provision remains as
a tribute to an older policy.

"Civic action" refers to the use of military forces in projects
which contribute to economic and social development. In many cases
projects of this type may resemble economic aid, and indeed, some
sharp congressional questioning has occurred in an attempt to prove
that it is economic aid hidden in defense programs. [33]

The emphasis on civic action projects, supported by United
States economic and military assistance programs, in large part
stems from one of the studies prepared for the President's Committee to Study the Military Assistance Program (Draper Committee)
in 1959. [34] This study concluded that:

The military establishments of our own and friendly nations
have the human and material resources for making important
contributions to economic as well as to military phases of
our foreign aid program--particularly in underdeveloped
areas.

and recommended use of military assistance funds to encourage this
type of activity. [35]

As the study pointed out, civic action was by no means a new
idea in the United States. In the early history of the United States
the Army had provided engineering instructors at civilian institutions, built roads and canals and opened the American West. The
United States Army Engineers even today continue to carry responsibilities for many dams and flood control measures as well as
harbor maintenance.

United States military assistance policy did not result in the
creation of civic action programs by the military in Latin America

or elsewhere in the world. Instead it assisted in projects which were
underway in many countries, encouraged new projects in those
countries and attempted to spread the idea to countries which had not
adopted it. The Draper Committee provided some typical examples
of civic action underway by 1959:

> In Argentina the Army has built bridges, cleaned canals
> and erected and repaired telephone lines. In Bolivia the
> armed forces conduct farming, lumbering, water transporta-
> tion and air freight operations. In Brazil, Brazilian Army
> engineers did more than 50 percent of all railway and highway
> construction and a naval gunfactory built automobile parts.
> The Dominican Republic navy operated a fishing fleet. In
> El Salvador the Air Force was being used for crop dusting
> and the Haitian Air Force operated all domestic passenger
> and cargo air services. In Paraguay the Air Force con-
> ducted mapping operations and the Army trained heavy
> equipment operators.

This type of activity was expressly approved by the Congress
which wrote into the Foreign Assistance Act the following section:

> To the extent feasible and consistent with the other
> purposes of this part, the use of military forces in less
> developed friendly countries in the construction of public
> works and other activities helpful to economic develop-
> ment shall be encouraged. [36]

For fiscal year 1965 the Administration requested an appropriation of almost $10 million for the encouragement of civic
action in 14 countries in Latin America. The assistance proposed
included such items as engineer equipment and training for
engineer battalions in various countries.

There is a general consensus on the part of journalists and
American scholars that by any standard of reasonableness the military budgets maintained by most Latin American governments are
much too large and the forces which those budgets support are an
unnecessary drain on Latin American economies. This consensus
has been reflected in United States policy. The only question for
American policymakers has been which segment of Latin American
forces should be reduced. During the 1950's, Administration
spokesmen were anxious to point out that the United States supported

only those forces designed for defense of the hemisphere. In 1960,
in no Latin American country did the local military units receiving
United States grant aid constitute more than one-sixth of the total
personnel of the local armed forces.[37] The shift in policy to internal security and civic action resulted in a change from the policy
of providing complete support to a fraction of the recipient forces to
providing a fraction of support to practically all of the recipient
country's forces. However, the drive for reduction of Latin American armaments continued.

In 1960 a Republican Assistant Secretary of State for Inter-
American Affairs stated publicly about military aid:

> ...I would like to make clear that this program is not
> designed to encourage participating countries to undertake
> heavy military expenditures. The program does not consti-
> tute U.S. endorsement, direct or implied, of the present
> size and character of Latin American military establishments.
> Although Latin American countries have the sovereign right
> to determine their own military requirements, we believe that
> most of them could reduce their military expenditures without
> jeopardizing their security.[38]

In 1963 a Democratic Coordinator of the Alliance for Progress
was saying:

> I know that much of the military spending is for such high
> priority missions as internal security and civic action. Yet
> I feel that money may be being spent for lower priority
> purposes, and expenditures for such purposes may result
> in the non-availability of resources needed for high
> priority economic and social development tasks.[39]

These judgments that the Latin American military forces are too
large are judgments which imply a determination that the forces are
larger than the military threat which they are designed to meet require them to be. By any quantative standard Latin American forces
are quite small in comparison to those of most nations of the
Middle East and the Far East. However, in the case of Latin
America there seems little probability of an overt communist attack
and in the event of such an attack, United States naval forces could
no doubt readily handle the problem. The last war fought among
Latin American states was that between Paraguay and Bolivia which

ended in 1935. Each year the probability of another such war seems to decrease. If one makes these assumptions, there is little or no reason for significant military forces in Latin America, either from the point of view of the United States or that of the nations themselves. As Senator Aiken put it after an inspection trip in Latin America:

> It is difficult, therefore, to make a military case for Latin American military establishments beyond the kinds of national guards which are maintained by Costa Rica and Panama. [40]

The critical question is not whether Latin American military establishments are overly large--this is widely recognized--but to what extent military aid has contributed to this situation. The normal criticisms of United States military aid to Latin America assume that there is a direct relationship between such aid and militarism in Latin America. Thus, military aid is held responsible for encouraging coups, diverting money from economic development to military purposes and encouraging an arms race in Latin America.

Essential to consideration of the impact of United States military aid is consideration of its magnitude in relation to the military budgets financed by the Latin American nations themselves. The following table compares the defense expenditures of Latin American countries in calendar 1963 with military assistance deliveries in fiscal year 1964 (July, 1963, to June, 1964--United States government statistics are generally only available on this basis).

DEFENSE BUDGETS AND MILITARY AID[41]
($ million)

	Defense Budget	FY 1964 Military Aid Deliveries	Military Aid As Percent of Country Effort
Argentina	$342.0	$ 2.5	.7%
Bolivia	8.5	2.4	28.2
Brazil	565.0	17.5	3.1
Chile	109.0	9.2	8.4
Colombia	62.0	5.9	9.5
Costa Rica	3.5	.4	11.4

	Defense Budget	FY 1964 Military Aid Deliveries	Military Aid As Percent of Country Effort
Dominican Republic	$ 33.0	$ 1.4	4.2%
Ecuador	19.5	3.1	15.9
El Salvador	9.2	1.0	10.9
Guatemala	11.0	1.6	14.5
Honduras	4.0	.3	7.5
Mexico	119.0	.4	.3
Nicaragua	8.0	1.1	13.7
Panama	1.3	.3	23.0
Paraguay	11.4	1.2	10.5
Peru	97.0	10.2	10.4
Uruguay	21.0	1.6	7.6
Venezuela	140.0	1.3	.9
	$1563.4	$61.5	3.9

As this table indicates, military assistance deliveries have amounted to less than 4% of the defense budget expenditures of Latin American nations receiving military assistance. [42] These estimates exclude the excess stocks given to Latin American nations, which even when valued at their original price were less than 10% of the Latin American military aid program in fiscal year 1964, and the costs of training not charged to the military assistance program. They also exclude the value of naval vessels transferred from the mothball fleet, but include the costs of repairing and overhauling vessels. They do not compensate for possible overcharges. These inclusions and exclusions probably cancel each other out. Sales are also excluded.

As is readily apparent from the table, military assistance was an insignificant part of the total effort of Argentina, Mexico and Venezuela. At the time the programs, which produced deliveries in fiscal 1964, were formulated, Argentina and Mexico had not signed military assistance bilateral agreements with the United States and were therefore ineligible for substantial grant aid. Venezuela meets its military requirements by purchase.

In the remaining countries military assistance represents a significant part of the country's defense effort, ranging from a low

of 3.1% in Brazil to a high of 23% in Bolivia. The United States contribution is particularly significant because it normally takes the
form of equipment and training. The Latin American national defense
budgets must absorb the costs of pay of military personnel, gasoline,
maintenance costs and the like, leaving little available for equipment.
As a result, although military assistance is only a comparatively
small portion of the country budgets it probably accounts for a large
portion of the new equipment introduced into the military inventory
of many of these countries. Thus, it must be concluded that although
the present emphasis on internal security and civic action may
change the situation, the United States emphasis on hemispheric
defense, the large American military missions in Latin America and
deliveries under the military assistance program have probably influenced at least some Latin American nations to maintain military
establishments larger than they would have maintained in the absence
of this assistance. On the other hand, however, it is clearly er-
roneous to assume that military aid has "caused" the high level of
defense preparations in Latin America or that these large expenditures
are required solely to maintain equipment furnished by the United
States.

MILITARY AID AND MILITARY COUPS

Substantial quantities of academic and Congressional criticism
have been heaped on the military aid program in Latin America for
causing military coups and hindering the achievement of economic
and social programs. Typical of the Congressional criticism is an
article written by Senator Ernest Gruening in 1962. Senator
Gruening asserted that ten years of military aid from this country
to our southern neighbors have actually hurt the Latin American
countries and made them even more unstable.[43] As examples the
Senator chose Argentina--where there was at the time no substantial
grant materiel assistance and military aid was less than 1% of the
defense budget--and Peru.

It is difficult to test the hypothesis that military aid causes
military coups. However, the attempt can be made by trying to
determine whether (1) the coups could not have taken place without
arms provided by the United States, (2) United States military
training given to Latin American students has encouraged them to
overthrow established governments and (3) whether the number of
coups has increased proportionate to increasing United States
military aid.

It is doubtful that the arms provided under military aid have ever been necessary for any military coup in Latin America. Use of American-provided arms, as in the case of Peru, has occurred, but as military assistance represents only a small part of the total military expenditures in Latin American countries, it can be assumed that other arms would be available. Given the political power of the Latin American armed forces, it can also be assumed that basic arms, such as rifles and machine guns, would have been purchased somewhere if not available from the United States. These factors are coupled with the fact that the military coup in Latin America seems to require only a small force for its execution. As the United States Commander in Chief for the Caribbean area put it:

> There are plenty of arms in Latin America to over-
> throw any number of governments if we had never given
> them one rifle, if we had never given them one truck. [44]

The exercise of comparing coups before and after military aid was performed by Secretary of Defense McNamara before a Congressional committee in 1964. He argued that in the last 15 years there had been 37 illegal and unscheduled changes of government, "not counting 5 assassinations." Only Chile, Mexico and Uruguay had no such experience during that period of time. In the preceding 20 years, prior to the beginning of our military assistance programs, there were 42 such changes of government. [45] Using McNamara's figures the pre-military aid rate of coups was 2.1 per year and the post-military aid rate was about 2.5 coups per year, all of which undoubtedly proves, as McNamara put it, that "This is a condition that existed before military aid." [46]

The final and most difficult question is whether the association with United States officers and men in the military missions and in training installations in the United States has encouraged the Latin American military forces to attempt to overthrow governments. Most of the evidence seems to be to the contrary.

The Defense Department has nothing but praise for the effect of the military assistance training programs. The Secretary of Defense said in 1964 that:

> ...The association of the Latin American military officers
> with the U.S. institutions and associations fostered by the
> training programs which are financed by the military

assistance program has introduced concepts of democracy
from which the Latin American nations have benefited. [47]

The Chairman of the Joint Chiefs of Staff has quoted an Argentine
official as stating:

> . . . one of the high spots of his association and that of
> his people with the U.S. military mission down there
> is the very fine professional attitude of our people and
> the influence that they have in directing the Argentines
> toward the professional part of their lives rather than
> toward the political. [48]

Academic writers, though generally quite critical of some of
the materiel programs, have on the whole lauded the impact of
military training. [49]

Some of the most fertile sources of unbiased evaluation of
military assistance training programs are the Congressional
groups which frequently visit countries receiving United States aid
and write reports evaluating those programs. These reports
have supported the training program and the influence of United
States military personnel without exception, though many have
been critical of the rest of the military aid program in Latin
America.

Senators McClellan, Mansfield, Smith, Bible and Hruska
visited seven Latin American countries in 1961 and concluded
that:

> Military officers who have been trained in the United
> States are among our staunchest supporters. They are
> a strong anti-Communist core. [50]

Senators McGee, Moss, Engle and Young reported, on their
return from Latin America, on support of training of Latin
American personnel in United States schools. They concluded:

> Moreover, the visiting military personnel are exposed
> to democratic principles and the American Way of Life.
> The United States of America--our democratic govern-
> ment, our mode of life--makes a deep impression upon
> those who see us at work and as we really are. Returnees

tell the story to their relatives and friends and it is believed. [51]

This report went considerably further than many by suggesting that the United States ought to take a more favorable stance toward the military in most Latin American countries. The Senators concluded:

While we carefully looked for evidence that military force was serving as a deterrent to democratic processes, our conclusions are to the contrary. In all instances the military groups seemed not only to be stabilizing influences but likewise to be actually promoting democratic institutions and progressive social and economic changes.

The group quoted Adlai Stevenson as having said that the Army is "providing democracy's strongest bulwark and most constructive promoter" in Latin America. [52]

On the basis of this evidence, it seems logical to conclude that the impact of the training portion of the military aid given to Latin American countries has not been to encourage military coups.

INTERNAL SECURITY ASSISTANCE

Providing military assistance for internal security purposes in Latin America presents a particularly difficult problem. Internal security assistance is, by definition, provision of arms and equipment to help the government in power stay in power. To some extent civic action serves the same purpose, as one of its announced and frequently achieved objectives is closer relations between the military and the local population, thereby permitting the military to be more effective in winning locals away from dissident elements.

In most Latin American countries the government in power is military or the government in power exists because the military has not chosen to exercise its "veto power" over who shall govern. Assistance for internal security purposes undoubtedly has the effect of propagating this system--although such assistance does not cause the situation and it is probable that Latin American military establishments would easily be able to maintain this situation without United States assistance.

The first policy problem--which can seriously be analyzed only on a country by country basis--is whether the existing system works to the advantage of the United States. The second problem is, assuming that the system is sufficiently to the advantage of the United States so that no serious United States effort should be made to change it, should the United States associate itself with the system by providing military aid for internal security?

On the whole, the present system, whereby the military has a veto power over the nature of governments in all but a few Latin American countries, tends to guarantee to the United States that few, if any, governments in Latin America will fall into communist hands. In the case of Guatemala in the 1950's and more recently, Brazil, military intervention, and only military intervention, prevented communist or fellow traveler takeover of these important countries. At least in the short run, the present role of the military establishments is a guarantee against disruption of these countries and permits attainment of economic development objectives on a reasonable schedule--though perhaps not as fast as would be the case if civilian authorities were in undiluted control. On the more Machiavellian side, those military establishments also tend to produce governments--both military and ostensibly civilian--which support United States policy in the United Nations and the Organization of American States. Because these governments do not tend toward measures which are "radical" in the American view, "expropriation" of United States mining and industrial interests is less likely under the "system."[53]

One of the most frequently stated criticisms of the "system" is the simple fact that it offends traditional Anglo-Saxon ideas of democracy. Another more practical objection is the argument that the system is likely, in the long run, to produce the opposite of the results intended. So long as the military, which is a relatively conservative force, effectively determines who shall govern, the non-communist left of peasant groups and labor groups is forced to make common cause with the communists. It is probably fair to generalize that communist movements have normally been successful or close to successful only when contesting a rightist government in conjunction with non-communist groups in circumstances that do not permit differentiation between communist and non-communist. Such circumstances present an ideal environment for identification of communist policy with aims and ideals shared by a wide range of the non-communist population and thus permit

infiltration of non-communist groups, such as trade unions, by communists. While the military may be capable of using force to control
such a combination, as in the cases of Bolivia, Brazil and Guatemala,
situations may arise when no conglomeration of troops and weapons
will be successful, as was the case in Cuba. [54]

If it is assumed that the "system" does not serve United States
interests in Latin America, it is clear that the United States should
neither support the "system" by military assistance for internal
security purposes, nor become identified with it by awards of de-
corations to members of military juntas or favorable treatment of
the leaders of governments established by military intervention.

If it is assumed that United States interests are served by the
"system," it does not necessarily follow that United States assistance should be provided for internal security. If the military in
these countries can command sufficient resources to take care of
their equipment needs (albeit at the expense of economic development),
United States assistance is not required to preserve the system, and
the cutting off of United States assistance would at least reduce the
identification of the United States with the system should it collapse
in any country.

However, easy abstention from the whole problem is probably
impossible in most countries as (1) United States assistance can
improve the odds that the military will be successful in maintaining
its position against dissident groups and (2) withdrawal of United
States assistance for internal security might well cause military
controlled governments to adopt a number of policies not associated
with United States desires for Latin America and to accept outside
assistance from European nations and perhaps from the communists
if it were offered. [55]

CONCLUSION

United States military assistance to Latin America began long
before the formal military assistance programs were inaugurated
after World War II. Prior to 1960 these programs stressed common
action for the defense of the hemisphere and were marked by the
absense of over-all policy control of the actions of Army, Navy and
Air missions to Latin American nations. Although some of the old
policies persist, there has been a sharp shift away from emphasis

on hemispheric defense against external attack toward defense against subversion. Programs for this purpose have concentrated on furnishing equipment and training for internal security and civic action.

Although the question is widely disputed, the weight of the evidence appears to be that military assistance has not "caused" military coups in Latin America. However, the tradition of military intervention in politics raises difficult questions of the extent to which the United States should permit itself to become identified with the Latin American military forces.

NOTES

1. The historical material in this chapter which is not specifically footnoted is taken from standard works on Latin American history and politics and from W. A. Brown and R. Opie, American Foreign Assistance (Washington: The Brookings Institution, 1953); Edwin Lieuwen, Arms and Politics in Latin America (New York: Praeger, 1960) and Mr. Lieuwen's various articles cited in the bibliography.

2. Brown and Opie, op. cit., p. 7.

3. TIAS 1838. All nations but Guatemala, Honduras and Nicaragua accepted without reservation.

4. See Brown and Opie, op. cit., Chapter 17 for a description of this legislation.

5. Quoted in Department of State Bulletin, April 9, 1951.

6. These estimates represent the cost of assistance to the United States and, therefore, differ from Lieuwen's statistics, op. cit., p. 202, which treat excess items as though they were newly purchased. The estimate shown for fiscal 1965 excludes regional costs included in the figures for prior years.

7. TIAS 2560.

8. This series, published by the Department of State, contains all significant treaties and Executive Agreements to which the United States is a party.

9. Much of the material in this section has been suggested by Morris Janowitz's challenging essay, The Military in the Political Development of New Nations (Chicago: University of Chicago Press, 1964) even though it is not intended to apply to Latin America. Articles by John Johnson, Edwin Lieuwen and Victor Alba in John J. Johnson (ed.), The Role of the Military in Underdeveloped Countries (Princeton, N. J.: Princeton University Press, 1962),

Lieuwen's Arms and Politics in Latin America, op. cit., William S.
Stokes' Latin American Politics (New York: Crowell, 1959) and
John Johnson's The Military and Society in Latin America (Stanford:
Stanford University Press, 1964) have also been useful as have the
innumerable Congressional studies, hearings, reports and other
books listed in the bibliography.

10. Data from the Selected Statistics, Appendix Tables 12 and
13 to the Report of the President's Committee to Study the Military
Assistance Program, (Draper Committee) (Washington: U.S. Government Printing Office, 1959).

11. TIAS 2442, TIAS 4455 and TIAS 4653.

12. Draper Committee Report, op. cit.

13. Executive Order 10893 of November 8, 1960.

14. Also November 8, 1960.

15. Letter to Chiefs of Mission, May 29, 1961. This letter and
other documents relating to the role of the Ambassador as well as
a summary of their contents are collected in a handy reference
pamphlet published by the Jackson Subcommittee, U.S., Congress,
Senate, Committee on Government Operations, The Ambassador
and the Problem of Coordination, 88th Cong., 1st Sess., 1963.

16. Testimony of Roy Rubottom, HAC, CY 60, p. 1880.

17. Testimony of Brigadier General Hartel, HAC, CY 60,
p. 2543.

18. Testimony of Brigadier General Enemark, HFAC, CY
62, p. 268.

19. HFAC, CY 62, p. 268.

20. HFAC, CY 60, p. 840.

21. HFAC, CY 62, pp. 269-279.

22. HFAC, CY 64, p. 98.

23. Testimony of General O'Meara, HFAC, CY 62, p. 271.

24. Ibid., p. 275.

25. HFAC, CY 64, p. 93.

26. HFAC, CY 64, p. 108.

27. Ibid., p. 402.

28. SFRC, CY 64, p. 542.

29. HFAC, CY 64, p. 92. The remainder was for naval defense
(24%) and for "general training" and "programs which have not been
developed in detail."

30. For a pre-Castro treatment of the problem, see Robert J.
Alexander's Communism in Latin America (New Brunswick, N.J.:
Rutgers University Press, 1957). More recent evidence is col-
lected in U.S., Congress, House, Committee on Foreign Affairs,
Castro-Communist Subversion in Latin America, Hearings of the

Subcommittee on Latin America of the House Foreign Affairs Committee, 87th Cong., 2d Sess., 1962 and the testimony of General
Andrew O'Meara before the full House Foreign Affairs Committee
in 1964. HFAC, CY 64, pp. 401-425.

31. Sec. 511(b) of the FAA of 1961.

32. Testimony of General O'Meara before the House Foreign
Affairs Committee. On April 14, 1964, General O'Meara stated
that only $3 million of $52 million had been approved. This was
only two and one-half months before the end of the fiscal year.
HFAC, CY 64, p. 403.

33. See an exchange between Congressman Passman and
Secretary McNamara, HAC, CY 64, pp. 341-342 and between
Congressman Passman and General Robert J. Wood, HAC, CY
64, pp. 531-533.

34. Annex D to the Draper Committee Report, op. cit. The
Annex, prepared by the Committee's staff, is entitled "Contributions of Military Resources to Economic and Social Progress."

35. Ibid., p. 119 in the version printed as a Congressional
document. House Document No. 215, Part 2, 86th Cong., 1st
Sess., 1959.

36. Section 505 (b). A similar statement appeared in the Mutual
Security Act.

37. HAC, CY 60, p. 1880.

38. Testimony of Roy Rubottom, HAC, CY 60, p. 1880.

39. Mr. Theodore Moscoso in a speech delivered on July 18,
1963 and reported in the press the following day.

40. U.S., Congress, Senate, Committee on Foreign Relations,
Latin America: Venezuela, Brazil, Peru, Bolivia and Panama,
Report of Senator George D. Aiken, 86th Cong., 2d Sess., 1959.

41. Defense budget estimates taken from HAC, CY 64, p. 515.
All figures are calendar year except those for Argentina, Colombia,
Guatemala and Nicaragua which are data for fiscal years ending in
October 1963, December 1962, June 1964 and June 1964, respective-
ly. Military assistance data is taken from Military Assistance Facts.
While the defense budgets and the military assistance deliveries do
not cover exactly the same time period, the data tends to be com-
parable as defense budgets do not rapidly change in most countries.
Military aid figures exclude "regional costs" and Jamaica.

42. Mr. Frank Sloan, a Defense Department Deputy Assistant
Secretary, estimated 6% before the House Foreign Affairs Committee in 1964. HFAC, CY 64, pp. 502-503.

43. Ernest Gruening, "Exporting Trouble," The Nation,
October 6, 1962.

44. Testimony of General O'Meara, HFAC, CY 64, p. 425.
45. SAC, CY 64, pp. 230-231.
46. Ibid., p. 231.
47. Ibid.
48. Testimony of General Wheeler, Ibid.
49. See, for example, Edwin Lieuwen, "Militarism and Politics in Latin America," in John Johnson (ed.), Role of Military in Under-Developed Countries, op. cit., pp. 162-163 and John J. Johnson, "The Latin-American Military as a Politically Competing Group in Transitional Society," Role of Military in Underdeveloped Countries, p. 129. Also see Johnson, Military and Society in Latin America, op. cit.
50. U.S., Congress, Senate, Committee on Appropriations, Special Report on Latin America: United States Activities in Mexico, Panama, Peru, Chile, Argentina, Brazil and Venezuela, 87th Cong., 2d Sess., 1962.
51. U.S., Congress, Senate, Study Mission to South America, February, 1962, (four different committees represented), 87th Cong., 2d Sess., 1962.
52. Ibid., pp. 10-11.
53. The line of analysis above is to be found in a wide variety of books and articles advocating "realism" and "national interest" in United States foreign policy. A number of other analyses have pointed to the fact that the military is, on the whole, more anti-communist than any other organized group in Latin America and can be a significant modernizing force. See, for example, the excellent analysis in Johnson, Military and Society in Latin America, op. cit.
54. This argument is presented in Robert J. Alexander, Communism in Latin America, op. cit. It is important to note that Alexander's argument is based upon the premise that the non-communist left may have to depose the military by force and that the United States should not hinder such action by strengthening the military. It is probable that many United States policymakers would not be entirely happy with the policies of the non-communist left which Alexander favors.
55. The reader looking for a conclusion will be disappointed as the author does not feel qualified to offer one. It should, however, be stated that conclusions on a regional basis are dangerous, as the relevance of the "system" varies markedly from country to country in Latin America.

CHAPTER 5   MILITARY ASSISTANCE TO EUROPE

The story of United States military assistance in Europe[1] is primarily a simple historical story of a program which was in the 1950's a cornerstone of United States policies, which has become in the 1960's an unhappy millstone left over from the past. The magnitude of this change can be seen from the fact that as recently as fiscal year 1957 military assistance deliveries to Europe were greater than the total military assistance request for all countries in fiscal year 1965.

The Mutual Defense Assistance Act of 1949 and the Mutual Security Act of 1951 stressed military aid to Europe almost to the exclusion of programs in other areas. The large military assistance authorizations made in 1950 for European military buildup were not translated into substantial deliveries until several years later because of inability of United States military production facilities to meet the demands of the Korean War and assistance to Europe at the same time. However, production capability soon began to increase and the large appropriations of the early 1950's began to be spent. Some indication of the downturn since that time can be seen from the following table of military aid deliveries to Europe:[2]

Fiscal Year of Delivery	Amount ($ Million)	Percent of Total Military Aid
1951	604.6	62
1952	1013.9	68
1953	2845.0	68
1954	2168.7	66
1955	1496.6	62
1956	1738.9	59
1957	1344.4	65
1958	906.3	39
1959	694.8	34
1960	796.0	42
1961	538.9	40
1962	411.6	29
1963	391.9	22
1964 (est)	369.3	27
1965 (est)	293.3	23

This decline is even more pronounced when programs (new commitments of funds) are considered. Europe accounted for 28% of the grant aid program in fiscal year 1961, 20% in fiscal year 1962 and only 4.7% in fiscal year 1966.

COUNTRIES CUT OFF FROM ASSISTANCE

The largest military assistance expenditures were for the purpose of developing adequate NATO forces, especially in the NATO Central Front. The primary recipients of this assistance were Germany, the United Kingdom, Luxembourg, France, Belgium, the Netherlands and Italy. The granting of equipment to these countries has recently been terminated due to the obvious ability of these countries to carry their own defense burdens.

As the increased economic strength of European nations became apparent in the late 1950's and the American public and Congress began to realize that the United States was spending a larger portion of its national budget and gross national product for defense than the European nations which were receiving large quantities of United States military aid, the continuation of military aid to these countries began to be sharply questioned. This questioning was reinforced by increasing recognition that the United States might soon face a significant balance of payments crisis. The continued spiraling costs of domestic programs required decreases in foreign aid if the federal budget were to remain close to being balanced. In addition to these factors, numerous members of Congress had been encouraging President Eisenhower to de-emphasize the military aspects of the foreign aid program.

The result of these pressures was a decision made during fiscal year 1960 "to cut off military assistance progressively to countries capable of providing and maintaining their own military forces."[3]

This decision, reinforced by the Kennedy Administration, resulted in termination of new commitments to give grant military aid materiel on the following schedule:

Fiscal year 1960: Germany, United Kingdom, Luxembourg

Fiscal year 1961: France

Fiscal year 1962: Belgium, Netherlands and Italy[4]

However, these decisions were not quickly reflected in the requests for new funds for military aid to Europe because of commitments previously made. The Executive Branch requested $314.6
million for military aid to Europe for fiscal year 1963. Of that
amount almost $250 million was reported to be to cover commitments
made before July 1, 1961. [5] In addition to the necessity to cover old
commitments, deliveries to these "cut off" countries continued to be
substantial because some of the equipment programmed in previous
years was just coming off the production line and being delivered.
As a result of these factors, estimated deliveries to these countries
as late as fiscal year 1965 (July 1, 1964, to June 30, 1965) were over
$150 million as shown on the following table:

Country	Value of Military Aid Delivered ($ millions)
Belgium	$ 6.3
France	4.1
Germany	.2
Italy	103.2
Luxembourg	0
Netherlands	50.2
United Kingdom	.4
TOTAL	$164.4

Even after June, 1965 the United States still had to make deliveries
of $13.5 million worth of equipment and services to these countries.
These deliveries are commitments in the sense that the recipient
countries have been advised that the United States will provide this
equipment and have no doubt taken steps to prepare for its use.

In light of the substantial programs which had been carried out
in the past for these and other European nations and the large back-
log of deliveries yet to be made from previous appropriations, the
Congress in 1962 added a provision to the Foreign Assistance Act
which stated:

The President shall regularly reduce and, with such
deliberate speed as orderly procedure and other relevant
considerations, including prior commitments, will permit, shall terminate all further grants of military equipment and supplies to any country having sufficient wealth

to enable it, in the judgment of the President, to maintain
and equip its own military forces at adequate strength, without undue burden to its economy. [6]

After hearing the programs proposed by the Executive Branch in
1963, Congress adopted a stiffer provision against assistance to these
nations which, unlike the 1962 provision, required termination instead of implying that it should occur. This provision flatly stated
that:

No assistance shall be furnished on a grant basis under
this Act to any economically developed nation capable of
sustaining its own defense burden and economic growth.

Exceptions were granted for commitments made prior to July, 1963,
and for limited training programs. [7]

The Congress in 1963 also wrote into law a provision which
prohibited the furnishing of assistance to any country which did
not take appropriate steps to prevent its ships and aircraft from
transporting goods to Cuba. [8] When this provision came into effect
in early 1964, all assistance was totally terminated to both the
United Kingdom and France which had refused to comply with its
provisions. [9]

Despite the phasing down of military assistance programs to
various economically developed nations of Western Europe, the
United States continued to maintain military assistance advisory
groups in most of these countries. The following table shows the
estimated average strength of these units for the period from
July of 1965 to June of 1966:

Country	U.S. Military	U.S. Civilians	Total
Belgium	25	7	32
France	9	1	10
Germany	96	22	118
Italy	38	7	45
Luxembourg (combined with Belgium)			
Netherlands	25	2	27
TOTAL	193	39	232

These groups, of course, have no responsibility for the planning
of grant aid, but are retained in these countries to observe and report on the utilization of materiel furnished and personnel trained by
the military assistance program, to administer military assistance
sales transactions and to arrange for the delivery of material from
programs funded prior to the cut-off of grant aid.

The military personnel in these groups are paid by the Army,
Navy or Air Force just as though they were assigned in the United
States. The civilians are paid from military aid funds. Some of
the expenses of these groups, especially in these countries, are offset
by contributions by the countries themselves. In the standard form
military assistance bilateral agreement, which these nations signed
at the beginning of grant military aid in 1950-51, there is a clause
requiring some country contributions. The clause in the agreement
with France is typical:

> Subject to the provision of the necessary appropriations,
> the Government of the Republic of France undertakes to make
> available to the Government of the United States of America
> francs for the use of the latter Government for its administra-
> tive expenses within France in connection with carrying out
> this Agreement...

Certain host countries also provide "assistance in kind" in the form
of housing and office space, services and equipment for use by the
Military Assistance Advisory Groups. The following table shows the
value of these reimbursements for fiscal year 1963.[10]

Cut-off Country	Currency Contributed by Host Country ($)	Estimated Value of Equipment and Services Furnished "in Kind"
Belgium	$179,860	--
France	151,760	$ 600
Germany	195,560	75,430
Italy	315,470	965
Luxembourg (no MAAG)		
Netherlands	135,490	42,570
United Kingdom	55,710	--
TOTAL	$982,850	$119,565

Although these contributions do not normally totally offset the costs
of United States Military Assistance Advisory Groups, the contribution, over $1,000,000 in fiscal year 1963, is certainly significant. [11]

These contributions are not available to the administrators of
military aid to reduce expenditures which are made from the foreign
aid appropriation. Instead the contributed currencies are given to
the Treasury which sells the local currencies back to administrators of programs using them--including military aid--in return for
dollars from regular appropriations. This procedure, required by
Section 1415 of the Supplemental Appropriations Act of 1953, is
designed to prevent "backdoor" financing of projects without the
Congressional review that is necessary in the case of regular appropriations.

Military assistance programs to these seven countries where
assistance has now been cut off totaled some $10,857 million, over
a third of all the military assistance ever provided by the United
States. The distribution of this amount among the countries is
shown below.

Grant Aid Programs
FY 1950-64
($ millions)

Belgium	$ 1,236
France	4,158
Germany	901
Italy	2,301
Luxembourg	8
Netherlands	1,218
United Kingdom	1,035
TOTAL	$10,857

Assistance to all these countries but Germany began shortly after
the passage of the Mutual Defense Assistance Act of 1950. Assistance to Germany did not begin until 1955-56 when German rearmament
was underway. This assistance was substantially less than that provided to France with roughly comparable forces because the aid to
Germany did not begin until a time when Germany was economically
in a position to pay for much of its own military effort.

Initially, United States military assistance to these countries
was designed to provide a modicum of military strength in NATO's
Central Front. The United States provided from United States or
European production large quantities of fighter aircraft, trainers,
naval vessels, and basic equipment, such as artillery, communications and transportation for ground forces. In the late 1950's in
recognition of increasing European defense budgets, United States
assistance was used to provide more sophisticated equipment, such
as missiles, and the Europeans themselves provided for more
standard weapons and much of the costs of maintenance and spare
parts for older equipment. The gradual decrease in the role played
by military assistance is evident from the fact that it dropped from
20% of the defense efforts to these countries to less than one percent in the ten years from 1953 to 1963.

Year (calendar)	Military Aid Deliveries	Country Efforts ($ millions)	Aid as % of Country Effort
1953	$2,056	$ 9,058	23%
1958	423	11,392	3%
1963	171	17,288	1%

When announced military assistance policy began to call for the
provision of more sophisticated equipment in the late 1950's, the
"nuclear issue" had to be faced. NATO tactical doctrine at the
time apparently called for more emphasis on the improvement of
tactical firepower with modern weapons, rather than the augmenta-
tion of existing forces with older weapons.[12] The Administration
reported to Congress in 1960 that it was delivering a variety of
nuclear-capable missiles to European NATO countries, including
CORPORAL surface-to-surface missiles, HONEST JOHN rockets,
MACE and SERGEANT surface-to-surface missiles, NIKE air
defense missiles and JUPITER and THOR intermediate range
ballistic missiles.[13] The intermediate range ballistic missiles
were withdrawn shortly after they were installed.

Under the Atomic Energy Act the United States cannot give
atomic warheads to foreign governments.[14] In compliance with the
Atomic Energy Act the United States began to negotiate two types
of agreements with various European countries. The first type were
agreements by which American forces maintain custody and control
of nuclear weapons. The second type are agreements for the
sharing of atomic information with these governments.[15] Agreements

for cooperation on the use of atomic energy for mutual defense purposes were signed with Belgium in May, 1962, [16] with France in May,
1959 and in July, 1961, [17] with Germany in May, 1959, [18] with Greece
in May, 1959, [19] with Italy in 1960, [20] with the Netherlands in May,
1959, [21] and with Turkey in May, 1959. [22] The United States and the
United Kingdom have had an agreement for cooperation regarding
atomic information for mutual defense purposes since 1955. [23]

     Although military assistance funds were used to provide a de-
livery capability, such as missiles, these funds were not used for
the procurement or positioning of warheads (which remain under
United States ownership and custody) nor were military aid funds
used to meet the custodial and maintenance costs of the warheads.
Similarly, the costs of classified equipment which remain under United States ownership and custody are not borne by foreign aid funds.
The construction of special ammunition storage sites was considered the responsibility of the NATO country concerned, although
apparently they could be considered a part of NATO infrastructure
costs. [24]

NORWAY AND DENMARK

     Norway and Denmark are both members of NATO. These nations
occupy strategic positions in the northern flank of NATO. As a
study of a map of Europe readily indicates, Russian access to the
waters surrounding the United Kingdom, and in fact to the Atlantic
Ocean itself, is heavily dependent on the ability to traverse the
Danish Straits. Rapid occupation of Norway would give the Soviets
a similar advantage in the event of war in Europe. Both these nations
have recognized the threat which the Soviet Union poses to them and
have decided accordingly to join NATO and to undertake significant
defense efforts.

     In the 1950's military assistance to these countries was based on
the necessity to improve ground forces for defense of the Danish and
Norwegian land masses. At the same time the United States encouraged
the development of air and naval forces in both countries. Later as
the economic capabilities of these countries increased, the United
States made longer term agreements with them under which these
countries and the United States shared the costs of additional defense.

The United States and Norway reached an agreement in 1962 which provides for a United States cost-sharing of ships for Norway and for assistance to the Norwegian Air Force. As late as fiscal year 1964 the United States was also providing army equipment such as M-48 tanks and armored personnel carriers for Norway. In return for the promise of continued United States assistance Norway agreed to increase its own defense budget from $165 million in fiscal year 1962 to at least $214 million by fiscal year 1965. It was anticipated that a substantial part of these increased expenditures would be spent in the United States. The United States portion of the program was expected to run through fiscal year 1967. The assistance to the Norwegian Air Force under this commitment included F-104 fighter bombers and was planned to include F-5 aircraft designed especially for military assistance recipients. [25]

Assistance to Denmark is similarly provided under a United States commitment entered into before July 1, 1963.

Since the initiation of military assistance programs, programs of military assistance to these countries have amounted to $843 million for Norway and $633 million for Denmark. The Norwegians and Danes are ineligible for new commitments to provide United States military aid by virtue of an amendment made in 1963 to the Foreign Assistance Act of 1961. [26] During fiscal year 1966 the United States planned to maintain a Military Assistance Advisory Group of 36 persons in Denmark and of 47 persons in Norway.

SPAIN AND PORTUGAL

Spain and Portugal were not as seriously damaged by World War II as were the countries occupied by the Axis powers. Because these nations were little affected by the war they did not share proportionately in Marshall Plan assistance and did not experience the striking economic growth which occurred in the rest of Europe. Assistance to Spain and Portugal was not cut off when other European nations stopped receiving new commitments for aid in the early 1960's, partly because these countries were less capable of paying the full costs of adequate defense.

Another influential factor in inducing continued United States aid has been the willingness of both countries to let the United States use bases on their territory. Spain provides the United States with

valuable naval and air bases, including a large naval facility at Rota
used for POLARIS submarines. Portugal owns the Azores Islands
which are a convenient stopping-off point for aircraft moving between
the United States and Europe.

Spain is not a member of the North Atlantic Treaty Organization
because some NATO members object to the present Franco government and to Spain's close relations with the Axis powers in World
War II. Portugal is a NATO member.

United States military assistance to Spain began after a mutual
defense assistance agreement was negotiated in connection with
agreements for the development of United States bases.[27] This 1953
agreement was extended for five years by an agreement reached in
September of 1963.[28] The first deliveries of military assistance
to Spain were made in fiscal year 1954. Portugal signed a military
assistance bilateral agreement in 1951 and has received military aid
ever since. Programs for both countries were proposed by the
Executive Branch for fiscal year 1965.

Programs through fiscal 1965 amounted to $327 million to
Portugal and $536 million to Spain since the initiation of military
assistance programs. In fiscal 1966 the Defense Department expected to maintain a Military Assistance Advisory Group of 24 in
Portugal and 103 in Spain.

The Congressional movement to terminate assistance to the
economically viable nations of Western Europe has not included
Spain and Portugal. The reason for this exception was stated by
the Senate Foreign Relations Committee to be the unique situation
regarding United States base rights. The committee did recommend
rapid reduction of the programs to those countries in its report
on the Foreign Assistance Act of 1963.

COMMITMENTS

Despite legislation looking toward termination of United States
military aid to European countries, programs are expected to continue for some time. In 1963, it was estimated that new funds would
be required to fill old commitments to European nations on the following schedule.

($ millions)

Fiscal Year	Amount[29]
1965	99.1
1966	98.6
1967	48.2
1968	14.5

Because deliveries of military equipment generally lag a year or two behind allocation of funds, it appears that the United States will still be delivering military aid to Europe in 1970.

As the years passed and the European nations benefiting from these commitments improved their economic position, these commitments began to be questioned in retrospect. As AID Administrator Bell put it:

I would not argue that this timing in Europe was impeccable. We ended up in the early sixties with some hangover commitments to some military assistance to Europe which were not really necessary by then.[30]

NATO COSTS

The grant aid provided to NATO allies is only a part of the United States contribution to the defense of Europe. The largest United States contribution is, of course, the continuing deployment in Europe of six United States divisions and the commitment in the NATO treaty to consider aggression against other members as aggression against the United States. However, there are also certain secondary costs associated with the United States membership in NATO.

When NATO was formed it was clear that a substantial construction job would be required to permit the buildup of both United States and European forces in Europe. The NATO nations, therefore, agreed that they would jointly finance construction of necessary facilities such as pipelines and airfields. Originally, the United States was responsible for almost half of the costs of these facilities, but the United States share has gradually been reduced, as the table indicates.

Formula Approved (Year)	U.S. %	U.K. %	Fr. %	Ger. %	Other Countries
1951	48.10	17.72	21.52	--	12.66
1952	42.76	13.16	13.16	--	30.92
1952	41.78	8.92	13.76	--	35.54
1953	42.86	11.45	13.75	--	31.94
1957	36.98	9.88	11.87	13.72	27.55
1961	30.85	10.50	12.00	20.00	26.65

The first appropriations for this NATO infrastructure program were made as part of the Mutual Defense Assistance Program, the predecessor of the present military assistance program. In 1953 the program was offered as part of the regular Defense Department budget, but the Senate Armed Services Committee recommended that it continue to be carried as foreign aid.

In 1963 Senator Sparkman questioned the rationale for continuing to carry contributions to NATO infrastructure in the category of foreign aid. Secretary McNamara agreed that there was no particularly strong reason for continuing to treat the program as part of foreign aid.[31] The Senate Foreign Relations Committee's report strongly recommended that the program be taken out of foreign aid and considered as part of the regular Defense Department budget. In light of the fact that no further aid was being provided to most of the European nations, this program did seem out of place in the military aid budget. However, the Defense Department presented the program as a part of the military aid budget when appearing before the Congress in 1964. No question about this action was raised in the Senate Foreign Relations Committee hearings and the Committee's earlier recommendation was not repeated.

As of the end of the fiscal year 1964 the United States expected to have $121.6 million tied up as undelivered balances connected with NATO infrastructure. This large tie-up of funds is the result of the United States system of obligating funds as soon as there is general agreement that a project should begin. Expenditures stemming from these obligations do not occur for some time after the incurring of the obligation.

In addition to construction under the infrastructure budget, NATO also incurs expenses for the operation of SHAPE headquarters and

other military headquarters spread throughout Europe. This budget
is primarily for housekeeping items--pencils, paper, rent, phone
bills, civilian wages and building and vehicle maintenance. Like infrastructure, the military headquarters budget is cost-shared among
the member nations of NATO. The present United States share is
24. 2%.

During the early years of NATO the United States incurred certain other costs for special projects in the NATO area. Major projects of this nature included the Facilities Assistance Program to
build up the military manufacturing capabilities of NATO allies,
cost-shared weapons production projects, a cooperative research
and development program called the Mutual Weapons Development
Program, contributions to the NATO effort to provide a common
supply system (the NATO Maintenance Supply Services Agency) and
the Central European Pipeline System.

CONCLUSION

Military assistance to Europe was designed to assist the European nations, which were recovering from the ravages of World War
II, to develop enough military potential to make NATO a meaningful
deterrent to communist aggression. Judged in these terms, this
assistance was undoubtedly successful.

Programs have continued in Europe due primarily to commitments made in the late 1950's and early 1960's. In retrospect it is
fair to conclude that some of these commitments should not have
been made, but it is likely that they will be fulfilled. Therefore,
some new programs for European nations will continue for some
years, though new commitments are presently prohibited by law.

The costs of United States participation in NATO construction
projects and military headquarters are paid from military assistance appropriations, largely by reason of historical accident. These
costs will continue so long as the United States remains an active
member of the NATO organization.

NOTES

1. For purposes of this discussion two NATO members--Greece
and Turkey--are being treated in a separate chapter.

2. Military Assistance Facts, published by the Department of
Defense, March, 1964, for estimates through fiscal year 1964.
Fiscal year 1965 data from the February, 1965, edition of the same
publication adjusted by the author for comparability.

3. SAC, CY 62, p. 150.

4. Ibid.

5. Ibid., p. 166.

6. Section 506(c) of the Foreign Assistance Act of 1961, as
amended, which was added by the Foreign Assistance Act of 1962.

7. Section 620(m) of the Foreign Assistance Act of 1961, as
amended, added by Section 301(e)(3) of the Foreign Assistance Act
of 1963.

8. Section 620(a)(3) of the Foreign Assistance Act of 1961, as
amended, as added by Section 301(e)(1)(B) of the Foreign Assistance
Act of 1963.

9. Testimony of General Robert Wood, SAC, CY 64, p. 263.
However, the Defense Department pamphlet, Military Assistance
Facts, as late as February, 1965, included funds earmarked for aid
to these two countries.

10. SAC, CY 62, pp. 135-136.

11. The total of contributed currencies in fiscal year 1963 was
estimated to be $3.9 million, including contributions of over $200,000
from Greece, Pakistan, Spain, Japan, Thailand and Italy. Worldwide assistance in kind for the same year was estimated to be $5.5
million. Ibid.

12. See the Legislative Reference Service Study, U.S. Foreign
Aid: Its Purposes, Scope, Administration and Related Information,
86th Cong., 1st Sess., 1959, House Document No. 116, for a
discussion of the military problems in NATO as they affected military aid, pp. 49-56 and material cited therein.

13. HAC, CY 60, pp. 2369-2370.

14. The only exception, a restricted one, is the United Kingdom.
The problem is discussed by former Secretary of State Herter in
hearings in 1960, HFAC, CY 60, p. 32.

15. Testimony of Major General Miller, SAC, CY 60, p. 251.

16. TIAS 5157.

17. TIAS 4268 and RIAS 4867.

18. TIAS 4276.

19. TIAS 4292.

20. TIAS 4764.

21. TIAS 4277.

22. TIAS 4278.

23. TIAS 3322.

24. This description of funding problems is taken from HFAC, CY 60, p. 922.

25. HAC, CY 64, pp. 537-542.

26. Section 620(m) of the Foreign Assistance Act of 1961, as amended.

27. A good short summary of the "Pact of Madrid" and U.S.-Spanish relations can be found in Appendix D to a Study of U.S. Foreign Policy in Western Europe prepared for the Senate Foreign Relations Committee by the Foreign Policy Research Institute of the University of Pennsylvania. All 13 of the special studies prepared for the Foreign Relations Committee are printed in a massive (1473 pages) compilation, U.S., Congress, Senate, Committee on Foreign Relations, United States Foreign Policy, 87th Cong., 1st Sess., Document No. 24, 1961.

28. Testimony of Frank Sloan, HFAC, CY 64, p. 503.

29. HAC, CY 63, p. 158.

30. SFRC, CY 64, p. 259.

31. SFRC, CY 63.

CHAPTER **6** MAJOR PROGRAMS IN THE
NEAR EAST AND SOUTH ASIA:
GREECE, TURKEY, IRAN,
PAKISTAN AND INDIA

Greece, Turkey, Iran, Pakistan and India, in geo-political terms, are important as the major sources of free world power in the so-called soft underbelly of the Soviet Union. These five countries all maintain large military forces. The cost of United States aid to India and Pakistan is kept classified but military assistance programs for the other three countries amounted to $173 million in fiscal year 1964. Four of the countries in this area present particularly interesting problems of military assistance policy because they are at each other's throats. Greece and Turkey have carried on a dispute centered around the status of persons of Turkish nationality on Cyprus, which has at times brought them to the brink of war. Pakistan was originally a part of the British territory of India and was partitioned from India more or less on religious lines. Religious animosities and the fact of partition have served to produce continuous discord between the two nations. This discord has been aggravated by the competing claims of both nations to Kashmir.

GREECE

The Greek-Turkish aid program was one of the first formal United States post-war military assistance efforts. After the end of the Greek-Turkish aid program as a separate entity, military assistance to Greece was continued under the Mutual Defense Assistance Program, Mutual Security Program and, finally, under the Military Assistance Program as part of a total Foreign Assistance Program. All told this military assistance has amounted to over $1.3 billion through fiscal year 1965 and in addition some $113 million worth of excess stocks has been provided. The United States currently maintains a military assistance advisory group in Greece composed of 114 military personnel and 11 civilians.

Of the nations in Western Europe, Greece is the least developed economically. It has a per capita gross national product of about $460. As a result of this comparative poverty, the United States not only provided substantial military aid to Greece, but also supported Greek forces indirectly through defense support. Defense support to Greece was terminated in 1961 but other economic aid

programs were continued at a reduced level. Greece was one of the
first nations which the Administrator of the Agency for International
Development could say was being cut off from economic assistance
by reason of its economic growth.[1]

Greece along with Turkey constitute the southern flank of NATO.
The tradition of Congressional reductions in Administration military
aid requests had significant effects on programs for Greece and,
thus, on NATO's strength in this area. For example, as a result
of a 29% cut by the Congress in fiscal year 1964, mitigated somewhat by a transfer to military aid from economic aid, the Greek
program was reduced by 25%. Similar reductions have occurred in
previous years. Because the United States provides most of the
military equipment used by Greece, these reductions have caused
considerable consternation in military circles.

In 1963 the Secretary of Defense read into the record of hearings
before Congressman Passman a report on the military capabilities
of Greek and Turkish forces. The unclassified version of this
document stated:

> Soviet bloc forces confronting Greece and Turkey
> have increased in capabilities during the past 2 years,
> particularly in Bulgaria. Bulgarian Army force structure
> has changed from one of defensive posture consisting of rifle
> divisions and armored brigades to one consisting of motorized
> and armored divisions with offensive capabilities.

> The serious and continuing problem centers around
> current inadequate army equipment levels in Greece and
> Turkey. Improved conventional capabilities of ground
> forces now deployed forward in both Greek and Turkish
> Thrace are essential. Impressive strides have been made
> by the Hellenic and Turkish armed forces in improving
> their combat capability. Greeks and Turks are more than
> willing to discharge their NATO responsibilities and are
> as sturdy allies as we can possibly ask for.

> ... Current posture of Hellenic and Turkish armed
> forces has required great effort and expenditures by the
> United States. It is economically as well as militarily
> unsound not to modernize the armed forces of Greece
> and Turkey in order that they can fulfill their missions
> which are vital from national and NATO viewpoints.[2]

A similar communication was received by the Department of Defense in 1964.[3]

In testimony given in 1964 the Chairman of the Joint Chiefs of Staff quoted a unified commander as having said that, with reference to the level of military assistance, "the armies and navies (of Greece and Turkey) will not be able to hold even their present level of over-all equipment."[4]

Secretary of Defense McNamara told the National Industrial Conference Board in May, 1964 of his concern over the military situation in the southern flank of NATO.[5] In this speech and testimony before Congressional committees, he reported that there has been a substantial improvement of Bulgarian forces along the border facing Greece and Turkey. He said:

Bulgaria now maintains about 10 divisions, some of which have been recently modernized and reinforced by the acquisition of Soviet medium tanks and tactical aircraft.[6]

The problem of the military posture of Greek forces was magnified by reductions made in the military assistance program as a result of a Congressional cut in the proposed program in fiscal year 1963 coupled with increased Vietnam costs and the beginning of a program for India. As a result of these factors a total of $7 million was cut from the fiscal year 1963 program for Greece causing curtailment of programs for vehicles, ammunition, missiles and engineer equipment.[7] The reduction in ammunition cut ammunition stocks in Greece below the level which United States commanders in Greece and General Norstad--then the NATO commander-- believed to be reasonable levels.[8] The following year the program for Greece was again cut substantially from the level which the Defense Department had recommended to the Congress, this time by 25%.

The situation was aggravated by the fact that large portions of the military aid given to Greece are required to maintain the equipment previously provided and for training. In fiscal year 1965, for example, two-thirds of military aid was for "operating" costs.[9] Much of the remaining third was to improve the Greek Air Forces, as was apparently the case in the preceding year.[10] The concern over the equipment of Greek forces quoted above did not include the Greek Air Force. The Air Force is presently equipped with F-84 and F-86 aircraft which the Department of Defense hopes to replace.

Two squadrons of aircraft were once given by Canada to Greece, but at the present time the United States is the sole source of aid for the Greek Air Force. In recent years the United States has been modernizing this force with both F-104 and F-5 aircraft.

Secretary of Defense McNamara told the House Appropriations Committee that:

(1) A percentage of the Greek Army's mobility depends on equipment nearly 20 years old.

(2) Communications capacity is limited by equipment produced in World War II and with only a small percentage of "recently equipped (sic) communications equipment on hand."

(3) The Greek Army was short of trucks, armored personnel carriers, trailers, helicopters, scores of tanks, howitzers and other items of equipment.

(4) The Greek Army, compared to the Bulgarian Army, is at a considerable disadvantage in mobility, particularly in tanks, and it is outnumbered and outranged in artillery.[11]

Another Defense representative stated that:

About 70 percent of army equipment and nearly all navy ships are of World War II type, for which repair parts are no longer available and maintenance costs are becoming prohibitive for continued operations.[12]

Despite pressing needs for economic development the Greek government has made a serious effort to overcome part of this military imbalance by its own efforts. The Greek military budget has been increased from $150 million in 1958 to $180 million in 1963. The seriousness of the situation in Greece also was recognized by NATO nations other than the United States. These nations have committed themselves to provide some military and economic assistance to Greece, and the United States has asked that the effort be "expanded greatly."[13]

TURKEY

Assistance to the government of Turkey began shortly after assistance to Greece as part of the same strategy (Truman Doctrine) of defending free countries against communist subversion or the threat of communist aggression. In the case of Turkey, internal subversion was not the problem as it was in Greece. The Turkish people have had a long history of unfriendly relations with Slavic nations, especially Russia. Little in communist doctrine or in the country principally espousing it appealed to the Turks. However, the end of World War II left Turkey almost powerless in relation to her Russian neighbor with whom she shares 370 miles of common border.

The first Russian initiatives came in the form of suggestions that the USSR and Turkey administer the Dardanelles jointly. The Dardanelles is a narrow passage from the Baltic Sea to the Mediterranean Sea which is controlled by Turkish territory on either side. Even with weapons of the range of those used in World War II, it was possible to cover the entire area with gunfire directed from the land. The nation which controlled the land on both sides of the Dardanelles would also presumably be able to install mines and submarine nets.

Control of the Dardanelles is important to Russia because it represents the only access to the Mediterranean for the Russian fleet. The only other alternative is going around all of Europe and entering through Gibralter Straits or proceeding from Asia through the Suez Canal. The Russian initiatives were rejected by the Turks. To make more clear the United States determination to prevent Russia from gaining control of Turkish territory by force, the United States sent a military mission to Turkey and provided $122.5 million of economic and $371.1 million of military aid under the Greek-Turkish aid program.[14]

The basic objectives of military assistance since that time have changed very little, although the missions of the Turkish forces are now spelled out in NATO force planning. A wide variety of military observers have spoken highly of the qualities of the Turkish fighting man and his determination to fight against communism.

Turkish economic development is considerably less than that of Greece in terms of normal indicators such as per capita gross national product or national income. The per capita gross national product of Turkey was estimated by the Agency for International Development in 1964 to be $209 compared to $461 in Greece. [15] Although economic assistance to Turkey has been reduced substantially from the high levels of the 1950's, in fiscal year 1963 Turkey received $127.5 million of United States economic aid and an additional $49.8 million in surplus agricultural commodities. Turkey received its last supporting assistance grant in 1964. The Turkish national defense budget in the latest year for which estimates are available was $381 million, compared to United States military assistance deliveries of $140 million. This budget was spent "almost entirely in accordance with" United States advice. [16]

The Turkish Army has received practically all of its present equipment and training from the United States. [17] This means that the basic equipment called for by tables of equipment and organization, such as vehicles, artillery, communications equipment, machine guns and individual weapons, has been provided by the United States. The Turkish Army is a regular force of some 400,000 men, about 40% of the size of the United States Army.

The Turkish Navy is composed primarily of vessels provided by the United States. United States Defense Department spokesmen have indicated that these vessels are rapidly becoming obsolete and difficult to maintain.

The Director of Military Assistance told Congressman Passman:

We have had in the program for the last 3 years naval vessels which we have had to delete because of lack of funds. We are trying to start a program to replace these vessels which are not combat worthy. They may or may not last until we are able to have ships to replace them. Meantime they are listed as being in existence and that is about all they are. [18]

The Turkish Air Force is composed of United States F-84 and F-86 aircraft. Some of these aircraft are being replaced with F-5 aircraft and F-104 aircraft. Other types of aircraft provided by the United States include trainers, utility aircraft, transports and helicopters.

Defense officials have been concerned by the continuing necessity to defer improvement in Turkish forces. For example, as a result of the reduction made by the Congress in the fiscal year 1964 military assistance request, the amount available for Turkey had to be cut by 22%. This action resulted in deferral of much of the improvement planned for Turkish forces, including artillery, vehicle spares, machine guns and rockets. [19]

Limits on the fiscal year 1965 program were expected to result in deferral of spare parts, training, ammunition, and attrition replacement. [20] This situation is aggravated by the high costs of maintaining existing forces--over 60% of the total request for fiscal year 1965. [21] The results of this situation have worried NATO commanders and the Joint Chiefs of Staff.

Secretary of Defense McNamara testified before the House Appropriations Committee on March 23, 1964 that: [22]

(1) Except for missile units, all major components of the Turkish ground forces are short a substantial part of their major mission equipment.

(2) Much of the Turkish Army equipment is below minimum NATO standards. Much of it is World War II or earlier, for which repair parts are no longer available or on which maintenance costs have become prohibitive to continued operations.

(3) Much of the outdated equipment will not satisfy requirements in a combat situation.

(4) Equipment shortages existed in trucks, trailers, armored personnel carriers, M-48 tanks, radios, helicopters, howitzers, mortars, etc.

(5) Maintenance cost of most ships in the Turkish Navy are very high in relation to their combat contribution.

IRAN

During the immediate postwar period the Soviet Union was actively threatening Iran. As a response to this Soviet action, the United States initiated a small scale military assistance program in Iran

long before the Korean War. After a period of turbulent politics the
present Shah assumed office and announced the beginnings of policies
reasonably favorable to the West. Military assistance was substantially increased after Iran joined the Baghdad Pact. This assistance was accelerated when a Middle Eastern crisis resulted from
the coup in Iraq.

On July 1, 1962 the United States entered into a long range military assistance agreement with Iran to last until June 30, 1967. [23]
The United States agreed to a combined grant and sales program.
The Shah agreed to a reorganization of Iranian armed forces which
resulted in a reduction in those forces. [24] Implementation of the
agreement depended on the Iranians' capability "to demonstrate by
their maintenance and by their training efficiency that they could
absorb and make proper use of the equipment." [25] Defense officials
saw the main advantage of this agreement as the assurance which it
gives to the Shah of continued United States support while the Shah
undertakes a variety of economic reform measures which are
creating substantial opposition within the country. [26]

In terms of military strategy, while initial Iranian assistance
programs postulated Iranian participation in collective defense
through the CENTO organization, the Secretary of Defense advised
the House Armed Services Committee that the prime purpose of
present assistance to Iran was "to help build up its military forces
to the point where they can insure internal security and provide at
least an initial defense against Soviet attack." [27] This strategy was
apparently based on the assumption that overt Soviet attack against
Iran is unlikely. [28]

The United States maintains a military assistance advisory group
in Iran, the strength of which was expected to be about 400 officers
during 1965.

INDIA AND PAKISTAN

Until 1947 India and Pakistan were both British possessions.
When the British relinquished control of them they permitted the
Moslem and Hindu populations to sort themselves out into two new
states, a newly created Pakistan and India, more or less organized
along the lines of existing religious distributions. The effect of this
action was to make Pakistan a nation divided into two widely separated

parts--East Pakistan and West Pakistan. The distance between the nearest points in Pakistan territory from East and West Pakistan is over 1,000 miles, making government and defense much more complicated than in a contiguous state.

Shortly after independence Pakistan began to realize that the pressures against it from its neighbors, India and Russia, would require it to solidify quickly alliances with other major powers or risk being wiped out. No nation was interested in aligning itself with Pakistan against India, but Pakistan did join two major anti-communist alliances--the Baghdad Pact and the Southeast Asia Treaty Organization. Even before Pakistan's entry into these organizations, the United States began to respond favorably to Pakistan's requests for assistance in building its military forces. Because Pakistan borders both Communist China and Soviet Russia, it was considered at the time desirable to develop at least a modicum of Pakistani military posture. Development of significant military potential in Pakistan also complicated the military problems which either the Russians or the Red Chinese would encounter in attacking either Burma or India.

Senator Chavez after visiting Pakistan reported on the extent of United States aid:

> Pakistan is being furnished equipment and material
> consisting of, though not limited to, naval ships and equip-
> ment, jet aircraft, trucks, tanks, electronic (including
> radar) equipment, artillery, ammunition, spare parts,
> technical publications, and training aids. The con-
> struction program has improved airfields and provided
> supply depots, maintenance shops, ammunition depots,
> hospitals and barracks, all of which add to the capability
> of the Pakistan military forces. Communication facilities
> have also been improved. [29]

The United States does not release estimates on the amount of military assistance furnished to Pakistan. However, Colonel Amos Jordan, who wrote on military assistance programs after studying them as a member of the staff of the Draper Committee, estimated that through 1960 United States military assistance had amounted to $390-440 million. [30]

The difficulties caused by overlooking the particular customs and habits of the military personnel in the nations receiving assistance are illustrated by the Pakistan program. In the 1950's, the United States constructed a large military training installation in Pakistan. This training installation included a number of features which are standard in such military construction in the United States but were ill-suited to requirements in Pakistan. For example, a cold meat storage facility was built even though Pakistani religion requires consuming meat shortly after it is killed, and the custom of the Pak Army is to slaughter, cook and eat meat in almost one continuous operation.

The magnitude of assistance to Pakistan has always been of considerable concern to India which believes that Pakistan's main desire in accepting the assistance is to prepare itself for military conflict with India rather than conflict with any communist country.

The United States currently maintains a Military Assistance Advisory Group of about 100 personnel in Pakistan. Assistance to Pakistan is furnished under aide-memoires signed in 1954, 1960, 1961 and 1962 in which the United States agreed to furnish maintenance, support and modernization training and equipment for specific units of the Pakistani armed forces. [31]

INDIA

Under the leadership of Gandhi and Nehru, India from the time of independence pursued a policy of non-alignment. Indian diplomats served as leading members of the neutralist bloc in the United Nations and India was a participant in most of the conferences of non-aligned nations. This Indian neutralism was based on the premise that neither free world nor communist countries would use their military might to threaten India's existence. One of the least militant members of all of the Indian government--Krishna Menon--was Indian Minister of Defense. Under his leadership, the Indian defense budget was kept at minimal levels and, because no large scale assistance was accepted from either the West or the Communist Bloc, Indian training and arms continued at a level which most nations had surpassed in World War II.

In October of 1962 the Chinese Communists gave up their continuing negotiations with India over the mountainous border areas between China and India. Communist Chinese armies attacking on various fronts in the mountains quickly drove ill-equipped and ill-trained Indian troops from the areas claimed by and previously occupied by India. It is generally agreed that it was Communist China restraint (however poorly motivated), not lack of military capability, which caused the Chinese Communists to stop their attacks short of securing all the disputed territory and substantial territories which were clearly Indian. The ease with which the Chinese Communist forces manhandled Indian defenses rocked the Indian nation and created a crisis in Indian defense policy.

India quickly turned to all possible sources of assistance, communist and non-communist. The United States and Britain, including the Commonwealth, each pledged $60 million worth of initial assistance to India. [32] The Soviet Union likewise agreed to provide assistance. United States initial assistance took the form of army equipment to develop six Indian mountain divisions, such as crew-served weapons and ammunition, communications equipment and radar, as well as Caribou aircraft, and 24 C-119 transport aircraft. The United States also expressed a willingness to assist India in the development of a defense production capability. [33] British and Commonwealth nations concentrated their assistance on the development of Indian air force combat capabilities.

In subsequent years the United States has provided continued substantial assistance. While the British and Commonwealth nations have also continued to assist, their contributions no longer match those of the United States. France, Germany, Japan and Italy have also provided assistance. [34] The Soviet Union, much to the consternation of Communist China, agreed to assist India with air force equipment and defense production.

By the end of 1964 the United States had over 100 people in its military mission in India. United States assistance has been furnished under a bilateral agreement signed in November of 1962.

NEPAL

In 1964 the Defense Department announced that it was developing a small military assistance program for Nepal as a joint effort with the British. [35] This program was to be for the equipment of some of Nepal's mountain troops. [36]

CONCLUSION

Military assistance to Iran, Pakistan, Greece and Turkey is part of an over-all United States forward strategy of assisting nations on the borders of the Soviet Union and Communist China to develop their military strength. This strategy was extended to India in 1962, after the Chinese Communist attack convinced India that military preparedness was necessary.

In the opinion of many military authorities a serious problem has developed in Greece and Turkey as a result of insufficient United States military assistance. Limited funds available for these countries have slowed military modernization although neighboring communist nations have apparently modernized their forces rapidly.

NOTES

1. SFRC, CY 64, p. 259.

2. HAC, CY 63, pp. 124-125.

3. Testimony of Secretary of Defense McNamara, HFAC, CY 64, p. 89.

4. HAC, CY 64, p. 325.

5. Speech by Secretary of Defense McNamara before the National Industrial Conference Board, May 21, 1964. Issued as a Department of Defense Press Release.

6. HAC, CY 64, p. 304.

7. Ibid., p. 310.

8. HAC, CY 63, p. 77.

9. HFAC, CY 64, p. 89.

10. HAC, CY 63, p. 438.

11. HAC, CY 64, p. 330.

12. Testimony of Deputy Assistant Secretary of Defense Frank Sloan, HAC, CY 64, p. 398.

13. Testimony of Secretary of Defense McNamara, HFAC, CY 64, p. 88.

14. U.S., Congress, House, U.S. Foreign Aid, House Document No. 116, 86th Cong., 1st Sess., 1959, prepared by the Legislative Reference Service, p. 106.

15. Agency for International Development, Proposed Mutual Defense and Development Programs, FY 1965 (Washington: U.S. Government Printing Office, April, 1964) p. 210.

16. Testimony of Secretary of Defense McNamara, HAC, CY 64, p. 331.

17. HAC, CY 64, p. 398.

18. Testimony of General Robert Wood, HAC, CY 64, p. 489.

19. McNamara Speech, National Industrial Conference Board, op. cit.

20. Testimony of Secretary of Defense McNamara, HFAC, CY 64, p. 89.

21. Sloan testimony, op. cit., p. 399.

22. HAC, CY 64, p. 344.

23. Ibid., p. 451.

24. Testimony of Secretary of Defense McNamara, SAC, CY 64, p. 227.

25. Sloan testimony, op. cit., p. 452.

26. Testimony of Secretary of Defense McNamara, HFAC, CY 64, p. 90 and Sloan testimony, op. cit., p. 397.

27. Testimony of Secretary of Defense McNamara, U.S., Congress, House, Committee on Armed Services, Hearings on Military Posture and H.R. 9637, (No. 36), 88th Cong., 2d Sess., 1964, p. 6908.

28. Ibid.

29. U.S., Congress, Senate, Committee on Appropriations, Report on United States Military Operations and Mutual Security Programs Overseas by Senator Dennis Chavez, 86th Cong., 2d Sess., 1960, p. 130.

30. Amos A. Jordan, Jr., Foreign Aid and the Defense of Southeast Asia (New York: Praeger, 1962), p. 214.

31. HAC, CY 64, p. 349.

32. Testimony of Secretary of Defense McNamara, HFAC, CY 64, p. 89.

33. It was originally expected that India would repay the United States for this assistance. HAC, CY 63, p. 382.

34. HAC, CY 64, p. 422.

35. Sloan testimony, op. cit., p. 397.

36. Ibid., p. 405.

United States military assistance to Africa can be considered as
two distinct sets of programs which have originated for different
reasons and continue to serve different purposes. The first set is
composed of the relatively large programs to the countries of North
Africa where the United States now has or recently has had major
military bases. This assistance is designed in large part to facilitate continued access to these bases on favorable terms. The remainder of assistance programs to Africa are smaller in size and
costs--frequently they are confined to training alone--and are designed to further the orientation of these nations toward the free
world and to encourage internal security. This is a prerequisite
for economic growth and a sine qua non for preventing forcible
communist-inspired takeovers of these governments.

NORTH AFRICA

By far the largest recipient of military assistance in Africa has
been Ethiopia which had been allocated $82.8 million of the $146
million programmed for Africa through fiscal year 1964. Ethiopia
was one of the first independent African states; although its history
(as Abyssinia) was a stormy one, it developed some technical skills
and industry which has provided a foundation for self-government.
Ethiopia has always been a pro-Western member of the African community and has generally exercised a restraining influence on newer
African nations which are less skilled and experienced in diplomacy.
Ethiopia has consistently provided relatively large contingents for
United Nations peace-keeping operations including the United Nations
operation in the Congo.

The present military capability of Ethiopia is primarily a 30,000
man force which performs the functions of a militia, an army and a
police force and bodyguard for the Emperor of Ethiopia. By African
standards this is quite a large force. Senator Church, on returning
from a visit in the area, indicated that the motivation for such a
large army was that the Emperor felt hemmed in by Moslem countries which might stimulate trouble among Ethiopia's large Moslem
population. [1]

The Imperial Ethiopian Navy is just beginning to develop into a
reasonably modern force. The main vessel in this force, a converted

United States seaplane tender, caused considerable press and Congressional comment as a result of the extensive and expensive modernization and modifications created to make the vessel a suitable flagship.[2] At one time the vessel was manned primarily by Norwegians, but increasingly, Ethiopians are developing the capability to maintain and operate it. It is being used to train Ethiopians in a variety of naval skills.

The Ethiopian Air Force has some F-86 jet fighters provided by the United States. Ethiopia's Air Force problems are aggravated by the fact that neighboring and often hostile Somalia receives Russian assistance.

The main United States facility in Ethiopia near Asmara is one of the world's largest communications centers. This facility has been described as very important[3] and as very valuable.[4]

Both Morocco and Tunisia have received military assistance from the United States. In both countries the United States had maintained military bases but has now given them up. The fiscal year 1965 program which the State and Defense Departments presented to the Congress included a "modest amount" for Morocco, but no grants of equipment to Tunisia. Assistance provided under earlier programs included training and basic communications equipment, transport and weapons for ground forces. Substantial economic aid has also been given to these countries.

Wheelus Air Force Base in Libya is one of the largest base complexes in North Africa. It is used both for air transport and training, and is expected to continue to be important to the United States for some years.[5] As a result, United States military assistance to Libya is based in part upon ensuring continued Libyan cooperation in permitting use of this facility. Libya has been subjected to some pressure from other Arab countries to eject the United States from this base. Military assistance is also intended to assist Libya in developing the military capability to maintain internal security.

Through fiscal year 1965 the United States had programmed about $11 million of assistance to Libya. Twenty-six United States military personnel were in the country as members of the Military Assistance Advisory Group during 1965.

SOUTH OF THE SAHARA

In the case of the newly emerging nations south of the Sahara Desert, military assistance serves entirely different purposes. The United States has no bases in any of these countries. All of these nations (except Liberia) are making the transition from colonial status to full economic as well as political independence. In most of these countries the coming of independence preceded readiness for independence in a military sense.[6] At the time of independence most of these nations had officers and technical specialists from the former metropolitan nations in the key positions in their armed forces and police. The rapid exodus of these personnel in some countries created a void of well-trained, responsible leadership. In those nations where the military leadership continued in the hands of the metropole, independence was clearly less than complete whatever political settlements had been made.

The United States initially took a dim view of extensive involvement in Africa through military assistance programs. There was considerable fear that such assistance would result in the development of an African arms race.[7] There was also the consideration that the primary problems in these countries were economic and political rather than military. United States policy has been that primary responsibility for assistance to these new nations remained with the former colonial ruler.[8]

Despite these considerations, military assistance to Africa began to increase in the early 1960's both in terms of the money spent and in terms of the number of countries assisted. This phenomenon is indicated by the following chart:

Africa South of Sahara (excluding Morocco, Tunisia, Ethiopia and Libya)	FY 1960	FY 1961	FY 1962	FY 1963	FY 1964	FY 1965
Number of countries aided	0	2	10	11	6	5
Cost in millions	0	$0.4	$1.8	$3.0	$6.6	$5.8

One of the major reasons for this increase in United States involvement was that these new nations did not feel themselves truly
independent so long as they were dependent upon the metropole for
their military training and equipment. To reduce this dependence
they sought United States assistance. Another factor was the unwillingness or inability of the former colonial powers to pay the
costs of extensive continued involvement.

Assistance to these nations began with an initial United States
survey team study of military requirements for internal security.
These surveys were followed in many cases by a decision that a
small program of equipment for internal security was required.
Frequently this type of program involves jeeps and trucks for mobility, communications equipment and considerable training both by
mobile training teams and in the United States.

The training program is of particular importance in the case of
these nations. In recognition of this fact, a leadership training program has been developed for the African states which goes beyond
the military assistance training available to other countries.
Selected African students, without military experience, are brought
to the United States to college. They spend their summers in United
States military installations and train further for a year following
the conclusion of their college studies.

The objectives of United States military assistance to Africa
south of the Sahara were elaborated by General Paul D. Adams,
Commander of United States Strike forces, who also is responsible
for administering military aid to Africa:

The U.S. objectives of military assistance in Africa
south of the Sahara are the realization of U.S. political
requirements and maintenance of free world orientation.
Specifically, military assistance is used as follows:

First, to foster an anti-communist, free world-
oriented military community;

Second, to assist in the development of an internal
security capability and political stability essential to
economic growth;

Third, to contribute to the existence of viable and
friendly governments;

Fourth, to provide recognition of new countries and
assist them in assuming the responsibilities of their
independence and sovereignty;

and Fifth, to prevent an African arms race. [9]

Later in his testimony General Adams phrased the objectives of
his programs more in terms of preventing communist encroachment
into Africa. As he put it:

We are trying to create a U.S. presence--as it is sometimes called--that will give these people an alternative to
the Chinese and the Russians who are competing to take
the countries over in time.

Normally, assistance is given to an African nation only after
a request for assistance is received from the country to be assisted.
That request is reviewed by a group composed of the economic aid
mission director, the military attache and the ambassador, who
then make recommendations to all agencies concerned in Washington. [10] In the Washington determinations, according to the Unified
Commander administering the program, the State Department picks
out which countries are to receive military assistance. [11] This
approach is consistent with the law governing the furnishing of
military assistance, which states:

Under the direction of the President, the Secretary of
State shall be responsible for the continuous supervision
and general direction of the assistance programs authorized
by this Act, including but not limited to determining whether
there shall be a military assistance program for a country
and the value thereof, to the end that such programs are
effectively integrated both at home and abroad and the
foreign policy of the United States is best served thereby. [12]

Despite attempts by the United States to limit its military assistance to Africa, it appears that with or without this assistance most
African states will develop some military capabilities, which may
in many cases go well beyond the forces required for internal security in their own countries. This trend has been encouraged by the

use of African forces for a variety of United Nations peacekeeping operations, especially that in the Congo. The tendency is in part attributable to the widespread belief in both the new African states and the older states of the world that a reasonable military force is an essential attribute of sovereignty, even though it may not necessarily be required to meet any foreseeable internal or external security threats. [13]

The United States, through its military assistance policy, or through any other policy, cannot expect to dictate to new African states to what extent they will develop military forces. The very attempt to do so could produce the opposite of the result intended. The attempt would no doubt be seen by African states as intervention in their policies, and the recommendations to limit armed forces might well be seen as a subterfuge to prevent these nations from taking what they consider to be their proper role in the affairs of the world.

Thus, the United States can expect that all African states will have military establishments. The only question for the United States is what attitude should be taken toward these newly developing military establishments, and what support should be given to them.

In this connection, it is important to realize the role which the military is likely to play in the development of many of these nations. Almost without exception the new African states have been granted independence before the development of an educated "administrative" class, before the development of national patriotism, and before the development of economic, political and social institutions which could facilitate national unity. Some former British colonies, such as Ghana, present a partial exception, [14] but are counterbalanced by extreme cases of disorganization and lack of national unity, such as the Congo.

The first problem of many of these new states will be developing a sense of "national identity" and overcoming parochial tribal and sectional differences. One of the most potent modernizing forces will be military forces which bring together the various tribal members and provide them with common objectives, national feeling and knowledge about the geography and other peoples of their own nation. In addition to this function, military training in new states can represent a substantial contribution to achievement of more widespread literacy and skill in the use of equipment such as vehicles, telephones and radios. It must be remembered that in the early years of the United States, the United States Military Academy was a major source of engineers for the whole nation.

In addition to these facts, the military organization in new African states is developing into one of the most powerful national forces. Military forces by their very nature develop an organization which is deployed throughout the nation, which has almost a monopoly of available force and which is one of the few disciplined nationwide organizations in new states. In these circumstances it appears inevitable that there will be many occasions during the next decade in Africa when the military will take control of some African governments. Neither United States military assistance nor that furnished by the nations of Western Europe, Israel or even the communists will have much influence on these political changes. In the older nations of Latin America and Asia the military have frequently intervened in politics before substantial military assistance was provided. [15]

With the exception of the extensive United States involvement, both bilaterally and through the United Nations in the Congo, present United States policy has been one of minimal involvement with the developing military in the new African states. Reliance has been placed in large part on the former colonial power for both economic and military assistance. When military assistance has been provided it has normally taken the form of training or of training combined with "impact" shipments of limited military equipment--primarily transportation and communications--on a "one shot" basis, rather than the development of continuing support of these forces with equipment and training.

Congressional leaders have been concerned that the United States not become too involved in the military affairs of African states, and particularly, that United States assistance not result in the development of an arms race in Africa. Accordingly, present law limits military assistance to Africa to meeting internal security and civic action requirements only, thereby excluding programs aimed at the development of capabilities to resist attack from other states. [16]

The Congress has also limited the value of grant programs of military equipment and supplies to Africa to $25 million each year. [17] Military assistance programs in 1964 and 1965 were well below this ceiling.

CONCLUSION

Military assistance in North Africa has primarily been connected with continued access to United States bases and facilities
throughout the area.

In Africa south of the Sahara, United States military assistance
has been limited to comparatively small quantities of equipment and
training for internal security and civic action purposes. Although it
is United States policy to discourage any type of arms race in Africa,
it is probable that the African states will develop military forces--
with or without United States assistance--and that those forces will
have much to say about who shall govern and what policies shall be
pursued in many African nations.

NOTES

1. U.S., Congress, Senate, Committee on Foreign Relations,
Committee on Appropriations, and Committee on Interior and In-
sular Affairs, Study Mission to Africa November-December 1960,
Report of Senators Frank Church, Gale W. McGee, and Frank E.
Moss, 87th Cong., 1st Sess., 1961, p. 16.

2. See for example, HAC, CY 63, pp. 329-331.

3. HFAC, CY 63, p. 1070.

4. Testimony of General Robert Wood, HAC, CY 64, p. 426.

5. Testimony of Assistant Secretary of State Talbot, HFAC,
CY 64, p. 264.

6. No value judgment as to whether the granting of independence
in any country was premature or tardy is intended by this comment.

7. Secretary Rusk used this argument in explaining why no
military aid is being furnished Somalia, though Somalia did request
it. HFAC, CY 64, p. 33.

8. Ibid., pp. 27-28.

9. HFAC, CY 64, p. 602.

10. HFAC, CY 63, p. 1080.

11. HFAC, CY 64, p. 616.

12. Section 622(c) of the Foreign Assistance Act of 1961, as
amended. (Emphasis added.)

13. See, for example, William Gutteridge's short book, Armed
Forces in New States (London: Oxford University Press, 1962).

14. David Apter, Ghana in Transition (New York: Atheneum,
1963), tells the story of a relatively smooth transition to

independence. Even in Ghana regional differences and tribal organizations and loyalties came very close to producing chaos at the time of independence and the present government is not "democratic"by Western standards.

15. This material summarizes the growing literature on the role of the military in underdeveloped countries. Some of the best examples are: Morris Janowitz, The Military in the Political Development of New Nations (Chicago: University of Chicago Press, 1964) on the general problem; John Johnson (ed.), The Role of the Military in Underdeveloped Countries (Princeton: Princeton University Press, 1962) which contains general essays and contributions on various areas of the world; Sydney N. Fisher (ed.), The Military in Middle Eastern Society and Politics (Columbus, Ohio: Ohio State University Press, 1963) on the Middle East; John J. Johnson, The Military and Society in Latin America (Stanford: Stanford University Press, 1964) on Latin America; W. Gutteridge, Armed Forces in New States, op. cit., on Africa; and S. E. Finer, The Man on Horseback (London: Pall Mall Press, 1962).

16. Section 512 of the Foreign Assistance Act of 1961, as amended. This section was added by Section 202(e) of the Foreign Assistance Act of 1963. The President may waive this requirement. Of course, there is nothing about United States provided bullets which makes them useless for external defense even though they were provided to meet internal security requirements.

17. Section 512 as cited above.

CHAPTER 8 — ECONOMIC AND MILITARY AID: FRIENDS OR ENEMIES

The relationship between economic and military assistance programs is quite complex. On the one hand, military assistance complements economic assistance by helping to develop internal security which is a prerequisite for economic progress. Economic assistance can provide the wherewithal for military assistance recipients to pay troops and purchase supplies and offers the promise of economic progress and eventual economic and military self-sufficiency. On the other hand, overemphasis on military assistance may encourage a recipient to divert resources from economic to military purposes and overemphasis on economic assistance may divert attention and resources from pressing military problems. The purpose of this chapter is to explore these interrelationships in detail and to indicate those fields where it is possible to use either economic or military assistance to achieve a policy objective.

THE ECONOMIC IMPACT OF MILITARY PROGRAMS

The United States military assistance program is presently concentrated in eleven countries on the border of the Sino-Soviet Bloc. These countries maintain large forces to counter the threat of communist aggression. By American standards the cost of these military establishments is not high, although in many cases these forces consume a significant portion of the total expenditures of these governments. The following table shows the dollar equivalents of defense expenditures of nine of these countries:[1]

Country	Defense Expenditure ($ Millions)
Greece	$ 180
Turkey	370
India	1,858
Iran	197
Pakistan	255
Korea	165
Philippines	79
Thailand	78
Vietnam	231

In considering the impact of United States military aid programs, it is essential to remember that these budgets do not resemble the United States defense budget. These countries do not conduct military research and development, a category which accounts for about 14% of the United States defense budget. With the exception of India they spend little for procurement of military equipment, as practically all of their equipment comes from the United States as grant assistance. Procurement costs account for over 30% of the United States defense budget. The major components of the defense budgets of these major military assistance recipients are the costs of paying troops and purchasing items like food, uniforms and petroleum on the local economy. The United States military assistance program never provides money and never pays troops of foreign governments. These costs must be borne by the countries themselves, assisted at times by United States economic aid programs. Except in rare cases the United States military assistance funds are not used for purchases of food, uniforms or gasoline for military use. These costs must also be borne by the recipient country.

It can be thus readily concluded that in the countries where extensive military assistance programs are provided, the burden of the forces being maintained on the country's economy is largely the cost of the military pay and allowances, as well as costs such as food and other local purchases connected with maintaining existing forces. This analysis is confirmed by data on the cost to maintain military forces in various parts of the world. The Department of Defense provided estimates to the House Appropriations Committee which indicate that the costs for a year of pay, allowances, subsistence (food), and individual clothing for the forces of Korea, the Philippines, Thailand and Vietnam was $515.9 million.[2] The published estimates of defense budgets for these same countries indicate that about $553 million was expended by them for defense. While these estimates may not be perfectly accurate, they serve to illustrate the extent to which the military budgets of countries supported by United States military aid programs are composed primarily of military personnel costs.

Several important economic conclusions follow from these facts about the distribution of military budgets in countries which receive most of their equipment from United States military aid, namely, Laos, Thailand, Vietnam, the Philippines, the Republics of China and Korea, Iran, Pakistan, Greece and Turkey. The most important economic fact is that the forces in these countries, as a result of our military assistance, do not require foreign exchange expenditures by their governments in any significant degree. The costs of pay and allowances of the armed forces, the costs of food and construction materials and locally procured items like oil and gasoline are all borne in the currency of the country maintaining these forces. Therefore, so long as the United States maintains roughly its present level of military assistance under policies now in effect, the level of these military forces will have no adverse effect on the balance of trade position of these nations.

However, it must also be noted that these countries do not maintain military forces because the United States assists them with military and economic aid. In some cases the United States has undoubtedly encouraged larger forces (1) by diplomatic and military pressures for them in alliance structures like SEATO and NATO and (2) by showing a willingness to support such forces. However, even without United States encouragement and aid these forces would exist because the countries themselves see a need for them. For example, given Communist China's avowed intention to capture Taiwan and the offshore islands, who can imagine that Chiang Kai-shek would immediately demobilize his forces if United States support were withdrawn? Similar situations exist in all of the other nine countries listed above.

Because these countries would maintain forces even without United States military assistance, it follows that they would have to develop sources of equipment and ammunition for those forces. Because these nations do not have the domestic capability to fabricate aircraft, tanks, sophisticated vehicles or artillery, it would be necessary for them to expend substantial amounts of foreign exchange to purchase either equipment for their forces or machinery and technical assistance to produce equipment for their own forces locally. Thus, in many cases the major impact of military assistance programs on the foreign exchange position of these countries is to preserve limited foreign exchange for expenditures beneficial for economic development by giving equipment, some of which would otherwise be purchased.[3]

Within the economy of an underdeveloped country the effects of military expenditure are felt both in the allocation of money from the central government's budget and in resource allocation.

Military expenditures by underdeveloped countries cause major changes in the allocation of resources, primarily manpower. The maintenance of large military forces requires conscripting manpower for military service which could otherwise be contributing to other economic tasks, or in a less than full employment situation might simply become part of a large pool of unemployed. For reasons discussed below, the training of military manpower can be used to the net benefit of the country concerned if military training is seen as an opportunity to teach skills such as reading, writing and vehicle maintenance which are useful in the civilian economy. Military expenditures also require the allocation of some land--maneuver areas, barracks, etc.--for military purposes and the diversion of some materials such as cement and gasoline to military uses. However, in general, these diversions of resources have not had a significant effect on economic development.

In terms of money allocation, which also can be called resource allocation as expenditures of funds obviously cause allocation of resources, the impact of military expenditures can be substantial. The following shows the percentage of total central government expenditures which defense budgets represent in some of the countries which are major recipients of United States military aid:[4]

Country	Defense Expenditures as Percentage of Central Government Expenditures
Greece	22.7%
Turkey	28.6
India	25.8
Iran	24.8
Pakistan	17.9
Korea	26.9
Philippines	11.8
Thailand	14.1
Vietnam	52.3

While these percentages may seem low in comparison with that of the United States, which spends over half of its total federal budget for national security, it must be remembered that the central budgets of these countries include many costs not in the United States federal budget. Many of the enterprises which are privately owned in the United States are conducted by governments in these countries and are a part of the national budget. Many of the social and educational expenses which state and local governments pay in the United States are paid by the central government in these countries.

These military expenditures are significant to the government involved and large enough so that the United States has generally seen fit to pay many of them. In the 1950's these costs were identified as defense support, the criteria for which was quite precise:

Defense support is supplied only when all of the following conditions are met:

---The country receiving defense support must be one which is also receiving United States military assistance.

---The military assistance must be in support of significant military forces.

---The purpose must be to secure a specific contribution by the recipient to the common defense.[5]

The countries listed for defense support in fiscal year 1959 were the same countries today categorized as forward defense countries, which receive the bulk of military assistance support. Only two countries which were to receive defense support in fiscal year 1959 were not on the list of 11 key countries to receive military aid in fiscal year 1965. Those were Spain, where economic development has ended the need for economic aid, and Cambodia, which asked the United States to end its programs. India is the only one of the 11 key countries for military aid in fiscal year 1965 which was not on the list of defense support recipients in 1958. India did not request United States military assistance until 1962. Thus, in 1958 the relationships between a large component of the economic aid program and the largest components of the military aid program were clear. Military assistance paid the costs of equipment, supplies and training and economic aid provided the budgetary support necessary for local purchases and pay and allowances of foreign forces.

By 1964 that situation had changed markedly. Defense support had been abolished as a category of economic aid programs. In its place a program labeled "Supporting Assistance" was established. Supporting assistance is more of a catchall of grant programs than a program of assistance to countries maintaining large military forces as part of an alliance structure.

Of the eleven countries which were scheduled to receive large grants of military assistance in the program which the Administration presented for fiscal year 1965, only three, Korea, Vietnam, and Laos, were scheduled to receive any supporting assistance at all. By 1963 "supporting assistance" had been divided into four categories, only one of which was related to support of forces which receive substantial military assistance. The four categories were:

(1) Funds to support the common defense. This is essentially the type of expenditure formerly called defense support.

(2) Maintenance of Economic Stability.

(3) An Alternative to Bloc Aid.

(4) U.S. military bases. [6]

Likewise the President's Contingency Fund, although justified to the Congress as "strategic assistance," is not clearly identifiable as a fund intended primarily to cover burdens associated with large forces supported by military aid. For example, the following is the complete list of projects included in the presentation of the Contingency Fund to the Congress in an Agency for International Development pamphlet in 1963:

---The most important use for the contingency fund has been for quick response to shifts in Communist pressure in Southeast Asia.

---The second major use of contingency funds is to meet emergency economic needs of politically vulnerable countries.

---In fiscal year 1962 the Dominican Republic faced an empty treasury. To help revive the economy and support the new liberal government $25 million was required from the contingency fund.

---In Ecuador last year and again this year budget support loans were required to forestall riots and maintain internal stability.

---Syria and Egypt faced acute balance of payments problems in 1962 and required supporting assistance loans which could not have been foreseen.

---Another important use of the contingency fund is to provide the flexibility to move into unforeseen situations where the alternative would be a dangerous dependence on Soviet Bloc assistance.

---The most frequent but smallest use of the contingency fund is for disaster relief. [7]

As a result of these developments in the structure of the economic assistance programs, there is now no single program identified with the support of the defense budgets of governments whose economies are overburdened by large military forces which the United States feels should continue to be maintained. This development is, of course, not necessarily an undesirable one as it has permitted the economic aid agencies to focus more clearly on the developmental objectives of economic aid.

This trend has not, however, affected the defense budget support which results from the sales of United States surplus agricultural commodities abroad under Public Law 480. This program, though administered by the Department of Agriculture rather than by the Agency administering economic aid, has traditionally made an important contribution to the financing of defense costs in several countries. The program involves the importation of United States surplus agricultural commodities into the recipient nation and introduction of those commodities into the country's normal distribution system by sale to distributors for local currencies which are paid to the government concerned under agreements established with the United States for use of the currency. From the distributor to the consumer these products are treated like products which had been purchased by importers from normal foreign sources. [8]

To stimulate the Administration to use the local currencies generated by these transactions--over a billion dollars worth per year--the Congress has permitted these currencies to be used without appropriations being made. One of the purposes for which this can be done is "to procure military equipment, materials, facilities, and services for the common defense."[9]

However, the local currency available under this section is only available for use within the country of origin, [10] so that these currencies cannot replace regular military assistance funds used for procurement in the United States. [11] Such funds can, however, depending on the exact agreements negotiated with the countries concerned, be used for local currency expenditures on specific defense projects such as the local currency costs of construction labor. They may also be used to supplement the defense budgets of the country. The total of local currencies generated by Public Law 480 which have been used for "grants for common defense" under Section 104(c) of Public Law 480 were $66 million in fiscal year 1961, $136 million in fiscal year 1962 and $113 million in fiscal year 1963. [12] Of the amount allocated in fiscal year 1963, $65 million was for Korea, $18.3 million for the Republic of China, $24.3 million for Vietnam and $5.0 million for Greece.

In summary, from the standpoint of actual contributions to defense budgets, there is at present little relationship between the economic aid programs administered by the Agency for International Development and military budget support. Only three countries of the key eleven which represent the most significant military aid recipients were scheduled to receive supporting assistance contributions in fiscal year 1964. In the case of local currencies generated by Public Law 480, which is administered by the Department of Agriculture, four countries of the key eleven were receiving such direct budget support according to the latest statistics available.

This development has meant that there is a decreasing relationship between requirements for military assistance and economic assistance requirements. This does not mean that there is decreasing economic aid in those countries--although the economic aid has increasingly been put on a loan rather than grant basis. It does mean there is less direct defense budget support of these countries. This trend is shown below for ten of the eleven key forward defense countries. India has been excluded because the objectives, nature and general magnitude of the economic aid program were established long before military assistance to India began.

Ten Forward Defense Countries
Economic Assistance
($ million)

	Fiscal Years			
	Average 1954–56	Average 1957–59	Average 1960–62	1963
Total Economic Assistance	748.3	710.4	647.7	626.1
Technical Cooperation, Development Loans	13.5	83.6	195.9	309.7
Other (including defense support and supporting assistance related to direct support of military budgets)	634.8	626.8	451.8	316.4

Despite the decreasing direct relationship between economic aid programs and military aid, there continue to be significant indirect relationships. Although the generalization requires some caveats, it is safe to say that any United States economic aid contribution will free resources for defense purposes whether or not this is the objective of the contribution.[13] The most obvious case in which this is true is when a country develops a budget or a five year program calling for expenditures for (a) economic development, (b) social welfare, (c) stimulation of investment, and (d) defense. The country then can measure its own resources against these needs and, in most cases, conclude that available resources will not meet needs. It can then seek external support in the form of foreign aid. Whether the external assistance takes the form of military aid, "defense support," direct contributions of food, or contributions to capital development projects is of little import.

The caveats to this generalization arise when the donor either (a) requires as a condition of his assistance that the resources freed by it not be diverted to defense, or (b) provides assistance to projects other than those contemplated by the plans of the country itself. There is undoubtedly considerable effort to ensure that such diversion of freed resources does not produce defense efforts beyond those which the United States considers necessary.

Coordination of United States planning for military aid requirements and economic aid requirements is complicated by the fact
that a number of highly significant economic programs are not controlled by the Agency for International Development. These include disposition of surplus agricultural commodities under Public
Law 480, Export-Import Bank loans, the Peace Corps, Treasury
stabilization loans and United States contributions to international
organizations. Edward S. Mason at the Elihu Root Lectures in
May of 1963 estimated these other programs at a value of $1 billion
per year by measuring Public Law 480 agricultural shipments at
world market prices, the Peace Corps, net loans of the Export-
Import Bank and contributions to those international organizations
engaged in development lending and technical assistance.[14]

However, a substantial effort is made to coordinate economic
and military programs. A statement by the economic aid agency on
the extent and method of this coordination is quoted in full below.

The coordination of economic and military assistance
programs is a major statutory and policy concern of the AID
Administrator. In accordance with section 622(c) of the
Foreign Assistance Act of 1961, as amended, the Secretary
of State, under the direction of the President, is responsible
for "the continuous supervision and general direction of"
foreign assistance programs. This responsibility was delegated
by the Secretary of State to the Administrator of the Agency
for International Development in State Department Delegation
of Authority No. 104 of November 3, 1961. Coordination in
the field in each country is the responsibility of the chief of
the U.S. diplomatic mission. Section 622(b) of the Foreign
Assistance Act of 1961, as amended, states that the chief of
diplomatic mission shall make sure that recommendations of
U.S. representatives pertaining to military assistance are
coordinated with political and economic considerations.

(1) Guidance to field agencies. --Joint coordinated
guidance on MAP and AID is provided annually to U.S.
country teams and unified commands as the basis for uniform
planning and programing in furtherance of established U.S.
interests and objectives in each country. In the case of
several of the forward defense countries, this has involved
major joint studies of the defense burden, its impact on
development, and the optimum mix of U.S. assistance in

the light of over-all security and policy needs. These studies have resulted in recommendations on assistance policy to the National Security Council.

(2) Field preparation. --The U.S. Military Assistance Advisory Group and the U.S. AID mission in each recipient country develop proposed multiyear assistance plans and annual programs under the leadership and subject to the over-all judgment of the Ambassador.

(3) Joint review in Washington. --AID and MAP proposals submitted by country teams are jointly reviewed by DOD/AID/ State and other agencies concerned in Washington. Country programs or projects involving joint AID and MAP funding receive special attention and examinations as a basis for achieving coordination and proper arrangements for timely funding. Major focus in these reviews is on the use of AID- generated counterpart funds for defense purposes, joint pro- jects such as civic action, and the appropriate allocation of country resources between defense and development needs.

(4) The Department of Defense proposes, and the AID Administrator approves, after consultation with the Under Secretary of State for Political Affairs and the State regional bureaus, the establishment, amount, timing, reduction, or termination of U.S. military assistance to each country within available funds.[15]

One serious problem which this material glosses over is the dif- ficulty of synchronizing economic and military aid even when programs for both are planned on the same time cycle. Economic and military aid programming cycles are tied to (a) the necessity to present a coherent request for new funds to the Congress, and (b) the neces- sity to develop programs to spend funds actually appropriated by the Congress. The emphasis in program reviews is therefore on the new programs planned and the dollar costs of those programs chargeable to new appropriations. However, the greatest inter- relationship of economic and military assistance occurs in the determination of how much local currency can be made available for the support of both military budgets and the local currency costs of United States military projects. Local currency available in any given year is normally available because of economic aid programs which were developed and funded about two years in advance of the

needs for local currency. Therefore, the decision as to whether
military assistance can fund in fiscal year 1967 the United States
produced materials for an air base, relying upon economic aid generated local currency (probably Public Law 480--agricultural
surplus--generated currency), will depend upon economic aid programs in fiscal year 1965, not those planned for appropriations in
fiscal year 1967.

MILITARY CONTRIBUTIONS TO ECONOMIC DEVELOPMENT

The preceding pages have considered the contributions, both
direct and indirect, which economic programs make to the maintenance of military forces in underdeveloped countries. There is also
a reverse flow of interrelationships. Military forces, and military
assistance, make contributions to economic development. These
contributions include (1) the use of military conscription as a device for training in literacy. For example, the Turkish Army
gives literacy training to more than 50,000 recruits per year;
(2) the by-products of military training in skills useful in the
civilian economy such as driving and maintaining vehicles, operation of communications and engineer equipment, piloting, seaman's
skills and the like; (3) the use of military units to perform functions
useful in the civilian economy (civic action) by building roads,
providing transportation services, etc.; (4) the use of military
medical capabilities for the civilian population; and (5) the use of
military personnel as part-time farmers.[16]

While these contributions are extremely valuable and there is a
general consensus that they should be expanded, they are not sub-
stitutes for economic assistance. If there is no military requirement for military forces, it is preferable to disband those forces
rather than keep them intact and occupy them with civic action type
projects. The military contributions to economic development can
be considerable, but rarely are they as great as they would be if
similar manpower and resources were applied directly in the civilian
economy. For example, training in repair of tank transmissions may
be valuable for a man who will repair Mack trucks when he returns
to civilian life, but the training will not have been nearly as valuable
as it would have had it been training in repairing Mack trucks.

TRADE-OFFS BETWEEN ECONOMIC AND MILITARY AID[17]

There are a wide variety of situations in which it is appropriate for either the economic aid program or the military aid program to bear certain costs. There is no necessity for this flexibility to be used by the Executive Branch as a device for allocating resources among various programs differently than the Congress has done in the appropriations process because existing law provides for transfers between the economic and military assistance programs to permit such reallocations.[18] Examples of this range of flexibility or trade-off are given below:

1. AID can fund equipment for military units which normally would be furnished under military aid. For example, equipment for Bolivian Army Engineer Battalions has been provided under economic aid programs.[19]

2. AID can pay part of the costs of training military personnel. For example, Georgetown University under a contract from AID assists in the training of Turkish Army recruits.

3. Military aid can pay for the costs of paramilitary units, as is the case with the Iranian Gendarmerie and the Vietnamese Civil Guard, or these units can be trained and equipped under AID programs. The extent to which economic aid funding can be used is indicated by the fact that AID had programmed over $2 million in arms and ammunition for Indonesia alone in fiscal year 1964.[20]

4. Military aid can be used for provision of consumable items which the country could purchase with AID import financing if military assistance did not provide them. For example, military assistance at one time provided nylon stockings,[21] and provides clothing, petroleum products and other consumables.

5. Economic aid funds can be used to build local production capabilities to manufacture items previously furnished by military aid or can be used to finance import requirements generated by a shift of funding from military aid to the recipient country. For example, during hearings in 1964 an AID witness indicated that the commercial imports in Korea--some of which are financed by economic assistance--would rise "in part as the result of the transfer of more military items from MAP (military aid) to the Korean economy."[22]

Thus, to a significant degree military and economic assistance programs are complementary in that one can be increased to pick up responsibilities formerly undertaken by the other.

Despite the fairly rosy statement quoted above on the coordination of economic and military assistance requirements in the field, it seems improbable that all can be peace and harmony in view of some of the built-in tensions between United States military and economic missions. Economic aid tends to draw, both as its administrators and field employees, personnel from the American liberal tradition, with its substantial distrust of the military as an institution.[23] In many this background produces a tendency to distrust anything coming out of the Pentagon, military aid included. To many of the people oriented this way the thought of military personnel from the United States fanning out all over the world to encourage the development of military traditions and the purchase and use of weapons is inherently distasteful. Coupled with this basic attitude are the simple facts that most military expenditures, whether by the United States or by recipient countries, do not encourage economic growth. Also, in many countries where the United States has both economic and military assistance programs, the military is often in control of the government and may not adopt as favorable a view toward the sacrifices required for economic development as United States economic advisors would prefer.

Military advisors, on the other hand, have devoted their entire adult lives toward problems of military preparedness and are probably more acutely aware than most other sectors of society of the aggressive intentions of the communists. These officers are likely to share with the military establishments which they advise the view that additional resources should be devoted to military preparedness, as they are more likely to be familiar with the country's military weaknesses than are economic advisors. Most undoubtedly believe that to increase economic programs at the expense of military preparedness without compensating increases in United States forces would be to fatten the calf for a greedy neighbor.

One observer wrote that such differences had resulted in sharp competition between the military assistance advisory group and the aid mission in Vietnam. Such competition, in one country, produced a situation where the MAAG chief and the aid mission chief did not even negotiate with each other over the distribution of available local currency resources.[24] He also suggested that instructions from

military channels were not always consistent with those received
in economic aid channels. [25]

The effects of these differences in background and philosophy
have probably been reduced by a number of events in recent years.
The increased stress within the American military forces on special
forces and guerrilla warfare, plus the experience of thousands of
United States military advisors in Vietnam, have vividly revealed
the impossibility of "military" solutions to internal security problems.
On the other hand, the Vietnam experience is also proof that economic development cannot proceed without internal security, which may
only be possible through the commitment of large military resources.

Typical of the problems which have plagued the relationships of
economic and military advisors in the field has been the control of
military budgets partially financed with defense support or the proceeds of sales of surplus agricultural commodities.   The General
Accounting Office discovered that, although such budgetary contributions had been made for almost a decade, not until October of
1959 did the Department of Defense and the economic aid agency
agree on which agency was responsible for, and the procedures to be
followed for, the review of the utilization of military budget support
assistance. [26] Presumably, until that time there was little or no
audit of the uses of local currencies generated by United States
economic aid programs.   The procedure adopted in 1959 was
quietly dropped in 1960 and by 1961 apparently forgotten. [27]

In addition to the complex of relationships between economic assistance designed to lead to economic development and military assistance, it must be remembered that the economic aid agency conducts a police program which, like many military aid expenditures,
is designed to promote internal security in the countries receiving
assistance.   These efforts are called the AID "public safety" program. [28]

This program, begun in 1954, is designed to strengthen the
capability of civil police and paramilitary forces to enforce the law
and maintain public order with the minimum use of physical force,
and to counter communist-inspired or exploited subversion and insurgency. As AID officials state it:

It is based on the premise that, to maintain internal
order, local governments depend primarily on their

police and gendarmerie, supported as necessary by the army. [29]

These programs reach almost a million police throughout the world. The program is operated from the present Agency for International Development, advised and assisted by an interagency police group with representatives from the Departments of Defense, Justice, State, Treasury and other agencies.

Emphasis is placed on limited furnishing of unsophisticated, and therefore relatively inexpensive equipment, technical assistance and training. In fiscal year 1964 some 198 United States police advisors were advising 33 countries, an increase of 89 advisors and 9 countries since fiscal year 1960. In fiscal year 1964 programs for public safety were estimated to cost $16.5 million. The largest recipients were Brazil, Thailand, Vietnam and Pakistan. Of the 33 countries receiving this assistance, 13 were in Latin America and 10 in Africa.

While much of the police training conducted by the United States is done in the recipient country itself, the United States does maintain a Police Academy in the United States. The Academy was expected to graduate some 450 students in 1964. As is the case with military assistance training programs, the United States pays the costs of training, domestic travel and per diem for trainees while in the United States, while the recipient country bears salary costs. However, recipient governments pay for about two-thirds of the cost of international travel for police training, while the United States normally picks up this cost completely in providing military assistance training to underdeveloped nations. In the earlier years of the program some training programs were conducted in foreign nations closer to the home of the trainees to save transportation costs. Some officers of Southeast Asian countries have been given training in the Philippines and some from Africa have been trained in Italy.

CONCLUSION

Economic and military assistance programs compete with each other for resources both in Washington and in each recipient country. In Washington, proponents of each program support greater allocation of resources to it within the fixed total available during each year for "foreign aid." Within the country there is also a problem of allocation of local currencies generated by surplus agricultural commodity sales or other economic aid programs. To some extent, although less than is generally assumed, economic aid is used to provide directly or indirectly for the pay and allowances and other costs of forces which receive their equipment through the military aid program. As a result of continuing shifts in the nature of the economic program the direct relation between economic and military aid is decreasing each year.

The military in any country can make significant contributions to economic development, but normally those contributions are not as great as would be made if similar manpower and funds were devoted directly to economic problems. There are a number of areas in which a choice exists as to whether to provide for a particular project from military or economic aid funds.

An extensive police training program is conducted by the Agency for International Development.

NOTES

1. Data provided to House Foreign Affairs Committee in 1964 Hearings. HFAC, CY 64, p. 262.

2. HAC, CY 64, p. 462.

3. This is not intended to be, and is not, an argument for providing aid, only an attempt to gauge the effect of that aid. If the United States did not see a military use for the forces maintained by a less developed nation, but wished to help it economically, it would seem more intelligent to provide economic assistance by financing imports of United States commodities or machinery. Such assistance is more likely to "reach the people" and improve the United States image (however defined) than are contributions of military goods and services.

4. HFAC, CY 64, p. 116.

5. Departments of State and Defense and ICA, The Mutual Security Program Fiscal Year 1959: A Summary Presentation, February, 1958, p. 41.

6. Agency for International Development, Department of Defense, Proposed Mutual Defense and Assistance Programs FY 1964, April, 1963, pp. 64-65.

7. Ibid., pp. 67-68.

8. This method of distribution means that to the consumer there is no difference between wheat, for example, given by United States grants and wheat purchased by the country from the United States or any other source. The grants involved are to the government, not the people, who pay about the same price that they would have paid had no such assistance been provided. This situation is one of the ones which leads to the allegation that United States aid doesn't "reach the people." However, there are many good arguments for the present system, not the least of which is the many disadvantages inherent in any other system.

9. Section 104(c) of Public Law 480, 83rd Cong., 68 Stat 454, 7 USC 1701.

10. HAC, CY 64, p. 430.

11. Section 105 of Public Law 480 requires agencies which wish to use local currencies for projects other than those specifically authorized under Section 104 of the same act to buy the local currencies at full value. Thus, from the standpoint of the administering agency these currencies are of no special value because, so long as the agency is willing to spend appropriated dollars, it can buy any local currency, whether generated from Public Law 480 or not, from the Treasury. A net total of $18.5 million of such currencies were made available, on the basis of reimbursement from appropriations, to the administrators of military assistance in the five year period ending in fiscal year 1964. HAC, CY 64, p. 432.

12. Agency for International Development, U.S. Overseas Loans and Grants, March 30, 1964, p. 5.

13. The representatives of AID and predecessor economic aid agencies do not concede this proposition. The question usually arises in a highly politically charged argument periodically carried out with members of Congress in which the Congressmen attempt to prove that economic aid to Egypt makes it easier for Egypt to attack Israel, and representatives of the economic aid agency argue that this is not the case.

However, this transferability has been recognized by practically every impartial study of foreign aid. The Draper Committee, for example, said, "It should be noted that both military and economic assistance increase the total resources available to the recipient country. Within the practical bounds of flexibility in movement of these resources, a recipient country may shift internal resources from economic to military uses or vice versa in accordance with the local government's appraisal of their relative importance, which may not always be the same as our own." Composite Report of the President's Committee to Study the United States Military

Assistance Program (Washington: U.S. Government Printing Office, August, 1959) pp. 149-150.

14. Edward S. Mason, Foreign Aid and Foreign Policy (New York: Harper & Row, 1964)

15. SFRC, CY 64, pp. 269-270.

16. These and other contributions are described and discussed in detail with examples in Annex D to the report of the Draper Committee, op. cit.

17. The comment in this section applies to all economic aid programs, not just those administered by the Agency for International Development.

18. Section 610 of the Foreign Assistance Act of 1961.

19. HAC, CY 64, pp. 531-533.

20. HFAC, CY 64, pp. 185-186. Shipment of this material was suspended.

21. HFAC, CY 60, p. 976. The stockings were part of the standard uniform for Korean WAC's.

22. HFAC, CY 64, p. 181.

23. The depth to which this tradition permeates American life is easily forgotten. For example, it is infrequently remembered that the founding fathers were so concerned over the threat to liberty from a standing army that Section 8 of Article 2 of the Constitution prohibits appropriations of money to raise and support armies for more than two years and two provisions of the Bill of Rights--the right of citizens to bear arms and the prohibition of sequestration of housing--are designed to reduce the power of such an army. There is a substantial literature on the American attitudes toward its military establishment. See Samuel Huntington, The Soldier and the State: The Theory and Politics of Civil-Military Relations (Cambridge: Belknap-Harvard, 1957) and material cited therein. A short bibliography on the question appears as pp. 257-258 of S. Huntington (ed.), Changing Patterns of Military Politics (Glencoe, Illinois: The Free Press, 1962)

24. Amos A. Jordan, Jr., Foreign Aid and the Defense of Southeast Asia (New York: Praeger, 1962), p. 144.

25. Ibid., p. 159.

26. HAC, CY 60, p. 2271.

27. Jordan, op. cit., p. 144.

28. The material on public safety programs is drawn primarily from material submitted by the International Cooperation Administration to the House Foreign Affairs Committee in 1960 (HFAC, CY 60, pp. 1019-1023) and by AID to the Senate Appropriations Committee in 1964 (SAC, CY 64, pp. 72-84).

29. SAC, CY 64, p. 72.

The most significant military assistance administrative processes are those by which military equipment and services are
planned, programmed, justified to the Congress, procured and
delivered by the Department of Defense. However, these processes are less often discussed than the general question of the
coordination of military assistance with foreign policy and economic
assistance programs. Most of the important administrative changes
affecting military assistance have occurred in the context of a
parade of new economic agencies and coordinating arrangements in
the State Department.

COORDINATION OF ECONOMIC AND MILITARY ASSISTANCE

The Congress and successive Republican and Democratic administrations have generally believed that military assistance should be
closely coordinated on the one hand with economic assistance and on
the other with the regular Department of Defense budget. While
these objectives are non-controversial, developing procedures and
administrative arrangements to achieve them has always triggered
controversy. This controversy is no reflection on those who administer the programs in question. To a substantial degree the two
objectives are contradictory.

For example, the Foreign Assistance Act makes explicit the
role of the Secretary of State and the relation of military assistance
to United States foreign policy. It states:

> Under the direction of the President, the Secretary
> of State shall be responsible for the continuous supervision
> and general direction of the assistance programs authorized
> by this Act, including but not limited to determining whether
> there shall be a military assistance program for a country
> and the value thereof, to the end that such programs are
> effectively integrated both at home and abroad and the foreign
> policy of the United States is best served thereby. [1]

The same law also states:

> In order to make sure that a dollar spent on military
> assistance to foreign countries is as necessary as a dollar

spent for the United States military establishment, the President shall establish procedures for programming and budgeting so that the programs of military assistance come into direct competition for financial support with other activities and programs of the Department of Defense.[2]

While the objectives implicit in these provisions are widely endorsed, implementation of the strict letter of the law of both of them at the same time can place two government agencies on a collision course. The Secretary of State is empowered in a legal sense to set the size of military assistance programs. The Secretary of Defense theoretically could not decide that military assistance should be reduced because of greater domestic defense budget needs without overruling the Secretary of State's determination regarding the sizes of country programs. Likewise, if the Secretary of Defense were to determine that a country's military requirements were so unimportant as not to merit the diversion of one single dollar when considered against regular Department of Defense requirements, the Secretary of State could not establish the value of a program for the country without overruling the Secretary of Defense. These provisions of the Foreign Assistance Act illustrate the difficulties which beset any attempt to find optimum organizational solutions to the coordination of the military assistance program.

With these factors in mind, a review of varying arrangements which prevailed during the first 15 years of military assistance can trace some of the perturbations in procedures for integrating foreign policy and military planning.[3]

The Greek-Turkish Aid Act of 1947 provided for a program of assistance to Greece and Turkey under the control of the President. The President delegated authority to administer the program to the Secretary of State who created a special coordinator's office to direct the program with the help of an interdepartmental committee. A special mission was established in Greece independent of the Embassy and serious frictions developed between the mission and the Embassy.[4] In Turkey special personnel for the assistance program were assigned to the Embassy and placed under the Ambassador's direction.

In April of 1948 the Congress passed the Economic Cooperation Act establishing the Economic Cooperation Agency independent of the

State Department to administer burgeoning economic assistance programs. The Economic Cooperation Agency was to consult with the Department of State on matters of foreign policy, but State was given no formal coordinating powers. This agency did not administer military aid.

In 1949 the Mutual Defense Assistance Act established a substantial United States military assistance program. The President gave the Department of State primary authority and responsibility for direction of the program. The Economic Cooperation Agency was to give advice on the proper balance between economic recovery and military assistance, but did not exercise control over the military program.

A Foreign Military Assistance Coordinating Committee, composed of the heads of the operating units in the Departments of State and Defense and the Economic Cooperation Agency, was charged with coordination of day to day administration of mutual defense assistance in these agencies. The heads of these agencies were constituted as a Foreign Military Assistance Steering Committee which never met.[5] The Coordinating Committee reviewed and approved detailed country programs.

The success of the committee was attributed to three elements by a Brookings Institution study:

(1) the delegation of authority from the President to the Secretary of State largely settled jurisdictional questions; (2) the authority of the Secretary was reinforced by his control over funds; and (3) real efforts were exerted to relieve the committee of problems that did not require the collective consideration or decision, such as problems of military procurement.[6]

By 1951 the major emphasis of the foreign aid program had shifted from economic to military objectives. This shift was thought to require better coordination of all the assistance activities then underway. As a first step late in 1950, the President directed the Secretary of State to assume the leadership and coordination of all foreign assistance programs. In January, 1951 the Secretary of State established the post of Director of International Affairs to provide coordination and direction both within the Department of State and interdepartmentally. An International Security Affairs

Committee with representatives from many agencies, including Defense, was established.

This device did not work well. The Congress still did not wholly accept a key role for the State Department in the administration of foreign aid, and the coordinating role of the Department became increasingly difficult. Although the basic framework of the International Security Affairs Committee may have been sound, the consensus was that it was ineffective in practice. The committee was therefore abolished and foreign aid planning and coordination was raised to the Presidential staff level.

This was accomplished by new legislation, the Mutual Security Act of 1951, which gathered into a single authorization all economic and military assistance activities except those of the Export-Import Bank. That act:

---Authorized the appointment of Director for Mutual Security in the Executive Office of the President;

---Gave the Director responsibility for continuous supervision, general direction and coordination of the military, economic, and technical assistance programs;

---Authorized the appropriation of all funds for foreign assistance to the President, who gave to the Director for Mutual Security the responsibility for the allocation and control of these funds;

---Established an independent Mutual Security Agency, located apart from the Executive Office of the President but placed under the Director for Mutual Security, to administer economic assistance programs.

---Made the chiefs of diplomatic missions responsible for coordination of all foreign aid activities in the countries to which they were accredited.

When President Eisenhower took office, he asked an advisory committee, chaired by Nelson Rockefeller, to study executive branch organization for foreign affairs. The committee made three major recommendations:

1. Delegation of full responsibility for the formulation and control of foreign policy to the Secretary of State, under the President;

2. Removal of operating functions from the Department of State, so far as possible; and

3. Consolidation of foreign assistance operations, except military assistance, in a single agency.

On the matter of coordination of economic and military assistance programs the committee recommended that:

The Secretary of State, and the Secretary of Defense, as appropriate, should have authority and responsibility to review plans and policies relative to military and economic assistance programs and foreign information programs, and legislative proposals of the foreign economic operations agency and the foreign information agency, to assure that, in their conception and execution, such plans, policies, and proposals are consistent with and further the attainment of foreign policy and military policy objectives. [7]

The new agency's relations with the Department of Defense were described as follows in the Rockefeller recommendations:

To assure to the new economic agency its proper role with respect to the coordination and direction of the military assistance programs, the Secretary of Defense would be required to keep the agency currently informed on the status of such programs, including military end item procurement and deliveries, both domestic and offshore. [8]

The independent agency recommended by the Rockefeller study was to be responsible for all foreign assistance and economic operating matters under the foreign policy guidance of the Secretary of State and to receive by transfer all assistance programs and operations still in the Department of State. To carry out these recommendations the President on June 1, 1953 submitted his Reorganization Plan No. 7 to the Congress. Because this plan would not become effective for 60 days, he also issued Executive Order 10458 and sent a memorandum to the heads of the executive departments and agencies putting much of the plan into effect immediately.

The President's memorandum envisaged a somewhat wider net-
work of coordinating relationships within the government than that
now existing. The Secretary of the Treasury was to review, as
appropriate, both military and economic assistance plans and policies and the Secretary of Defense, again "as appropriate," was to
review economic programs.[9]

On August 1, 1953 when Reorganization Plan No. 7 went into
effect, the Mutual Security Agency was succeeded by the Foreign
Operations Administration. On the same day, Executive Order
10476 delegated most of the Presidential power under the Mutual
Security legislation to the Director of the Foreign Operations Administration, including the power to allocate all assistance funds.
The President also directed the Secretary of Defense to exercise
his responsibility and authority for military assistance programs
subject to the coordination, direction, and supervision of the Director of the Foreign Operations Administration. However, the Congress
in the Mutual Security Act of 1954 took this power to supervise military programs away from the Foreign Operations Administration.[10]

The Mutual Security Act of 1954 vested authority to administer
foreign assistance programs in the President. The President in
turn delegated that authority to the Departments of State and Defense (for military assistance). Under a series of Executive Orders
and internal State Department directives[11] the International Cooperation Administration was established to administer economic
assistance programs.

The Director of the International Cooperation Administration
was given, subject to the concurrence of the Secretary of State,
responsibility for coordinating economic and military assistance and
for determining the value of country military assistance programs.
During the latter part of the Eisenhower Administration this function
was vested in C. Douglas Dillon in the position of the Under Secretary of State for Mutual Security Coordination.[12]

On assuming office in 1961 President Kennedy established a
foreign assistance task force to consider improvements in the foreign
aid program. The work of that task force was embodied in the President's foreign aid message in 1961.[13] In that message the new President recommended more emphasis on long range development and
less on use of economic aid for short term political advantage. The
new look in foreign aid was to be administered by a new agency--

the Agency for International Development. President Kennedy's
proposals for foreign aid were embodied in the Foreign Assistance
Act of 1961, which, though frequently amended, remains the basic
legislation governing foreign aid.

The new foreign assistance legislation continued the provision
of the Mutual Security Act which gives the Secretary of State the
authority to determine the value of military assistance programs
to particular countries.[14] This authority has been delegated by the
Department of State to the head of the economic aid agency.[15]

From time to time questions are raised as to whether it is
appropriate to (a) give the Secretary of State this authority and (b)
for the Secretary of State to delegate authority of this type to the
head of the economic aid agency. A Brookings Institution study in
1957, after extensive discussion of the problem,[16] concluded:

> The evidence indicates that this authority and the
> procedures surrounding it have contributed substantially to
> effective coordination. Their effect on administrative
> efficiency is less clear. Protection of the program against
> narrowness and specialization associated with the particular
> interests of the military services has been achieved at the
> cost of considerable interdepartmental negotiation, leading
> to friction and delay.

> The question of appropriateness turns on the issue
> whether foreign military assistance should be governed
> within the framework of general foreign policy or within
> the narrower framework of defense policy. The President's
> delegation of this approval authority to the Secretary of
> State was based on the assumption that foreign policy
> should take precedence in guiding defense policy when
> military assistance programs are to be carried out through
> other governments. This study has revealed no basis for
> reversing this assumption.[17]

Another study prepared at the same time by the Systems Analysis
Corporation concluded that policy frictions had occurred in the past
between the Departments of Defense and State, but made no recommendations in light of the fact that the State Department had recently
established a new organization for mutual security coordination
and it was too early to see what the effect of that change would be.[18]

The Draper Committee in 1959 concluded that the Department of State should have the authority to disapprove programs for inconsistency with foreign policy and to propose programs on the basis of foreign policy considerations. However, the committee indicated that the language of the then existing Mutual Security Act (the same as that in the present legislation) that the Secretary of State can determine the value of military aid programs "appears to be unnecessary and subject to misinterpretation."[19] The committee pointed out that the vesting of this authority in the Secretary of State was not entirely consistent with the vesting of other functions in the Secretary of Defense. Rather than attempt amendment of this legislation, the committee recommended that the President issue appropriate clarifications of the roles which he expected the Secretaries of State and Defense to play in the administration of military assistance.

The latest study of foreign aid programs--that of the Clay Committee--did not comment on these problems.

ADMINISTRATION OF MILITARY ASSISTANCE
WITHIN THE DEPARTMENT OF DEFENSE

When military assistance began, the military aid functions were carried out by the Army, Navy and Air Force acting more or less independently. The Mutual Security Act of 1947 had established an organization superior to all of the military departments, but at the time that organization had little power. Subsequent amendments to the National Security Act tended to concentrate more authority over regular defense programs in the Secretary of Defense and the Joint Chiefs of Staff. An Office of Military Assistance was established under Brigadier General Lyman Lemnitzer, within the Office of the Secretary of Defense. Programming and planning functions, however, continued to be carried out by the military departments.[20]

Continuing developments increasing the power of the Secretary of Defense and his office at the expense of military departments[21] led to a larger and more powerful military assistance organization within the Office of the Secretary of Defense. During the later Eisenhower years this organization was administered within the Office of the Assistant Secretary of Defense (International Security Affairs) by a civilian Deputy Assistant Secretary.

Likewise, the military role in administering the program was increasingly coming under the cognizance of the Joint Chiefs of Staff although in military aid programs, as in regular Department of Defense programs, the tendency of this organization to recommend actions far beyond the budgets available gave considerable power to those who administered the program within the Office of the Secretary of Defense.

The typical pattern became one of (1) the development of "requirement" programs by military assistance advisory groups, calling for expenditures far in excess of those which the Congress was likely to provide for, (2) the endorsement of those programs by military authorities including the Joint Chiefs of Staff and (3) last minute realization of the necessity to cut programs to fit them within existing appropriations or the President's budget, resulting in all critical decisions being made without benefit of military advice and in ignorance of the recommendations of the military assistance advisory groups on which programs should be given greatest priority. The continued recommendations of high force goals and unrealistically expensive programs by military authorities had de facto transferred the power to make important decisions to the Office of the Secretary of Defense, in consultation with the State Department.

The magnitude of the problem is shown in the development of the military aid program for fiscal year 1959. The military departments, on the advice of military assistance advisory groups, developed proposed aid programs to meet prescribed force objectives. The cost of these programs was estimated to be $6.5 billion, which had to be cut to the $1.8 billion presented by the President to the Congress.[22] This situation was considered highly undesirable by practically all concerned. Accordingly, when the Draper Committee studied the military assistance program at the request of President Eisenhower in 1958-1959, they were quick to recommend sweeping changes in program administration.

Recognizing the dearth of military judgment which had been applied in program administration, the committee recommended changes within the organizational structure of the Office of the Secretary of Defense and that a high ranking military officer be appointed as Director of Military Assistance. This recommendation was accepted and in 1960 a four-star Army General (W. B. Palmer) was appointed to head the program.

The committee also recognized that one of the factors inhibiting the application of military judgment to the program was that much military planning was conducted under unrealistic assumptions as to the funds which could be, or would be, made available. The committee recommended that military assistance be planned on a long range basis under realistic "dollar guidelines" setting maximum programs for planning purposes. This system was installed and more attention was given to selecting among recipients and among weapons systems within a fixed available fund. Military assistance planning was developed to provide long range lists of requirements and indications of key decisions which had to be made in the future.[23] In addition, this type of planning by the United States and implementation of certain other Draper recommendations permitted closer cooperation in planning between recipient nations and their United States advisors.

As the Joint Chiefs of Staff, the Office of the Secretary of Defense and the Unified Commanders increased their power at the expense of the military departments, the departments began to lose their value as planning and administering organizations. The Draper Committee also recognized this trend and emphasized it by recommending that Unified Commanders be given control of programs in the areas under their jurisdiction. These commanders report through the Joint Chiefs of Staff rather than through a military department.

THE PRESENT MECHANICS OF THE PROGRAM

The present procedure for planning and programming as well as implementation of military assistance occurs in the following steps:[24]

(1) Policy objectives and order of magnitude dollar guidelines[25] are transmitted to the Unified Commands by the Director of Military Assistance accompanied by appropriate procedural guidance. The Director of Military Assistance also provides the Unified Command with a detailed listing of the articles and services which are available for the Military Assistance Program (in effect, a catalog).

(2) Strategic guidance is transmitted to the Unified Commands by the Joint Chiefs of Staff. That guidance is precisely the same as that used for the establishment of worldwide requirements for United States forces.[26]

(3) Based on this guidance and the supplementary instructions of the Unified Commands, each Military Assistance Advisory Group, with the assistance of the other members of the Country Team, provides the Unified Command with information required for development of the country plans and programs.

(4) The Unified Command military assistance plan and program recommendations are submitted to the Director of Military Assistance.

(5) The Director of Military Assistance distributes these plan and program recommendations to the military departments for review of pricing, lead time, and availabilities; to the Joint Chiefs of Staff for review for consistency with United States strategic plans; and to the Department of State, the Agency for International Development and the Bureau of the Budget for policy review and coordination. This proposed program is reviewed by the Secretary of Defense and forwarded to the Administrator of the Agency for International Development for further review and coordination in connection with the economic assistance function. It is then recommended to the President, through the Bureau of the Budget, as part of the President's budget.

(6) The President establishes the amount of new obligational authority to be included in his budget, and submits it to the Congress.

(7) After completion of Congressional action, the annual program is adjusted to conform to the actual appropriation and revised as necessary to reflect any changes in world conditions. Approval to implement the annual program is then obtained from the Administrator of the Agency for International Development and necessary apportionments are obtained from the Bureau of the Budget.

(8) The Director of Military Assistance issues military assistance program orders and other instructions to the military departments, together with appropriate fund allocations.

(9) The military departments take supply and procurement action, effect deliveries of material to the countries, and provide training and other services. Utilization of materiel by recipients is supervised by the Military Assistance Advisory Groups.

(10) As the occasion demands, the Director of Military Assistance receives recommendations for program changes from the Unified Commands, the Joint Chiefs of Staff and other agencies, and
proposes to the Secretary of Defense, the State Department and the
Agency for International Development organization adjustments in
the program to conform with changes in supply availability, the international situation and in United States national security objectives.

(11) Forecasts and reports of deliveries and supply performance
are submitted periodically by the military departments to the Director of Military Assistance and distributed to the Unified Commands
and Military Assistance Advisory Groups.

The role of the Joint Chiefs of Staff in administering military
assistance is provided by the official statement of the Department
of Defense on the subject:

> With respect to military assistance, the Joint Chiefs
> of Staff recommend military objectives, force objectives,
> scale of equipping, and priorities both on a country and
> area basis. Accordingly, the JCS is charged with continuous
> review to assure that Military Assistance Programs are in
> consonance with global security plans, and that military
> assistance resources are being distributed most effectively,
> in promoting U.S. strategic concepts. In instances where
> the supply situation is such that priorities for allocation
> of materiel among the recipient nations, or between the
> recipient nations and U.S. forces must be established, the
> recommendation of the Joint Chiefs of Staff is obtained.

> All military assistance guidance, plans and programs
> are referred to the Joint Chiefs of Staff for comment and re-
> commendation, continuing a close coordination that has existed
> since early in the history of the program. All directives
> and communications to the Unified Commands, the Military
> Departments, and to the Military Assistance Advisory Groups,
> which pertain to military assistance affairs and have strategic
> or military operational implications, are coordinated with
> the Joint Staff. Likewise, JCS directives and communications
> to the same agencies, which pertain to military assistance
> affairs, are coordinated with the Office of the Assistant
> Secretary of Defense (International Security Affairs).[27]

The Unified Commanders still perform the major role envisaged for them by the Draper Report. At the present time the commanders directly engaged in military assistance activities are:

Commander	Area of Responsibility
Commander in Chief, Europe (CINCEUR) (Also the NATO Supreme Allied Commander Europe)	Europe including Greece and Turkey plus North Africa
Commander in Chief, Middle East, Africa and South Asia (CINCMEAFSA) (Also Commander in Chief, Strike Command)	Africa south of the Sahara, Middle East and South Asia, including India and Pakistan
Commander in Chief, Pacific (CINCPAC)	Far East, including Southeast Asia
Commander in Chief, Southern Command (CINCSO)	Latin America

Some indication of the extent of Unified Command military assistance activities can be seen from the number of persons employed in military assistance work in command headquarters. For the fiscal year ending on June 30, 1964 the average number of these people was estimated as follows:[28]

Command	Military Personnel	Civilian Personnel
CINCEUR	60	29
CINCPAC	80	--
CINCMEAFSA	36	14
CINCSO	24	7

The Unified Commands command and supervise the activities of the Military Assistance Advisory Groups in their area of responsibility. These functions include: recommendation to the Joint Chiefs of Staff and Director of Military Assistance on the appropriate size and functions of Military Assistance Advisory Groups; direction and supervision of submission of military assistance planning and programming data and budget data for administrative support programs;

provision of necessary technical assistance and support (in conjunction with the military departments); and general supervision of the
Military Assistance Advisory Group's exercise of assigned functions.
In short, in military assistance organization since the Draper Report,
the Military Assistance Advisory Groups work for the Unified Commands.

The Unified Commands submit priority lists in their program recommendations so that if reductions must be made in a program,
these reductions can be made in the order the Commander suggests.

PERSONNEL FOR MILITARY ASSISTANCE

In the early years of the military assistance program no special
training was required for military assistance assignments and the
selection of personnel was somewhat haphazard. As a former Director of Military Assistance put it:

In the early days we gathered officers for military
assistance assignment from all over, largely on the basis
of availability. They received no preliminary course of
instruction, and when they got out to the end of the line
they found themselves in a very confused situation-- confused at the Washington end, confused at the country's
end and the Military Advisory Group was in the middle.[29]

This situation produced, as might be expected, considerable
criticism of the operation of the military assistance program,
especially because the combination of short tours of duty in military
assistance assignments and the lack of instruction in detailed programming and requisitioning procedures produced a variety of mistakes which the General Accounting Office and the auditors of the
three military departments were quick to discover. As a result
of this criticism it was decided in October of 1957 to establish a
Military Assistance Institute to train officers being assigned to
military assistance advisory groups.

The Institute presently operates in suburban Virginia with a
small staff, primarily composed of retired military officers.
About 50% of the officers scheduled for duty in military assistance
advisory groups abroad take the one-month course. The quantity
of instruction to be crowded into a single month is indicated by the

following description of the course provided to a Congressional Committee:

> The program of instruction includes background on
> U.S. government policy, U.S. military strategy, U.S.
> agencies in foreign countries, U.S. personnel in foreign
> countries, American capitalism and democracy. It also
> covers communism and the cold war, to include communist
> tactics and propaganda, foreigners' attitude toward the
> United States, the cold war, the role of civic action in
> winning the cold war. It includes technical instruction
> in the military assistance program. It includes the or-
> ganization of the unified commands and the MAAG's and
> the organization for military assistance here in Washington;
> the military assistance programming concept, force ob-
> jectives and priorities, MAP levels of support, MAAG
> functions, materiel program, training program, area and
> country subjects, including regional briefings, country
> briefings, something about the culture, the religion, and
> so forth, and health hints abroad.[30]

The Draper Committee recommended that all officers being assigned to military assistance duties be required to attend this
school, but this recommendation has not been implemented.

Foreign language training for military officers being assigned
to military assistance advisory groups abroad has not been common.
Such training is furnished where considered absolutely necessary,
but most officers sent to advise local personnel do not know the local
language. The effects of this lack of training are less than might be
expected because in most countries where the United States has a
large military assistance program, foreign military personnel at
senior levels have received English language instruction in preparation for taking military schooling in the United States. However, the lack of training undoubtedly does reduce the effectiveness
of the United States advisory effort. For that reason the Draper
Committee also recommended that expanded language training be
made available to military assistance personnel.

Many who have commented on the United States military assistance program have recommended basic changes in the military
personnel system designed to improve the effectiveness of the military assistance advisory groups. These recommendations form a

general pattern of indications that (a) personnel assigned be given
more extensive training in foreign languages, in the host country's
culture, in United States foreign policy and in military assistance
procedures; (b) personnel be selected only from the finest officers
and men available in the United States armed forces with emphasis
on tact, military competence, suitability for assignment and impeccable personal traits; (c) once assigned that personnel be retained
in their assignments beyond the normal tour of about a year in posts
where families are not permitted to accompany officers and two
years in other posts. Some implementation of these types of recommendations has taken place, for example, by reducing the
number of one-year tours by constructing housing for dependents in
Korea, but on the whole, these types of recommendations have not
been adopted.

The reason that recommendations of this type have not been
adopted to a greater extent is adopting them would distort the present military personnel system. The assumption which underlies
this system is that officers should be rotated often so that they
develop a wide range of experience which will lead to the optimum
development of officers to fulfill their major function. That major
function is not the administration of the military aid program, but
the command and control of United States forces in time of war.
Although persons interested in special problems--such as administration of education programs, particular weapons systems, research and development, and military assistance--frequently
recommend greater specialization and longer tours in the programs
in which they are interested, it is impossible to implement completely these types of recommendations without destroying the basic
military personnel system in the United States.

AUDIT OF MILITARY ASSISTANCE ACTIVITIES

As is the case with most government activities, some arrangement exists for post audit of military assistance activities. In the
case of military assistance, as distinguished from most audits of
private firms, these audits are more than a mere accounting for
funds. Instead the auditors cover performance in achieving objectives and even evaluate the objectives as part of their audits.
Because military assistance is both a defense program and a
foreign aid program, it is subjected to audits by both the regular
foreign aid auditors and the regular Department of Defense auditors

as well as the General Accounting Office auditors. Most of these
audit reports are classified, but on occasion the General Accounting
Office issues an unclassified report on the military assistance program.[31] This complex auditing system led a Defense Department
spokesman to state that the program was probably the "most audited
program in the entire government...."[32] Extensive procedures
exist to ensure that deficiencies and problems spotted by auditors
are corrected.

CONCLUSION

The most frequently considered military assistance administrative problem has been the question of what organizational arrangement best facilitates the coordination of economic and military aid.
Over the past twenty years a variety of organizational arrangements
have been tried, none of which have proved to be perfect. Within
the Defense Department military assistance administration has
been improved by replacing the military departments with the
Unified Commands as the level of review above the Military Assistance Advisory Groups, and by designating a senior military officer
as Director of Military Assistance within the Office of the Secretary of Defense. Several steps have been taken to improve the
effectiveness of United States military advisors, but problems
persist.

NOTES

1. Section 622(c) of the Foreign Assistance Act of 1961.
(Note: Emphasis added.)
2. Section 504(b) of the Foreign Assistance Act of 1961.
3. This summary is drawn primarily from the Brookings Institution, "Administrative Aspects of United States Foreign Assistance Programs," Study No. 6 in U.S., Congress, Senate, Special
Committee to Study the Foreign Aid Program, Foreign Aid Program: Compilation of Studies and Surveys, 85th Cong., 1st Sess.,
1957.
4. Ibid., p. 421.
5. Ibid., p. 422.
6. Ibid., citing Brookings Institution, The Administration of
Affairs and Overseas Operations (June, 1951) (prepared for the
Bureau of the Budget).

7. Portions of the Rockefeller Committee Report are printed in U.S., Congress, Senate, Subcommittee on National Security Staffing and Operations, Government Operations Committee, The Ambassador and the Problem of Coordination, 88th Cong., 1st Sess., 1963, p. 125.

8. Ibid.

9. Presidential memoranda are available as (a) press releases from the White House, (b) in the Federal Register and, therefore, in the Code of Federal Regulations, or (c) in special publications of the agency affected; in this particular case, for example, in International Cooperation Administration, Mutual Security Legislation and Related Documents (December, 1955), pp. 97-99.

10. Section 525 of the Mutual Security Act of 1954. (69 Stat 283).

11. E.O. 10575 of November 6, 1954, E.O. 10625 of August 2, 1955, E.O. 10610 of May 2, 1955, Department of State Delegation of Authority 85 of June 30, 1955 with subsequent amendments. 20 Federal Register 4825.

12. Section 523(a) of the Mutual Security Act of 1957 and E.O. 10610, as amended November, 1957.

13. March 22, 1961.

14. Section 622(c) of the Foreign Assistance Act of 1961.

15. State Department Delegation of Authority No. 104 of November 3, 1961.

16. Brookings, "Administrative Aspects of United States Foreign Assistance Programs," op. cit., pp. 463-468.

17. Ibid., p. 529.

18. Systems Analysis Corporation, "Military Aid Programs," Foreign Aid Program: Compilation of Studies and Surveys, op. cit., pp. 1037-1038.

19. Report of the President's Committee to Study the Military Assistance Program (Draper Committee) (Washington: U.S. Government Printing Office, 1959), p. 41.

20. The organization for administering military assistance and general procedures for control of foreign policy and military programs in the Eisenhower years are outlined in Timothy W. Stanley, American Defense and National Security (Washington: Public Affairs Press, 1956).

21. The strengthening of the Joint Chiefs of Staff and the Secretary of Defense vis-a-vis the military departments continues to be highly controversial. A number of books, articles and Congressional hearings provide details. See U.S., Congress, Senate, Subcommittee on National Policy Machinery, Committee on Government Operations, Organizing for National Security: A Bibliography, 86th Cong., 1st Sess., 1959.

22. Amos A. Jordan, Foreign Aid and the Defense of Southeast Asia (New York: Praeger, 1962), p. 43.

23. The early implementation of the Draper recommendations is described by one who helped implement them in Arnold Kotz's "Planning for International Security," Public Administration Review, Vol. 22, December, 1962, pp. 213-220, and by one who helped to formulate them in Amos A. Jordan, Ibid., pp. 59-68.

24. This description is taken primarily from the United States Air Force publication, Information and Guidance on Military Assistance, 8th ed., June, 1964.

25. Although President Kennedy and President Johnson have instructed the Secretary of Defense to disregard arbitrary budget ceilings or predetermined financial limits in the regular Department of Defense program (U.S., Congress, House Committee on Armed Services, Hearings on Military Posture (No. 36), 88th Cong., 2d Sess., Testimony of Secretary of Defense McNamara, p. 6897), this has not been the practice in military assistance.

26. Testimony of General Taylor, HFAC, CY 64, p. 96.

27. Information and Guidance, op. cit., p. 19.

28. Department of Defense, Military Assistance Facts, p. 35.

29. General W. B. Palmer, "Military Assistance Program: A Progress Report," Army Information Digest, Vol. 17, No. 4, April, 1962, pp. 40-46.

30. Testimony of Colonel Enemark before the House Appropriations Committee, CY 60, p. 2614. It can be assumed that some of these subjects were not covered in depth in the four weeks. This assumption is supported by the criticisms of the Military Assistance Institute made by a member of the Draper Committee staff. Jordan, op. cit., pp. 161-162 and 165-166.

31. Eight GAO reports on military aid were issued in fiscal 1962, of which 3 were unclassified. Four of 9 were unclassified in fiscal 1963. SFRC, CY 64, p. 278.

32. SAC, CY 60, p. 273.

CHAPTER 10 GRANTS OF EQUIPMENT

Military assistance expenditures consist of amounts spent for equipment and supplies ("defense articles" in legal terms), for services such as repair and rehabilitation of equipment or shipping costs ("defense services" in legal terms), and training and administrative costs. In the most recent year for which estimates are available, of the total program of $1,200 million, equipment and supplies accounted for 60% of the total or $768 million. This does not include the acquisition value of excess stocks furnished at no procurement cost to the military assistance program.

SOURCE OF SUPPLY

Equipment and supplies furnished as military aid can come either from existing stocks of the Army, Navy, Air Force or Marine Corps or from new procurement directly from a manufacturer. In the fiscal year 1963 program presented to the Congress, it was estimated that 22% of the equipment and supplies to be purchased with military assistance funds would come from service stocks and 78% from new procurement.[1] In the program for fiscal year 1964, the 36% was to come from service stocks.[2]

In fiscal year 1965 the Defense Department estimated this amount in slightly different fashion. The estimate which was given to the Passman Subcommittee is shown below:

Fiscal Year 1964-65 MAP Anticipated Source of Supply[3]
(Dollars in millions)

Service Code	Definition	FY 64 Value	%	FY 65 Value	%
"K" procurement or replacement	Articles provided by military departments from procurement or inventory.	$ 653	54	$ 601	52
"I" special	Materiel and services procured solely for MAP and financed by direct citation of MAP funds (includes training).	416	35	480	41

Service Code	Definition	FY 64		FY 65	
		Value	%	Value	%
"L" replacement, not in kind	Articles provided from military departments, to be replaced, but not in kind (materiel only).	$ 72	6	49	4
"O" offshore	Procurement offshore, solely for MAP (materiel only).	48	4	21	2
"E" excess	Articles excess to military departments (Materiel only).	*10	1	*8	1
	NOTE.--Acquisition value of excess, not a charge to MAP and nonadditive in this table.	(28)	(2)	(20)	(2)
"R" redistribution	Articles originally supplied by MAP but now excess to holding country requirements (materiel only).	*1	1/	*2	1/
"N" NMSSA	Articles from the NATO Maintenance Supply Service Agency.	1/	1/	--	--
	TOTAL	$1,200	100	$1,160	100

* Cost of repair and rehabilitation only.
1/ Less than 0.5.

Although it is sometimes alleged that military assistance is a dumping ground for excess stocks of the United States military establishment, that comment is not generally borne out by the actual use of excess stocks in the program. Through fiscal year 1964 excess stocks with an original cost of $2,611 million were provided under the military assistance program. During the same period equipment and supplies were provided from new procurement or non-excess stocks with a value of approximately $25 billion. In fiscal year

1963 a total of $1. 6 billion was used for military assistance, sup-
plemented by excess stocks valued at acquisition cost of slightly over
$100 million.

Historically, the excess stocks provided have been the greatest
in comparison to the non-excess in grants to Latin American nations.
However, in absolute terms the largest quantities of excess have
been provided to nations of the Far East as indicated below:

FY 1950-64 Excess Stocks and Non-Excess
Equipment and Supplies
($ million)

	Grant Aid	Excess at Original Cost	Excess as % of Grant Aid	% of all Excess to Region
Europe	$15,775	$ 778	5%	30%
Africa	146	18	12	1
Near East and South Asia	5,270	312	6	12
Far East	8,582	1,297	15	51
Latin America	540	152	28	6

The relationship will differ in future years as European nations no
longer receive excess stocks without charge. In fiscal year 1964,
for example, it was estimated that $27.5 million of excess stocks
(at original price) would be provided as military aid of which $10
million were to go to the Near East and South Asia and almost $12
million to the Far East.

In testimony presented to Congressional committees during
1964 military assistance witnesses pointed out that a declining
level of excess stocks is becoming available for use as military
assistance. [4] However, there is a tendency, because of the timing
lag between preparation of a program and implementation, for
items to be excess, which, at the time programs are developed, are
assumed only to be available at full price. For example, the Department of Defense estimated that $30 million of excess would be
usable in fiscal year 1962 and $48 million in fiscal 1963, but found
that over $100 million was available in each of those years.

REPAIR AND REHABILITATION OF EQUIPMENT

Under the terms of the Foreign Assistance Act excess stocks
are stocks which are "excess of the mobilization reserve" at the time
these stocks are provided as military assistance.[5] Such stocks can
be given to foreign governments eligible for military aid with no
charge to the military assistance appropriation. However, the program does have to pay for the costs of repair and rehabilitation of
equipment and supplies coming from excess stocks. The Secretary
of Defense has estimated that these costs are about 30% of the
original costs of the excess materiel.[6]

Costs for repair and rehabilitation may arise even though equipment is not excess. Excess equipment is excess because it is no
longer needed. Such equipment or supplies may never have been used
(ammunition, for example) or may have been needed and used at one
time but became excess because of changes in equipment levels in
United States forces or because of replacement by more modern
models. In some cases military departments are willing to turn
over equipment not technically excess to the military assistance
program because it is not being used or it is about to be replaced.
In such case repair and rehabilitation may be required. In many
cases this repair and rehabilitation cost can be quite large. Preparation of naval vessels may run into millions of dollars.

The cost of repair and rehabilitation of equipment depends on
how high the standards for spit and polish are. Policies of the various military departments have differed on this point. The Army
standards, for example, are that:

Articles provided to Grant Aid recipients under the
Military Assistance Program will possess the required
serviceability and appearance to insure that the articles
delivered will reflect credit upon the United States.

All materiel, except aircraft, furnished from the Department of the Army inventory will meet the serviceability
standards provided by appropriate technical instructions
for the same materiel furnished to operational units of the
Army. All equipment is provided complete with the acces-
sories needed to perform the mission for which it is intended.

All used major items of equipment are cleaned and
painted or otherwise refurbished to present a good uniform
appearance. This good appearance is intended not only to
create an immediate favorable impression, but to provide
tangible evidence that the equipment has been overhauled
and is in condition for immediate operational use. These
appearance standards are normally applied only to external
surfaces and appurtenances such as tires, canvas, glass,
floor mats, etc. and should not be construed as being designed to create a false "like new" appearance. (Emphasis
supplied.)[7]

By contrast the Air Force follows a less strict standard dependent upon "serviceability."[8]

A practice similar to that of the Army is followed in the over-
haul of naval vessels. The General Accounting Office criticized the
practice of bringing vessels to be given to foreign governments up
to higher standards than those used in the United States Navy. In
response to this charge, the Department of Defense listed as one
of its reasons:

It is recognized that to transfer a ship in good condition
is politically sound in that it prevents possible dissatis-
faction by recipient countries. It avoids the feeling that
the United States is unloading inferior or obsolete materiel
and fosters the desire to standardize to U.S. equipment.[9]

Through fiscal year 1964 the Department of Defense had programmed about half a billion dollars for repair and rehabilitation costs.
The program for fiscal year 1964 included $25.9 million for this
purpose. Using the estimate that the cost associated with repair and
rehabilitation of equipment is about 30% of the original cost of the
equipment, about two-thirds of this repair cost was for non-excess
equipment.

AIRCRAFT

Equipment furnished under military aid reflects the fact that the
peak years of military assistance programs and deliveries occurred
in the 1950's. As a result, equipment presently held by United States
allies is somewhat older than that now used by United States forces.

The comparative obsolescence of forces which have been dependent upon military assistance is particularly noticeable in the case of aircraft. The following is a complete list of fighter aircraft provided under military aid through June of 1964.

Type	Number Delivered	To be Delivered After 1 July 1964
F-84F	1,505	--
F-86D	298	--
F-86E	430	--
F-86F	1,701	4
F-86K	343	--
F-86L	18	--
F-104 (All types)	218	159
F-5 (All types)	10	158

Only the F-104 and F-5 are considered modern aircraft. Many of the others were first produced during or before the Korean War.

In addition to these aircraft, the United States has provided large numbers of transport, training, liaison and utility aircraft. Those provided in the largest quantities include the following:

Type	Number Programmed through 1964
L-19 (liaison)	822
T-28 (trainer)	250
T-33 (trainer)	1081
C-47 (transport)	421

All of the above types are obsolescent or obsolete, but funding limitations have precluded more extensive provision of modern types.

The effects of the declining level of appropriations and increasing costs for military assistance can be seen in the number of aircraft being procured. Over the 14 years from fiscal year 1950 to fiscal year 1963 an average of 519 aircraft was procured each year. In fiscal year 1964 the Defense Department was able to only procure 276 aircraft within the limits of available funds. Part of the cause for this drop is the ever increasing cost of maintaining older equipment now in country inventories, resulting in a reduction of the total available for modernization.

SHIPS

The United States has provided the following ships as grant military assistance since 1950.

Type	Number since 1950
Destroyer	35
Destroyer/Escort	61
Submarine	25
Minelayer	18
Minesweeper	326
Landing craft	522
Patrol vessels	158
Other	113

Under 10 U.S.C. Section 7307 major combatant vessels cannot be given as grant aid by the United States. Such vessels are normally "loaned," with special authorizing legislation required for each loan or loan renewal. Proposals for such legislation are considered by the Armed Services Committees of the House and Senate, not by the committees which pass on military aid.

Most of the vessels provided as military aid were the types built for the United States immediately preceding or during the Second World War. Since the beginning of military assistance a total of $1,833 million has been used for ships.

VEHICLES AND WEAPONS

Some $6.9 billion has been programmed for vehicles and weapons, primarily for ground forces in nations receiving assistance. This sum of money has purchased what would be considered astounding quantities of equipment until it is remembered that military assistance has been provided at one time or another to over 70 countries, with armed forces in excess of 5 million men. Some examples are given below:

Vehicle or Weapon	Programmed since 1950
Jeeps	119,465
2 1/2 ton trucks	129,204
3/4 ton trucks	55,069
Tanks	17,605
Armored personnel carriers	8,199
Howitzers, 105mm	4,793
Mortars	23,166
30 caliber carbines	1,253,071
30 caliber rifles	2,061,400
Machine guns	65,220

The effects of declining appropriations and increasing costs can also be seen in purchasing trends for these weapons. From fiscal year 1950 to fiscal year 1963 an average of 8,395 jeeps and 1,257 tanks was procured each year. In fiscal year 1964 funds were available for only 1,928 jeeps and 111 tanks.

AMMUNITION

Another large expenditure of military assistance funds for materiel is made in the purchase of ammunition. Ammunition for training and initial stockage is required as well as ammunition which becomes part of a "war reserve" to be drawn upon in time of war until additional ammunition can be delivered from the United States or local production. Programs through fiscal year 1964 provided for $4.1 billion of ammunition, including $115.6 million in fiscal year 1964. Although precise figures are not available, active fighting in Vietnam has certainly caused a sharp increase in ammunition costs.

MISSILES

During the late 1950's and the early 1960's the United States was continuing substantial military assistance to the technically sophisticated nations of Western Europe. This assistance was increasingly taking the form of providing, usually under cost sharing agreements, sophisticated weapons like missiles, which could only be produced in the United States.

During the period from the beginning of the program to fiscal year 1964 the missiles provided by the United States cost $1.4 billion in addition to an unknown amount of electronics and communications equipment associated with these missile systems.[10] Defense accounting procedures do not reveal in unclassified form the number of missile "systems" given to allies under military aid, but some idea can be gained from the table below of individual missiles.[11]

JUPITER (Strategic Intermediate Range Ballistic Missile)	57
THOR (Strategic Intermediate Range Ballistic Missile)	72
TARTAR (Used from ships to hit airplanes)	116
TERRIER (Used from ships to hit airplanes)	152
BULL PUP (From aircraft to the ground)	918
NIKE (Surface launched against aircraft)	2,914
HAWK (Surface launched against aircraft)	1,466*
SIDEWINDER (Launched from planes against planes)	13,121
HONEST JOHN (Surface launched to surface targets)	3,648

Some of the above listed missiles are designed for use with nuclear warheads, but these warheads are not charged to military assistance appropriations.

The shift from providing aid to Western Europe to the less technically sophisticated underdeveloped nations resulted in a decrease in the quantity of military assistance funds spent for missiles. In fiscal year 1964 only $20 million was programmed for this purpose.

COMMUNICATIONS AND ELECTRONICS

Communications and electronic equipment is traditionally an expensive item of military procurement. Military assistance funds have been used to procure some $1.9 billion worth of such equipment since the beginning of the program. The inflation of costs of such equipment is clearly shown by the fact that in fiscal year 1964 such costs represented slightly over 6% of military aid costs while in the preceding 14 years such costs were less than 3% of the total program.

OTHER

Figures released by the Defense Department also show programs of over $2.5 billion for "other" equipment and supplies, a
category ranging from materiel handling equipment, engineer equipment, and language laboratories to clothing, machine tools and the
like.

HOW EQUIPMENT IS PROCURED

Military aid includes some equipment designed especially for
the military aid program, such as the F-5 fighter. This equipment
is procured by one of the United States military departments acting
as an agent for the Director of Military Assistance. This procurement takes place within the normal military procurement mechanism
and is governed by the procedures which control procurement for
United States forces under the Armed Forces Procurement Act of
1947.

The remaining quantities of equipment and supplies used in the
military assistance program may be procured by the military departments as extensions of their own contracts. For example, if
the Army is buying 700 tank transmissions on a contract and plans
to renew the contract for the following year for 700 transmissions,
the planned uses for military aid are added on (normally before the
contract is negotiated) so that the total buy might be 900 transmissions. From the point of view of the supplier, however, his sale
is to the United States Army not to the military aid program.

Another frequently used alternative method is for the Army to
turn over to foreign governments as military aid some tank transmissions from existing Army stocks. In that case the contract with
the supplier could be increased to replace the items taken from the
Army's stock. In such a case the demand that created part of the
order was caused by the military aid program, but from the point of
view of the manufacturer he is producing solely for use by the United
States Army. For this reason it is difficult to pinpoint the impact
of military aid on the United States economy.

For the reasons outlined above, contractors wishing to sell
equipment for use in the military aid program need only watch the
procurement announcements of the United States military departments

to be assured that they will have full opportunity to bid on all military assistance contracts.

In the early years of the military aid program, defense planners believed that the world's capability to produce armaments was far below what was required to meet the communist challenge. Also in this period there was a real problem of "dollar gap," the reverse of a United States balance of payments deficit. European economic recovery had not reached the point where large quantities of goods were being produced which could be sold in the United States. On the other hand, the European demand for consumer goods (like automobiles and appliances) could not be filled from European production sources and the European capacity for producing capital goods (machine tools, steel plants, heavy machinery, etc.) had been largely destroyed during the war, forcing the European nations to purchase such equipment in the United States. As a result, there was a great demand in Europe to purchase goods produced in the United States and Canada, but European nations did not export enough to have sufficient dollars to meet their needs.

One of the methods used to put dollars into European hands was to expand military procurement in Europe greatly. This action was considered at the time to be an ideal method because (1) it provided for a large European weapons production capability, (2) the results of the production were given to various nations and, therefore, resulted in immediately increased military capabilities, and (3) the whole arrangement put dollars in European hands so that Europeans could purchase other goods in the United States.

In addition to this effort, the United States undertook a separate program to encourage the development of production facilities in Europe. This effort, known as the Facilities Assistance Program, built many weapons production facilities in Europe.

PRICING POLICY

When the military assistance program first began as the Mutual Defense Assistance Program, the prices which the military assistance program and foreign governments purchasing equipment under the military sales program paid for United States produced equipment were the "replacement costs" of the items, that is, the costs which the military department would incur in replacing them. This

policy, designed to protect the military department budgets, resulted in exorbitant charges to the military assistance program.
For example, if the United States Army had a used older model
howitzer which was given to Greece, the Army would not be reimbursed for the market value of the weapon, nor for the original
costs of the weapon minus some allowance for depreciation, nor
for the actual cost to the Army. Instead, the Army was given the
amount which would permit replacement of the item--not with a
like item but with whatever item was currently replacing items
of a like type. Thus, the replacement price might be the price
of a new model, a much more expensive howitzer with greater
capabilities than the one being replaced.

Small wonder with prices determined in this fashion that foreign
governments showed little enthusiasm for purchasing equipment and
supplies from the United States when other sources could be found.
This policy so inflated the costs of military assistance that several
studies have estimated that it resulted in excess charges to the
foreign aid program of about $1 billion before it was changed in
1957. [12]

The present law specifies that the military assistance program
(and purchasers under the sales program) shall pay the same price
for military equipment and supplies that the military departments
pay in getting such goods from each other. [13] However, the Secretary of Defense is authorized to negotiate prices for major items
to be furnished under military assistance provided that such items
are not excess and that the price is negotiated at the time that a
firm order is placed on the military department for the item. [14] No
evidence that this provision has been used appears in Congressional
hearings on military assistance in recent years. Navy regulations
for the determination of price of non-excess items include provisions for reducing the prices of items of which the Navy has a long
supply. The Air Force maintains a special board for the pricing of
aircraft and missiles.

Even after these revisions in pricing policy, the Department of
Defense continued a procedure which resulted in substantial costs to
military assistance funds for equipment, which, though technically
not excess, was not being replaced by the military departments.
The then Director of Military Assistance estimated that the fiscal
year 1961 military assistance fund included $285 million to pay mili-
tary departments for equipment which they were not planning to replace in kind. [15]

This practice was severely criticized in a General Accounting Office audit report.[16] The Department of Defense response to this report indicated that while the military departments might have misunderstood relevant directives resulting in some overcharges, "MAP was undercharged in other instances."[17]

Another problem developed by this report concerned the price charged military assistance for items not excess. The General Accounting Office found that military aid was being overcharged for many of these items. The Department of Defense response indicated that in some cases--when items are no longer being procured--the price to be charged is that of the last procurement, which generally means the highest price at which the item was ever bought, a price considerably higher than the actual price of the particular item furnished under military aid.

Frequently in the production of military assistance items a question arises as to whether allied nations or United States military departments should get the first items off the production line, or how a limited number of items shall be allocated among allies and military departments. These questions are considered by the Joint Chiefs of Staff.[18]

EQUIPMENT STILL IN SERVICEABLE CONDITION

Military equipment delivered under the military aid program deteriorates just like any other equipment. Some simply falls apart as a result of adverse climatic conditions or hard use. Some is lost in training or combat operations; other types of equipment, such as aircraft, are destroyed by accidents. As a result much of the military equipment supplied to United States allies under previous programs is no longer in serviceable condition and much of it has also been dropped from country inventories as excess or by other means. The rate of serviceability losses has increased as the number of years since the high levels of military aid in the 1950's has increased. The following table shows the percentage of equipment still serviceable in various regions of the world.[19]

As of 30 June	Percent Serviceable of Equipment and Supplies Delivered Under Military Aid		
	1961	1962	1963
Europe	65.3%	61.6%	56.9%
Near East and Africa	67.2	66.8	65.8
Far East	59.8	58.5	57.4
Latin America	74.2	78.9	78.9
Worldwide	64.2	61.9	59.0

As the table indicates, new deliveries of equipment have outpaced aging and losses in Latin America, but in no other area of the world. A high proportion of equipment supplied to the Far East is no longer serviceable undoubtedly because (a) climatic conditions are more conducive to rust and deterioration than in Europe, (b) local forces are less skilled at maintenance, and (c) equipment has been destroyed or lost in combat, such as the shelling of the offshore islands, the French War in Vietnam, the present war in Vietnam and the actions in Laos.

The peak years of deliveries of military assistance to Europe were from fiscal year 1953, when over $4 billion worth of supplies and services was delivered, to fiscal 1959, the last year when deliveries exceeded $2 billion. It is reasonable to expect that most of this equipment will be phased out of European inventories during the period a decade later from 1963 to 1969. This conclusion is borne out by the fact that in the two years ending in June of 1963, $1.2 billion worth of equipment and supplies provided to Europe became unserviceable or was dropped from inventory, leaving only $6.4 billion worth. A continuation of this rate would indicate that European nations will continue to be using material provided by the United States until the early 1970's, but that most of the equipment will have been removed from inventory by the late 1960's.

The Congress in passing the Mutual Security Act was convinced that equipment which the United States provided should be returned to the United States when the recipients no longer had a use for it. The requirement imposed at that time was similar to that which appears today in the Foreign Assistance Act:

Section 506(a). In addition to such other provisions as the President may require, no defense articles shall be furnished to any country on a grant basis unless it shall have agreed that...

(4) unless the President consents to other disposition, it will return to the United States Government for such use or disposition as the President considers in the best interests of the United States such articles which are no longer needed for the purposes for which furnished.

Assurances to this effect by countries receiving military assistance are contained in bilateral agreements which deal with over-all military assistance programs and their implementation, or in special agreements which deal solely with the excess problem. Typical of the latter is the agreement with Japan, [20] which provides that (a) Japan will report to the United States when military assistance furnished equipment is no longer required for the purpose for which originally intended, (b) the United States may accept title and, if this is done, the Japanese will move the material to a Japanese port. If the United States does not wish to take back the material, the agreement provides for disposition to be accomplished after consultation between the United States and Japan.

One of the theories underlying this Congressional requirement was that military equipment could be transferred from one country to another after it became excess in the first country, thereby getting double return for many military assistance dollars. To a substantial extent this requirement has had the result which was expected, especially in the early years of the military assistance program when the quality of European weapons was increasing rapidly and material and weapons previously provided to Europe could be transferred to underdeveloped nations. Also, after the French left Indochina over $230 million worth of equipment was recovered in fiscal year 1956 for redistribution to meet requirements in other countries. However, the value of such redistribution is limited by a predictable string saving tendency on the part of the nations which have received United States equipment. Because there is no return to the country giving up the equipment when it is redistributed by the United States, there is a tendency to hang on to equipment until it is clear beyond doubt that it is useless to that country. [21]

Material reported as excess is screened against military assistance requirements in all other countries of the world. If no requirement exists for redistribution, a determination is made as to whether
it would be profitable for the United States to take the material back
and sell it as surplus. If it is determined that a profit can be made,
the United States disposal agencies sell the material in the same
manner as excess generated abroad by United States forces and the
proceeds are returned to miscellaneous receipts of the Treasury--
not for further military assistance activities. If it would not be
profitable to take such material back, the holding country may be
authorized to dispose of the property involved. The recipient country applies the proceeds from the sale of such scrap and surplus
to support of its defense effort. [22]

An indication of the magnitude of transactions in excess stocks
reported by recipient countries was given in hearings on the military
assistance program in 1960. By the summer of 1959 Belgium had
declared to the United States equipment and supplies with an original
cost of $115.9 million of which $7.8 million had been turned over
to Belgium for Belgium to sell and deposit the proceeds in a special
account supplemental to the Belgian defense budget. By that summer, Belgium had received about a quarter of a million dollars from
such sales with a rate of return of about 3% of the original cost of
the equipment sold. [23]

DIVERSION

The Foreign Assistance Act and predecessor legislation impose,
and military assistance bilateral agreements have embodied, several conditions designed to prevent improper use of military assistance. Recipient countries are not permitted without the consent of
the United States to allow private parties to use the equipment, to
give away or sell the equipment or to use such articles "for purposes
other than those for which furnished." [24]

Military assistance agreements spell out with some specificity
the exact purposes for which assistance is furnished. In the case of
the NATO countries, the agreements generally conform to that with
Belgium which states that Belgium undertakes to make effective use
of assistance:

(a) for the purpose of promoting the integrated defense of
the North Atlantic Area, and for facilitating the development
of defense plans under Article 9 of the North Atlantic Treaty,
and (b) in accordance with defense plans formulated by the
North Atlantic Treaty Organization recommended by the
North Atlantic Defense Committee and Council, and agreed
to by the two Governments. [25]

In the case of non-NATO countries the agreements are somewhat
different. The agreement with Pakistan signed in 1954 provides:

    The Government of Pakistan will use this assistance,
exclusively to maintain its internal security, its legitimate
self-defense, or to permit it to participate in the defense of
the area, or in the United Nations collective security
arrangements and measures, and Pakistan will not undertake any act of aggression against any other nation. The
Government of Pakistan will not, without the prior agreement of the Government of the United States, devote such
assistance to purposes other than those for which it was
furnished. [26]

It has been extremely difficult for the United States to make
nations which have received military assistance comply with the
terms of these agreements. This situation, although perhaps impossible to foresee when the equipment was provided, arises because
many countries such as the Netherlands, Belgium, France and the
United Kingdom have extensive worldwide commitments. Without
doubt, it is impossible to segregate completely, in any logistics
system, equipment provided as grant aid by the United States and
equipment purchased from various sources. It is unrealistic to
expect a Belgian paratrooper, for example, before landing in the
Congo to remove a part from a purchased pistol if the part was provided by United States grant aid.

A second problem arises because the United States has furnished
practically all the military equipment in use by some nations. The
result is that unless these nations agree to renounce completely the
use of force no matter how serious they consider the threats to their
interests to be--and this is unlikely--they will be using United States
equipment for purposes for which the assistance was not intended.
For example, the Secretary of Defense testifying before a Congressional committee stated that, in any shooting war between Greece

and Turkey, 'almost certainly they would be using United States weapons. "[27]

Diversions from intended uses usually occur at times when the problems confronted by United States policymakers are far greater than diversion of United States provided equipment. As a result, the United States interest may not always be served by sole concern with the equipment being used, especially when it may be possible to encourage the termination of military action entirely rather than simply to suggest that it should not be carried out with United States weapons. These factors have combined to produce many situations in which military assistance furnished equipment has been used by recipients outside the scope of the undertakings made by those countries before equipment was furnished. The Greek and Turkish situation has already been mentioned. The French Government used equipment furnished by the United States in the war in Algeria[28] and India periodically accuses Pakistan of using United States furnished equipment against India.

CONCLUSION

Most of the equipment furnished under the military assistance program is taken from the stocks of the Army, Navy and Air Force. Unless such equipment is excess to United States requirements, the military assistance program pays the military department concerned for the equipment. Procurement for military assistance purposes is handled by the Defense Department in the same manner as procurement for United States forces. Deliveries of equipment under military assistance have declined sharply since the peak years in the mid-1950's due to decreased funds available for purchase and the inflation of military equipment prices. Over half the equipment provided since the beginning of the military aid program is still considered serviceable.

Military assistance agreements with recipient governments require them to declare equipment excess when no longer needed for the purposes for which furnished and to refrain from using such equipment for purposes other than those spelled out in agreements with the United States. Enforcement of both these conditions has been difficult.

NOTES

1. Testimony of General W. B. Palmer, HAC, CY 62, p. 398.

2. Testimony of General Robert Wood, HAC, CY 63, p. 169.

3. HAC, CY 65, p. 512; detail may not add to totals due to rounding.

4. See, for example, the statement of the Director of Military Assistance before the House Appropriations Committee during 1964. HAC, CY 64.

5. Section 644(g), 22 USC 2403.

6. HAC, CY 64, p. 342.

7. Department of the Air Force, Information and Guidance on Military Assistance, 8th ed., June, 1964, p. 31. Prior to 1962 the Army had provided even more spit and polish to produce a like new condition. This practice was severely criticized by the General Accounting Office.

8. Ibid., p. 49.

9. HFAC, CY 60, p. 973.

10. A missile system consists of all the ground support equipment associated with maintaining a missile, launching it, finding targets for it and in some systems, determining its success.

11. Department of Defense, Military Assistance Facts, except for item marked * which is listed in Information and Guidance, op. cit.

12. Systems Analysis Corporation, "Military Aid Programs," in U.S., Congress, Senate, Special Committee to Study the Foreign Aid Program, Foreign Aid Program: Compilation of Studies and Surveys, 85th Cong., 1st Sess., 1957, stated that the overcharges were in excess of the $1 billion which had been estimated by the Government Accounting Office.

13. Section 644(m) of the Foreign Assistance Act of 1961.

14. Section 644(m)(3) of the Foreign Assistance Act of 1961.

15. SAC, CY 60, p. 268.

16. U.S., General Accounting Office, "Review of the Pricing of Materiel Delivered to the Military Assistance Program by the Military Departments," February 29, 1960.

17. The Department of Defense response is contained in the hearings of the Senate Appropriations Committee, CY 60, pp. 269-273.

18. Information and Guidance, op. cit., p. 19.

19. Estimates from HAC, CY 62, p. 403 for 1961; HAC, CY 63, p. 159 for 1962; and HAC, CY 64, p. 404 for 1963.

20. TIAS 2958.

21. Several reports of the General Accounting Office have been critical of United States Military Assistance Advisory Groups for lack of aggressiveness in getting countries to declare this material excess.

22. Information and Guidance, op. cit., pp. 32-33.

23. HAC, CY 60, pp. 2431-2433.

24. Section 506 of the Foreign Assistance Act of 1961, 22 USC 2314.

25. Article 2 of the agreement which entered into force in 1950, TIAS 2010.

26. Article 2 of the bilateral agreement with Pakistan. TIAS 2976.

27. Testimony of Secretary of Defense McNamara before the House Appropriations Committee, CY 64, p. 330.

28. HAC, CY 60, pp. 447-448.

CHAPTER **11** THE MILITARY ASSISTANCE
TRAINING PROGRAM

United States military assistance is currently provided primarily
to those nations which face a significant military threat but which do
not have the economic capability to maintain the forces required for
their own defense. The absence of economic development in these
countries coincides with a lack of familiarity with complex machinery
and the management of large complex organizations. It is, therefore, not enough in these countries for the United States to provide
weapons, communications equipment, and transportation equipment.
The members of the armed forces of these countries must be taught
how to utilize and maintain this equipment. Accordingly, the United
States provides approximately one-tenth of the total value of its military assistance in the form of training.

The most frequently discussed aspect of this training is training
of foreign military personnel within the United States. Some 16,500
foreign military personnel were expected to be trained under the
auspices of the military assistance program within the United States
in fiscal year 1963.[1] More foreign students are trained in the
United States under this program than under all other United States
government programs combined.[2] This training varies from simple
training in such skills as military engineering to firing and maintenance practice with advanced missile systems. Fifty percent of
those trained are officers; the remainder, enlisted men and a few
civilians.

Military assistance trainees attend practically all United States
military schools with the exception of a few senior service schools
such as the National War College and the Industrial College of the
Armed Forces, which are normally reserved for United States nationals alone. There are some 350 different installations in the
United States where foreign military trainees take formal courses.[3]
Normally, training in the United States is conducted in the English
language with language training being provided before the trainees
reach the United States. Most of the training is given to single individuals although occasionally whole units, such as a ship's crew,
are trained. This unit training concept is particularly useful with
weapons like missiles where training ranges and complex instrumen-
tation are involved. In such training of units in the United States,
the training is less costly than building training facilities abroad.

The United States provides the full cost of the student's training, transportation to and from the United States and a per diem allowance. Most foreign trainees are given quarters at the United States installations where they are studying. In the case of European nationals, the United States does not bear the full cost of training. Recipient governments are asked to pay the cost of transportation and per diem allowances as well as the trainee's salary. Although many military assistance trainees are other than Caucasian, substantial difficulties in acceptance in the United States have not been encountered despite the fact that many of the installations used for military assistance training are in the deep South. This acceptance is partly attributable to public relations campaigns conducted by local base officials.[4]

TRAINING IN OVERSEAS UNITED STATES SCHOOLS

To minimize the costs associated with extensive travel of trainees to and from the United States from geographically distant nations, the United States has utilized United States schools established for the use of United States personnel in foreign countries and special schools established solely for the military aid program to train foreign students. The major schools utilized for this training are Fort Gulick and Albrook Air Force Base in the Canal Zone. As of March 15, 1964, a total of 21,825 Latin American personnel had attended these schools. Instruction for Air Force, Army, and Navy personnel is given in counterinsurgency and civic action. Instruction is conducted in Spanish.

Some personnel from the Far East are trained in United States military installations in Okinawa and some from Europe in the schools utilized by United States forces in Germany.

TRAINING IN THE RECIPIENT NATION

The United States maintains large military assistance advisory groups throughout the world. Typical examples of the size of these groups in countries where the United States has large assistance programs follow:

| Country | Average Strength June 30, 1964–June 30, 1965 | | |
	U.S. Civilian	Military	Local
Greece	11	112	–
Turkey	53	426	230
Iran	11	409	–
Pakistan	3	103	–
Korea	105	1,402	772
Republic of China	4	842	121

These military assistance advisory groups have as part of their
function the administration of the military aid program, from determining what equipment is to be given to making sure it is properly
utilized. However, the substantial size of these missions or military assistance advisory groups is primarily attributable to the fact
that most of the personnel in them are assigned to the training of
foreign military personnel within the country. For example, in
fiscal year 1964 training personnel were about 90% of total military
personnel assigned to the military assistance advisory group in
Korea, 75% in the Republic of China, 56% in Iran and 30% in Greece.[5]
These training personnel who are permanently assigned to military
assistance advisory groups may carry out roles as unit advisors
(actually stationed with their units), headquarters advisors or as
managers of the training effort responsible for assisting local officials involved in training and providing training manuals and similar
materials.

The efforts of the military assistance advisory groups are sup-
plemented by United States mobile training teams which are called
upon for special skills not normally within the competence of persons
permanently assigned to foreign countries. Such teams are usually
composed of senior enlisted and junior officer skilled military personnel. Typical examples of the work conducted by mobile training
teams are counterinsurgency advice in the Far East, use of armored
tactics in Greece or utilization of new air force concepts in Latin
America.

In some cases the United States needs to teach foreign governments to use highly complex equipment manufactured in the United
States, such as F-104 aircraft, extensive communications systems
and the like. The United States military departments may not have
trained personnel available for these types of assignments and must
therefore call upon the contractor which produced the equipment or

other skilled contractors. These contractor groups, paid for by military aid funds, are normally called contract technical service personnel teams. The cost of these teams has been somewhat in excess of $10 million each year.

SELECTION OF PERSONNEL
FOR UNITED STATES TRAINING

United States military training, especially the more costly kind conducted within the United States, is most effective when given to persons who have an extensive career in their country's armed forces ahead of them. Likewise, the United States presumably benefits more if its training is given to up and coming leaders rather than to "duds" within the country's military forces. Accordingly, it is the policy of the Department of Defense in selecting these trainees to insist upon the cream of the crop from the recipient country's military establishment.

After these personnel have completed their training, it is customary for the United States to follow up to determine that the trainees are in jobs that properly utilize their training and to maintain effective contacts with trainees through alumni programs of the military schools concerned and occasional contacts with United States personnel trained in the same institutions.

ORIENTATION TRAINING

In addition to training in specific skills and officer training such as that given in the Command and Staff College, the United States brings large numbers of senior foreign defense officials (both military and civilian) to the United States for what is known as orientation training. This training normally consists of tours of United States military installations and local points of interest and includes entertainment at various bases and social contact with United States officers, as well as military briefings. The theory of this training is that it provides an opportunity for the emerging leaders of these nations to understand the American military establishment and the American people. It presumably also leaves them more oriented towards the United States and its policies than they were when they began the training. During fiscal year 1963, 1,430 individuals were given these orientation training tours. [6]

COST

According to estimates of the Department of Defense, military assistance training was expected to cost $102 million in fiscal year 1964, but only $72 million in the budget proposed for the following year. [7] This cost includes not only the costs of training teams and contractor teams but also the costs associated with administration of the training program.

The Congress normally imposes a ceiling for administrative expenses on the Department of Defense. This ceiling is in a sense an artificial figure because the line between program administration and training administration is difficult to draw, especially in the case of personnel in military assistance advisory groups who may carry out both functions. The cost of military assistance training also includes charges made by the military departments for the use of their military schools. These charges tend to vary widely depending largely on how much of the school's overhead is pro-rated as a charge to military aid.

TRAINING OUTSIDE THE MILITARY AID PROGRAM

In addition to the programs described above, the Army, Navy, Air Force and Marine Corps have authority to train certain foreign personnel with their own funds. The Draper Committee estimated that some 4,400 men received such training from 1950-1958. [8] These programs are normally administered by military attaches in the field and by United States military departments in Washington.

Training like equipment can be sold. The United States does sell a substantial amount of training in connection with sales of equipment to foreign governments. [9]

TRAINING FOR IMPROVED MANAGEMENT

In recent years the General Accounting Office has made about ten reports per year about the military assistance program. These reports generally point to mistakes in requisitioning of spare parts and other equipment producing surpluses in recipient countries, poor supply management in recipient countries, inadequate maintenance and storage of United States equipment and the like. Unlike

most reports of the General Accounting Office these reports in large
part consider and criticize the actions of foreign officials rather than
United States officials. The United States officials are held responsible only inferentially because they have not succeeded in training
the military personnel in various countries to handle military equipment perfectly.

When the primary concentration of military assistance was to
the well-developed nations of Western Europe, little problem was
encountered in supply and maintenance procedures within recipient
countries. Many of these countries, particularly the United Kingdom and Germany, had personnel familiar with complicated military equipment and fully capable of operating a logistics system as
complicated as that of the United States. Mistakes were made by
both the United States personnel who programmed assistance and by
the country officials receiving it, but on the whole the situation was
not bad. These problems were similar to those discovered by the
General Accounting Office in the operations of the United States
Army, Navy and Air Force, and similar to those occurring in private industry. [10]

As the emphasis of military assistance shifted from the nations
of Western Europe to less developed countries like Korea, maintenance and logistics operations became much more of a problem.
The magnitude of the problem can be seen by a comparison of the
technical sophistication which conscripts in these countries have
with that of conscripts in the United States. The average American
boy by the time he is drafted knows how to drive a car and may
know how to keep it in repair. He understands that engines burn
gas, need oil and that motor blocks will freeze unless antifreeze
is used. He can operate and perhaps repair or change tubes in
television and radio sets. He can read and write in English and may
be accustomed to reading and talking about technical data such as
that found in popular magazines about cars and perhaps boats. He
can add and subtract, divide and multiply and may know algebra.
He is at least aware of the complex accounting systems involved in
credit cards, charge plates, automated billing machinery and the
like. He has at least been exposed to elementary physical concepts
such as gravity, inertia and centrifugal force. He has played with
electric trains, or go-karts, or model airplanes with motors, or
model cars. Such a boy, when he enters the training program of the
United States armed forces, is ready to learn how to drive trucks,

jeeps, and tanks, how to operate and maintain radios, how to keep
stock records and even financial records.

On the other hand, a student receiving military training in a less
developed country will have had none of this training in the use of
sophisticated equipment and accounting systems. It is fair to assume that military training in these countries is much more difficult
and much less likely to be successful in producing qualified officers
and men than in the United States.

In the United States, a new recruit assigned to supply or logistic
duties becomes a part of a system that has developed by trial and
error for over a hundred years. A similar recruit in a less developed country will probably have to become a part of a system which
is in the midst of transition from an antiquated system or none at
all to one patterned on the American model.

The combination of these factors makes the military job which
United States training must accomplish a major effort. The Defense
Department's appraisal of how well it is doing in this effort is indicated by an article written by General Williston B. Palmer, who
was at the time it was written the Director of the Military Assistance Program. He said:

> Even with ever-increasing technical help from the
> United States forces, the struggles of our friends to develop
> competent supply and repair systems have been painful
> and difficult. Gradually, as more of their younger men
> receive our training and as more of their older men retire,
> things begin to get better. But it has been a harrowing
> experience for both sides, the giver and the receiver.
>
> . . . .
>
> And it is the fact, in my professional judgment, that
> our military assistance is being used with steadily improved
> efficiency to produce increasingly effective forces, even
> though that same judgment also tells me that there is hardly
> a country where the forces are yet up to the standards of
> United States forces in tactical and logistical effectiveness.
> They started practically from zero effectiveness and they
> are immensely more effective than they were. [11]

The task of improving supply and logistics systems and training
to use new and sophisticated military equipment is itself a formidable one, and much of the money spent for military assistance
training is devoted to it. This training is designed to increase military capabilities--the primary purpose of the military aid program.
Devotion to these purposes is sufficiently time-consuming so that
many officers responsible for training in any country and for determining what equipment will be provided to the country do not have
the time, or perhaps the inclination, to go beyond those jobs and
perform essentially political work. Thus, Janowitz noted that
officers in military assistance advisory groups are generally
"hardware" oriented. [12]

The possibilities of the military assistance training program as
an instrument for teaching officers of the new nations such American
concepts as the meaning of democracy, the non-political role of
the military and the necessity for economic development have been
stressed in many studies of the military assistance program.
Generally, the suggestions for expanding this function of the training
program are made only in the case of formal training received in
United States schools rather than in the case of training performed
within the recipient country. [13]

In 1959 the Draper Committee conducted a special study of training programs as part of their review of the whole military assistance
program. [14] This study pointed out that, unlike the situation in the
United States, the military forces of the countries receiving military
assistance play a substantial role in the maintenance of internal
security and in politics in their own countries. This fact, it was
said, should be recognized in the training provided by the United
States. The study recommended expansion of orientation tours by
foreign officers in the United States, better procedures for "the
identification and grooming of future leaders," and suggested that
relatively few foreign military officers of middle and upper rank have
been provided instruction in concepts or doctrines governing the employment of the military instrument both in peace and war.

A study of underdeveloped countries by the Center for International Studies of the Massachusetts Institute of Technology made similar
recommendations in 1960. [15] This group concluded that:

We have looked at military assistance too much from the
point of view of its military effectiveness alone; its

relationship to social, economic, and political change, and
to the overall policy objectives of the United States in the
transitional societies has been given too little consideration.[16]

In addition to suggesting greater use of military forces as a training
ground for the development of skills usable in the economy and to
perform projects contributing to economic development, the study
recommended:

Opportunities should be expanded for foreign officers,
especially at the middle and junior levels, to travel and
study in the United States.[17]

Some studies of the role of the military in developing countries
have indicated that the effects of training in the United States are
not exactly what they are expected to be. The United States may
attempt to train foreign military officers to the concept that the
military should remain completely out of politics. However, the
teaching of the ways in which the military can contribute to economic
and social programs may encourage the officer returning from
training to participate in politics at least to the extent necessary
to undertake these programs in his own country. Also the mere
exposure to the American standard of living may kindle desires to
move faster toward economic development, which may tempt military officers to deal harshly with governments not adequately pur-
suing policies to accelerate economic growth.[18]

CONCLUSION

About one-tenth of the annual expenditures of the military assistance program are made to train foreign military personnel to use
equipment provided by grant aid. This training takes many forms
including providing United States training personnel to the recipient
country, bringing foreign students to special schools abroad or to
the United States and sending contractor technical teams and military mobile training teams to the recipient country. The fact that
most military personnel in the underdeveloped countries do not have
the technical and accounting skills associated with more complex
societies makes the work of the trainer much harder, especially in
the logistics management field. However, progress is being made.

Some observers have recommended that the United States expand
the use of its training programs as a tool for teaching political attitudes toward democracy, toward the role of the military and toward
economic growth and social responsibility. While some changes in
this direction have been made, training tends to be "hardware"
oriented--that is, oriented toward specific military problems rather
than general social and economic ones.

NOTES

1. HAC, CY 63, p. 68.

2. Statistics on foreign students in the United States are published by the Institute of International Education. See the Institute's
pamphlet, Open Doors (New York: Institute of International
Education, 1964)

3. These installations are listed in an appendix to the Institute
of Internation Education, Military Assistance Training Programs of
the U.S. Government (New York: Institute of International Education,
1964). Much of the material in this chapter is taken from that report.

4. Ibid., p. 20.

5. Administrative strength from HAC, CY 63, p. 550; total
strength from Military Assistance Facts, 1964, pp. 34-35.

6. Military Assistance Training Programs, op. cit., p. 25.

7. FY 64 estimate from Military Assistance Facts, 1964; FY
65 from HAC, CY 64, p. 298.

8. Report of the President's Committee to Study the Military
Assistance Program (Draper Committee) (Washington: U.S. Government Printing Office, 1959), Vol. II., p. 348.

9. The Institute of International Education found that over one
thousand men received such training each year. Military Assistance Training Programs, op. cit., p. 8.

10. Secretary of Defense McNamara frequently has responded to
criticism of the logistics management of countries receiving military aid by pointing out that similar problems occur in spare parts
management, for example, in firms like Ford, which he headed,
and General Motors.

11. General W. B. Palmer, "Military Assistance Program,"
Army Information Digest, April, 1962, Vol. 17, No. 4.

12. Morris Janowitz, The Military in the Political Development
of New Nations (Chicago: University of Chicago Press, 1964), p. 97.

13. An excellent description of just what is included in the present training programs in the United States is provided by Lieutenant Doyle C. Ruff, USAF, "Win Friends--Defeat Communism," Instructors Journal, II, No. 1 (July, 1964), 25-34. C. Windle and T. Vallance, "Optimizing Military Assistance Training," World Politics, XV (October, 1962) 91-107, is an example of these suggestions.

14. Draper Committee Report, op. cit. The study "Training and Education under the Assistance Programs" appears as Annex E to the committee's report.

15. Center for International Studies, Massachusetts Institute of Technology, "Economic, Social and Political Change in the Underdeveloped Countries and Its Implications for United States Policy," printed as Study No. 12 in U.S., Congress, Senate, Committee on Foreign Relations, United States Foreign Policy: Compilation of Studies, 87th Cong., 1st Sess., 1961.

16. Ibid., pp. 1247-1248.

17. Ibid., p. 1249.

18. For example, see Janowitz, op. cit., pp. 62-63.

CHAPTER 12   THE MILITARY SALES PROGRAM

As its title implies, Lend Lease, America's first experience with a large program of military assistance, was designed to be on a sales, or reimbursement, basis. The lend lease concept was that America's aid should consist of making available the products of America's factories, not of making them available without charge. Accordingly, the Lend Lease Program contemplated reimbursement for American assistance.

After World War II, it was becoming increasingly obvious that the countries which needed United States assistance were not in a position to pay for it either in cash or on easy terms. In fact, these nations were not able to cover their obligations under the Lend Lease Program. As a result, American postwar assistance, economic and military, was generally made available on a grant basis. The Marshall Plan and Greek-Turkish aid furnish examples.

However, in the case of military equipment, it was also recognized that many countries which were friendly to the United States would not be included in the early grant programs because they were not considered vital to the military posture of the free world. Latin America provides an example. Thus, although no provision for grants of military equipment to Latin American nations was made in the Mutual Defense legislation in 1949, provisions were included in that law to permit sales to these nations. These sales continued to be considered as aid and were called "reimbursable assistance."

Until about 1958, the sales program was of little importance in relation to grant military assistance. There were several reasons for this lack of emphasis on sales. First, most of the nations receiving assistance were not in a financial position to buy the military equipment which both they and the United States thought was required. Second, most of the nations which were receiving grants of military assistance were also beneficiaries of the economic aid program. To have shifted military assistance from a grant to a sales basis would only have increased the burdens which the United States was carrying under its economic aid program.

The third and most important reason for the failure to expand sales was the pricing policy then in effect for military equipment. Because both military sales and military grants to foreign governments are, and traditionally have been, authorized by the same piece of foreign aid legislation, the methods for determining prices to be charged to the military assistance program were also used for the determination of the price at which United States-produced equipment should be sold to foreign governments. The price which the United States was asking foreign governments to pay during this period for equipment then in the inventory of United States forces was the cost of replacement of that equipment. Therefore, if the United States were offering to sell a tank built in 1940 at a cost of $18,000, the asking price would be the price of a new tank--probably more complicated and powerful than the one being sold-- at prevailing prices at the time of the offer to the foreign government.

The theory of this policy was that if military assistance sales or grants were going to be used to take equipment away from United States forces, the programs should pay the costs of replacing the equipment they took. This policy was, however, indiscriminately applied to equipment which had already been used by United States forces and to equipment which the military departments were planning to replace, whether or not it was sold or given away under military aid programs. The result of this policy was to place the price of United States-produced military equipment well above that asked by other suppliers. A number of extremely valuable new contracts were lost by this policy. [1] Most of the purchases of military equipment which were made in the United States were made only because no other country produced the equipment desired.

By the late 1950's, the situation was becoming more favorable to expanded sales of United States military equipment and training. A number of countries, especially in Europe, which had become accustomed to United States equipment and training while they received grant aid, were no longer receiving enough grant aid to meet all their requirements. Pricing policy had been revised so that United States-produced goods were available at competitive prices. Finally, the former European shortage of dollars and hard currency had ended, and the situation was beginning to be reversed as the flow of gold from United States reserves began.

The increasing balance of payments problem was undoubtedly the greatest incentive for increases of military export sales, both by private exporters and by the United States Government. By 1964 the United States Government was extensively engaged in a

wide variety of efforts to reduce the outflow of dollars from the country by such devices as keeping procurement by the economic aid
agency and the Defense Department within the United States and by
taxing the income from foreign securities. At the same time efforts
were being made by all government agencies to increase the inflow
of dollars to the United States by encouraging tourism in the United
States, by encouraging commercial exports and by increasing military sales.

The resulting growth of military assistance sales can be vividly
seen from the following comparison of deliveries under the sales
program with deliveries under the program for grant aid. [2]

($ millions)

Fiscal Year	Credit Sales	Total Sales	Grants
1950		2	56
1951		19	980
1952		72	1481
1953		161	4159
1954		121	3296
1955		118	2396
1956	7	119	2920
1957	7	72	2078
1958	39	353	2325
1959	60	222	2050
1960	21	256	1697
1961	30	268	1344
1962	21	323	1427
1963	46	861	1765
1974 (est.)	62	960	1391

Because of the long lead time associated with many of the articles
purchased under the sales program, the above table showing deliveries does not reveal completely the marked increase in military
sales after 1960. The following table shows firm orders placed (purchases) by foreign governments during the fiscal years covered.

($ millions)

Year	Total Purchases
1960	234
1961	327
1962	892
1963	922
1964 (est.)	1604[3]

As a matter of normal commercial practice, and to avoid unnecessary pressures on purchasing governments to buy from other
sources, the United States Government does not release figures
for the cash purchases on a country by country basis. However, it
is apparent that the bulk of the increase shown above in sales is a
result of German purchases in the United States. Under Secretary
of State Douglas Dillon and Secretary of the Treasury Robert
Anderson began in late 1960 to obtain German cooperation in increasing military export orders. This action ultimately led to the
Strauss (the German Minister of Defense)/Gilpatric (then United
States Deputy Secretary of Defense) German Offset Agreement of
1961. [4] That agreement accounted for $600 million of sales in the
United States in fiscal year 1962[5] and presumably comparable
amounts for later years.

Information provided by the Department of Defense indicates
that the total of direct sales purchases were divided by region as
follows. [6]

	Through FY 1964 ($ Millions)
Europe	$4,023
Africa	52
Near East and South Asia	142
Far East	501
Western Hemisphere	771
TOTAL	$5,490

NOTE: Detail may not add to total due to rounding.

The number of countries expected to purchase equipment or services from the United States during fiscal year 1965 was 51, a reduction from 61 listed as having made purchases in the peak year of 1960. In sales, of course, it is not the number of countries purchasing but the amount purchased which counts.

DIFFERENT TYPES OF SALES

There are a variety of ways in which a foreign government can purchase military equipment and supplies from United States sources. From the seller's viewpoint, these various methods are available to stimulate sales of his product.

1) Direct Sales from Private United States Supplier to Foreign Government: Military equipment can be sold by United States suppliers directly to foreign governments or through a foreign subsidiary or middleman to those governments. Much of the equipment and supplies used by military forces in foreign countries, as is the case in this country, are commercially available items which are useful to a variety of purchasers other than military forces. Examples are clothing and cloth, canteens, vehicles, such as bulldozers, cranes, and materials handling equipment, office supplies, mapping equipment, small aircraft and helicopters, oil and oil products and medical supplies. These types of items are of no intrinsic military value, and export of them is similar in its problems to export of any other commercially available item.

Some of these types of items are currently furnished under grant military assistance, primarily to countries like Korea, the Republic of China, Greece and Turkey, Vietnam and Thailand. Engineer equipment (graders, trucks, bulldozers, etc.) is also provided under military assistance to the large number of countries where the United States is encouraging military civic action by assisting engineer units. Sale of items to be given to foreign nations under the military assistance grant program must be made to the military department acting as the procurement agent for the Department of Defense for the commodity or item. Military assistance requirements for these items are normally lumped into total Department of Defense requirements and not separately identified in invitations to bid.

Equipment and supplies of this nature are not normally sold through the military sales program of the Department of Defense. The Congress has actively discouraged replacement of commercial exports by government to government sales, even though the effect of the sale on the balance of payments and the profit of the seller would be about the same whether the sale were direct or through the United States Government to the purchasing military forces. Thus, the Foreign Assistance Act of 1961, as amended, in which the authority for the government to sell military equipment and supplies to other governments is contained, states:

No sales of unclassified defense articles shall be made to the government of any economically developed nation under the provisions of this subsection (sales) unless such articles are not generally available for purchase by such nations from commercial sources in the United States: Provided, however, That the Secretary of Defense may waive the provisions of this sentence when he determines that the waiver of such provisions is in the national interest.

This provision, by its terms, applies only to sales to economically developed nations, but as a practical matter it affects all such sales because at the present time less developed nations do not purchase such material in significant quantities from the United States for use by their armed forces. Either the material is provided as grant assistance or it is procured locally to avoid exacerbation of the chronic foreign exchange shortages in these countries.

The policy of this section has made it difficult for United States businessmen to sell these commercially available items to foreign military establishments. Smaller United States businesses find it difficult to maintain a sales organization capable of effectively representing them with foreign military forces. These military establishments are hesitant to undertake to procure abroad what is available within their own country. Even when these countries are desirous of procuring material of this type in the United States, they may find it difficult, unless they buy through the Department of Defense because they do not maintain the capability to negotiate contracts, set and alter specifications and inspect and accept merchandise in the United States. When these countries can procure through the Department of Defense, they benefit from the lower costs associated with the large purchases of the Defense Department or the General Services Administration as well as in the inspection and negotiation costs which are saved by combined procurement.

In the case of items which are clearly military in their
origins and applications, such as tanks, artillery, military communications equipment, weapons, military aircraft and military vessels, special procedures are in effect. From the point of view of
both buyer and seller the problems of sales and procurement are the
same except that applicable laws and regulations require the approval
of such sales by the Department of State. [7]

2) Direct Cash Government to Government Sale: As described above the United States Government is authorized to sell
military equipment to foreign governments, both from existing stocks
of the Defense Department and from new procurement. Because
these sales are considered complementary to grant military assistance and are covered in the same legislation as grant aid, many of
the conditions applicable to giving grants have been applicable to
sales for cash.

Prior to the passage of the Foreign Assistance Act of
1961 countries wishing to purchase equipment and supplies from the
Department of Defense were required to consider such "assistance"
as falling within the terms of the bilateral agreements governing
grant assistance. Countries which did not receive grant aid were
required to sign sales agreements incorporating the relevant portions of the grant agreements. In such instances, it was usually
provided that the country agrees that the equipment is required for,
and will be used, solely to maintain internal security, for legitimate
self defense, or to permit the purchasing country to participate in
regional or collective security arrangements that are consistent with
the United Nations Charter. Although no longer required by legislation, the United States continues to make most of its military sales
under the terms of such agreements. Such sales are made to allied
and friendly nations, but are not, of course, provided to communist
countries. [8]

The procedures for processing military sales requests
differ with the political importance of the request. Although procedures change frequently, the basic pattern involves a separation of
buyers into two categories. The first category is that of allies who
present no policy problems to the policy levels of the Defense Department and the Department of State by their normal requests to purchase
equipment. These countries may seek information on what is available for purchase either by consultation with the military assistance
advisory group in their country or by a request for information from

their attaché in the United States to the United States military department (Army, Navy or Air Force) responsible for the item. The prospective purchasers are given necessary information on the characteristics of the item, necessary ancillary procurement or training--i.e., radios for tanks, training for pilots, spare parts supply, etc.--the price and delivery timing. The transmittal of this information and the sales transaction including all arrangements for delivery, payment and the like are handled by the supply organization of the military department concerned under procedures designed to make the United States a reasonably quick and intelligent supplier.

Certain logical expedients have been developed to permit better handling of sales requests. For example, to handle continuous requests for parts for United States equipment, the Air Force encourages the submission of a "blanket" order under which rapid action can be taken to prevent military deficiencies caused by lack of critical parts or equipment. Timing of sales requests to permit integration of planning of purchase for resale with purchase for United States use for grant aid is also encouraged. [9]

In the case of countries not allied to the United States, significant sales normally present substantial political problems. Examples are requests to purchase from countries in much of Latin America and Africa and from nations involved in the Arab-Israeli disputes. In these cases the original request to purchase may be made to the State Department and even if not submitted originally to State will undergo Department of State review for the political acceptability of the proposal. If the proposal is accepted on political grounds, the actual supply operations and relations between supplier and consumer are similar to those of the United States and allied countries purchasing from the United States.

In many cases the purchasing country includes cash or its equivalent (certified checks or other forms of commercial paper) with an order for United States equipment. In such cases the payment is always made in United States dollars. If the United States agrees, countries can also purchase on a "dependable undertaking" to pay the United States within 120 days after delivery. Under these arrangements the buyer must first agree to pay upon delivery and second, agree to reimburse the United States for all costs which may be incurred incident to terminations of contract, etc. In either case the funds appropriated for military assistance are not

now involved in these sales. Cash sales result in direct and immediate reimbursement to the military department concerned. Under
the "dependable undertakings" the United States military departments
accept the tying up of their funds which occurs during the period between the time when they pay the contractor and the time when they
are reimbursed by the recipient country. [10]

      3) Credit Guarantees: Under legislation passed in 1964 the
United States government is authorized to guarantee credit extended
by private institutions to foreign governments to permit them to
purchase military equipment in the United States. Under these arrangements a private United States institution--a bank, for example--
loans funds to a foreign government to permit it to purchase equipment from the United States. The United States Government agrees
to pay the lender if the foreign government defaults on the loan and,
to insure the fiscal soundness of the guarantees, maintains a reserve
of 25% of the outstanding guarantees.

      An example of the operation of these guarantees follows:
The Government of Protonia, after consultations with the United
States military assistance advisory group in Protonia, becomes interested in buying the XYZ radar system which several of the officers of Protonia have seen in operation while in the United States
receiving training under the military assistance program. Both
the military assistance advisory group and the Jones Radio Com-
pany--manufacturer of the system--provide information to Protonia, which begins to conclude that it needs the system but cannot
afford to pay cash for it. In time Protonia is advised that the United
States is not prepared to give the system to Protonia, but that the
Department of Defense can make arrangements with private banks
in the United States to permit Protonia to purchase the system and
pay for it over five years at 5% interest.

      Protonia accepts the United States offer and the First
City Bank and the Third New York Bank loan Protonia $5 million,
which along with an additional $1 million from the Protonian
treasury, Protonia turns over to the Air Force which then begins
delivery on the $6 million XYZ radar system. The banks did not
make the loan until they had received notification from the government that Protonia's payment of interest and principal on the notes
was guaranteed. At the time of the loan to Protonia the Defense
Department put into reserve $1.25 million. When Protonia paid
back its first $1 million installment a year later, the Defense

Department reduced its reserve by $250,000 so that the reserve continued to be 25% of the unpaid principal.

From the point of view of the government, these credit guarantees permit the encouragement of sales of military equipment on credit terms without tying up government funds for the transaction. From the point of view of the lender, these loans provide a potentially large source of paper guaranteed by the full faith and credit of the United States. From the point of view of the purchasing government, the loan provides a method to purchase military supplies and equipment on reasonably favorable terms. In presenting the credit guarantee proposal to the Congress, the Department of Defense indicated that it was intended for financing sales to "non-industrial countries."[11]

4) Credit Assistance: Under Section 507 of the Foreign Assistance Act of 1961, as amended, the United States can sell military equipment and services to foreign governments on credit with payment to be made within three years from the date of delivery of the equipment or service. These sales must be financed from funds available for military assistance grant aid or from repayments from prior sales. Section 508 of the same act permits reuse of receipts from sales under the credit sales provision, but only for the financing of further sales.

In practice the system begins when a credit sale is negotiated. Then the military department is paid[12] from the account built up from repayments from prior sales if funds are available from this source. If the revolving fund has no funds left for additional transactions in the year in question, the grant program is reduced to free funds to pay the military departments. Thus, the supplying military department is paid just as though grant aid were involved, but the sales revolving fund does not get its money back until the customer pays. As of mid-1964 no credit sales recipient had ever defaulted on any payments, although there had been some tardy payments.[13]

Through fiscal year 1964 the Defense Department estimated some $548 million of credit sales had been made, including $132.1 million in fiscal year 1964 itself.[14] The major recipients of this credit are listed below:

	($ Millions)
Australia	$107.6
Brazil	20.0
France	79.9
Israel	31.2
Japan	29.8
Peru	17.7
Venezuela	70.5

Collections from prior sales have been increasing on a fairly steady pattern as repayments from earlier sales are received and reused and received and reused again. By fiscal year 1964 it was estimated that $91.8 million would be available from collections, an increase from $79.3 million available in the preceding year.[15] This availability can be expected to continue to increase.

These collections have been generally insufficient to finance the full costs of credit provided, so that funds have had to be used from the grant aid account to supplement them. For example, in fiscal year 1962 over $20 million was taken from grant aid programs to use for sales promotion, $50 million was taken in fiscal year 1963, over $30 million in fiscal year 1964 and the Executive Branch program submitted for fiscal year 1965 to the Congress assumed that an additional $50 million of the military assistance appropriation would be required for credit purposes.

The law does not require that interest be charged for these credit sales, but in some cases interest is charged.

FUTURE SALES EFFORTS

In a presentation made to the House Foreign Affairs Committee in 1964, Mr. Henry Kuss, the Deputy Assistant Secretary of Defense in charge of military sales, explained the government's future plans for promoting sales of United States-produced military goods and services. Mr. Kuss indicated that there were three objectives of the military export sales program: (a) promote the defensive strength of our allies, consistent with our political-economic objectives; (b) promote the concept of cooperative logistics and standardization with our allies; and (c) offset the unfavorable balance of payments resulting from essential United States military deployment abroad.[16]

To achieve these objectives Mr. Kuss presented a program of planned export sales which would involve selling enough equipment so that about 25% of our allies planned expenditures for equipment in the 1962-71 time frame would be used to buy from the United States. The estimates for the total effort to sell United States-produced military equipment and supplies in the three years 1964-66 are shown below:[17]

Program	Total Sales
Cash governmental and private sales (including dependable undertakings described above)	$3,600 million
Sales from both United States Government and private sources where purchasing country finances through Export-Import Bank and the private banking system without guarantees.	1,000 million
Credit guarantees and credit assistance.	400 million
TOTAL	$5,000 million ($5 billion)

Military assistance sales programs also include various types of cooperative logistics arrangements under which the United States provides supply services to other countries on a continuing contractual basis. The official publication of the Defense Department on military assistance describes these arrangements as follows:

Military assistance sales include various types of cooperative logistics support, ranging from one-time direct procurement services to full support where all logistics functions are provided by the U.S. in support of the country requirement. In its more sophisticated form, military assistance sales of spare parts to an ally may be regularized and provided on a full support basis under the terms of a cooperative supply support arrangement concluded

between the U.S. Department of Defense and the Ministry
of Defense of the customer country. Under these arrangements, the U.S. purchases, stores, manages and issues
spare parts in response to the customer's request, utilizing
the U.S. logistics systems and providing support familiar
(sic; presumably "similar" was intended) to that given U.S.
forces. This support is provided on a reimbursable basis
and in accordance with the terms of the specific arrangement
between the U.S. and the country concerned. 18

SALES PROMOTION TRAINING

Although new commitments for grants of military equipment and
supplies are no longer being made to most of the countries of Europe,
the United States is continuing to provide some training to officers
of some of these countries. The theory of providing this training
is that these officers, in addition to continuing to be acquainted
with changes in United States military doctrine, will become familiar with and want to buy equipment manufactured in the United States.
These foreign officers are brought to United States military installations where they may receive general training along with United
States officers, or they are given the opportunity to learn how to
use specific equipment. In other cases orientation training is provided. This type of training involves visiting a number of United
States military installations, receiving briefings and watching
United States equipment in actual use in training and maneuvers.
For the fiscal year ending in June of 1965 the Defense Department
planned to spend about half a million dollars for this purpose. 19
These costs must be paid out of the appropriation for military aid,
because there is no similar account in the regular Department of
Defense budget.

POLICY PROBLEMS IN EXTENDING CREDIT

The obvious, but frequently forgotten, characteristic of arms is
that they are generally designed to cause death. This single fact
means that transactions in arms have considerably more political
potency than those involving oatmeal or machinery. Because sales
of arms can have critical impacts on the United States political
position throughout the world, sales in arms by private United States
sellers are regulated and State Department clearance is required

before such sales are made. In the case of sales made by the
United States government a similar control is exercised.

When arms are to be sold and the sale facilitated by the extension of United States credit, even more difficult problems arise. In
theory, perhaps, the United States should only extend credit for
arms purchases when United States policy calls for the country
planning the purchase to have the weapons involved. However, in
most cases a country willing to purchase can purchase essentially
the same material from Britain or France should the United States
refuse to sell it. Under present policy the requirements which must
be satisfied before credit will be extended are quite extensive and
go far beyond the requirements for cash sales. For example, the
Secretary of Defense has stated that in cases where the credit
guarantee provisions of the new law are involved that he or his
deputy will review each transaction and will want assurance that:

> (a) the military equipment is required in the country
> at hand and is not excess to its requirements and will not
> be used in a way to reduce the stability of relations between
> that country and its neighbors or reduce the political
> stability of that particular government, (b) we will wish
> to be assured that the country can afford the diversion of
> resources from economic expansion to the procurement
> of military items; and (c) we will wish to insure that they
> have cash flows that will permit repayment on the terms
> that we agree upon. [20]

ORGANIZATION FOR SALES

At the time of this writing the program for the stimulation of
military export sales was being managed by Mr. Henry Kuss, acting
within the Office of the Secretary of Defense in the Pentagon. Mr.
Kuss has a staff of his own and also utilizes the specialized skills
of the Army, Navy and Air Force, each of which has offices specifically concerned with cooperative logistics and military sales.
Much of the detailed work in supply and shipment of items purchased
is handled by the standard logistics operations of the United States
military departments. Demonstrations of equipment and provision
of specifications, technical data and the like are handled either by
the contractor or the military department concerned or both. Sales
negotiations may be handled in the country planning to do the

purchasing or in the United States. If the transactions are to be negotiated in the country doing the purchasing, the military assistance
advisory group will usually make its best efforts to facilitate the
transaction and arrange for necessary meetings between the country
officials and the prospective seller and/or the United States military
department from whose stocks the material to be sold will come.

CONCLUSION

Until about 1958 the military sales program was of little importance in relation to the grant program. After that time as a result of changes in pricing policy and aggressive sales efforts to
help alleviate the nation's balance of payments problem, the sales
of United States-produced military equipment to foreign governments
expanded rapidly. Sales can be made directly from a United States
firm to a foreign buyer or indirectly through the Defense Department to the foreign buyer. Sales through the Defense Department
are made for cash, for credit or under the new credit guarantee
program. The Defense Department has extensive plans for further
increasing United States sales of military equipment.

NOTES

1. Several examples are given in the study prepared by the
Legislative Reference Service of the Library of Congress. U.S.,
Congress, House, Committee on Foreign Affairs, U.S. Foreign
Aid, 1957.
    2. Sales figures through FY 1963 from United States Air Force,
Information and Guidance on Military Assistance, 8th ed., June,
1964. Grant aid deliveries and FY 1964 sales from Military Assistance Facts, March 1, 1964, published by the Department of Defense.
    3. Military Assistance Facts, ibid.; estimate subject to down-
ward revision.
    4. HFAC, CY 64, p. 410.
    5. HFAC, CY 63.
    6. Military Assistance Facts, op. cit., p. 29.
    7. From the point of view of the seller, these regulations are no
doubt considered quite complicated and burdensome. The operation
and criticisms of these rules are beyond the scope of this book. The
State Department's regulation "International Traffic in Arms" describes present policy and procedures.

8. Yugoslavia was for many years an exception to this policy.

9. See Information and Guidance, op. cit., pp. 53-54 and the relevant directives of the Army, Navy and Air Force.

10. The use of the "dependable undertaking" mechanism in new procurement was added to the law by the Foreign Assistance Act of 1964.

11. HFAC, CY 64, p. 510.

12. Because the governmental accounting system is so complex, "paid" is used here to describe "obligated" in technical fiscal language.

13. Testimony of General Robert Wood, SAC, CY 64, p. 265.

14. Military Assistance Facts, op. cit., p. 30. The FY 64 amount which is included in the over-all figures included some cases under consideration which may not have been consumated.

15. Under a special financial procedure the collections available for use in the credit sales account include some collections expected to be made in future years. For example, the FY 1964 collections available for new credit were composed of actual collections minus an amount already applied to the preceding year's collections and plus some collections actually expected in the following year. This procedure permits accelerated use of funds by "obligation" of funds not to be received before the following year on the theory that cash will be received from the debtor before actual cash is required to pay for new equipment ordered in anticipation of receiving the cash from the debtor.

16. Mr. Kuss's testimony appears as pp. 509-515 of HFAC, CY 64.

17. This chart is one presented by Mr. Kuss and printed by the Committee on p. 513 of the hearings, expanded slightly by the author to show the interrelationships of these various programs.

18. Information and Guidance, op. cit., p. 25.

19. Testimony of General Robert Wood, HAC, CY 64, p. 573.

20. SAC, CY 64, p. 228.

CHAPTER **13** MILITARY AID AND
DOMESTIC POLITICS:
THE UGLY DUCKLING

Since 1951 military aid has been presented to the Congress and
the people of the United States as a more or less integral part of a
total "foreign aid" program. The result of this combination of
military and economic aid has been to increase the totals which
are bandied about in public debate as "foreign aid." On the other
hand, it has been argued that including military assistance in the
foreign aid budget may well have increased the palatability of the
foreign aid program to the American people and to the Congress.

CONGRESSIONAL SUPPORT FOR MILITARY AID

The Marshall Plan and the Greek-Turkish aid program received near unanimous support from the Congress. In the early
years of the foreign aid program the United States was actively
engaged in combating communist aggression in Korea. During
that period foreign aid appropriations were also enacted without
serious opposition. Since that time, however, there has been a
marked deterioration in Congressional support for foreign aid.
The gap between what Presidents Eisenhower and Kennedy asked
for and what the Congress and the people of the United States were
willing to support is a measure of this deterioration. "Foreign
aid" has been one of the most hotly debated issues in the Congress
year after year. The situation was aptly summarized by a former
Congressman who said, upon retirement as Deputy Director of
the economic aid agency:

> I know of no other major national policy which has
> endured so long without. . .a consensus.[1]

The wide divergence between Executive Branch and Congressional opinions on the foreign aid program in general and the military aid program in particular is reflected in the following table:[2]

Military and Economic Assistance Requests and Appropriations 1950-65
(\$ Millions)

FY	Economic Aid Request	Actual Appropriation	Military Aid Request	Actual Appropriation	Total Request	Actual Appropriation
1956	\$2,142	\$1,998	\$1,125	\$ 705	\$3,267	\$2,703
1957	1,860	1,749	3,000	2,017	4,860	3,766
1958	1,787	1,429	1,600	1,340	3,387	2,769
1959	2,150	1,783	1,800	1,515	3,950	3,298
1960	2,830	1,926	1,600	1,300	4,430	3,226
1961	2,275	1,916	2,000	1,800	4,275	3,716
1962	2,891	2,315	1,885	1,600	4,776	3,915
1963	3,461	2,604	1,500	1,325	4,961	3,929
1964	3,120	2,000	1,405	1,000	4,525	3,000
1965	2,461	2,195	1,055	1,055	3,516	3,250

As the above table shows, despite a frequently assumed popular and Congressional preference for military over economic aspects
of foreign aid, the military assistance program has fared rather
badly before the Congress, even in comparison to economic aid.
In the nine year period ending with fiscal 1964 economic aid and
military aid requests were each cut a total of 21% by the Congress.

It is not necessary in a book of this type to explore the general
question of the advisability of a foreign aid program. This debate
has focused on "foreign aid" considered as an entity rather than
as a military program and an economic program. This debate has
been carried on to an alarming degree in generalities and in argu-
mentation for previously conceived positions.[3] Within the Congress
of the United States there has been widespread acceptance of the
concept that the foreign aid program does not enjoy the confidence
and support of the American people. Even those Congressmen who
assume that there is public support for foreign aid have a tendency,
amply justified by their own surveys of opinion and mail, to believe
that this public support is for lesser effort, measured in dollar terms,
than traditionally recommended by the Executive Branch.

The magnitude of this opposition is indicated by the fact that
over a third of the members of the House of Representatives normally
vote against the annual bill to authorize foreign aid for the coming
year. The strongest opposition in recent years has come from

Southern Democrats and Midwestern Republicans as shown by the table below:

Congressmen Voting or Paired Against
Foreign Aid Authorization for FY 1963

Region	Democrats	Republicans	Total
Northeast	--	2	2
Mid-Atlantic (N.Y., N.J., Pa., Md., Del.)	--	12	12
Midwest (West Va., Great Lakes States, Kansas, Neb., and the Dakotas)	4	56	60
South (Deep South plus Texas, Ark., Mo., Ky., and Tenn.)	64	9	73
West (inc. Okla.)	5	21	26
TOTAL	73	100	173

One of the interesting facts suggested by the above table is that most of the Congressmen voting against foreign aid come from "safe seats." Most of the Southern Democrats and Midwestern Republicans who make up five-sevenths of those voting against foreign aid do not normally stand in serious fear of not being re-elected. Thus, the common assumption that Congressmen vote against foreign aid because of fear of retaliation at the next election is at best a half truth.

Occasionally, roll call votes have been taken on the question of reducing or increasing the amount for military aid within the foreign aid bill. Unfortunately, the last roll call which presented this type of question in the House was taken in 1961. However, it can be assumed that the political factors and opinions of most Congressmen have not changed too much since that time. The following table is an analysis of those Congressmen who voted for the foreign aid bill as a whole, but also voted not to increase the amount for military assistance and also those who voted to increase the amount for military assistance, but voted against the foreign aid bill as a whole.

The amendment was to increase military aid from the level approved by the Appropriations Committee. The committee recommended $1.3 billion; President Eisenhower's budget had called for

$1.8 billion and President Kennedy's revision of that budget called for $1,885 billion. The amendment, which passed, was to increase the appropriation to $1.6 billion.

Net Changes by Region and Party
35 Congressmen Supporting Foreign Aid but not Military
Aid at $1.6 billion Minus 10 Congressmen Supporting
Military Aid but not Foreign Aid[4]

Region	Democrats	Republicans
Northeast	--	--
Mid-Atlantic	--	2
South	9	1
Midwest	1	7
West	--	5
TOTAL	10	15

The table shows, in substance, Congressmen willing to vote for foreign aid, but not for $1.6 billion in military aid were drawn from the same parties and areas--Southern Democrats and Midwestern Republicans--as those who vote against foreign aid. The same facts lead to the same conclusion when the constant voters, rather than the shifters, are considered. Almost 90% of the Congressmen who were opposed to or in favor of the total foreign aid bill maintained their opposition or support in a vote on military aid alone. The inescapable conclusion is that military aid is supported by those in the Congress who support foreign aid and opposed by those who oppose foreign aid. The same factors that affect consideration of foreign aid in the House tend to be brought to bear in the Senate. However, the lesser number of Senators prevents the quantitative approach from being used with any degree of reliability.

The reactions by the Congress and the American public to the total foreign aid program have had an extremely significant effect upon the emphasis placed by this country on its military assistance efforts. First, and most significant, from fiscal year 1956 to fiscal year 1965 a total of $3.3 billion requested by the Executive Branch for military aid has been rejected by the Congress.[5] The effect of these reductions is greater than their absolute magnitude because of the tendency of some major reductions

by Congress to force the Executive Branch into making a lower request for the succeeding year. This effect is compounded because of
the apparent necessity for Congress to cut any Administration request for foreign aid no matter how large or how small. It seems to
be assumed that an alert Congress will and should cut foreign aid.
For that reason, any foreign aid request is likely to be cut. In recognition of this situation, which they themselves have created, members of Congress have accused the Executive Branch of recognizing
this phenomenon and mitigating its effects by padding their requests.
No tangible evidence of padding has ever been given and because of
the political necessity for the President to hold his total budget request to a minimum, padding is unlikely. [6] However, Secretary of
State Rusk, in defending the Administration's request for fiscal year
1965, said:

> It does pull away from 10 or 15 years of procedure by which it
> was more or less anticipated there would be successive re-
> ductions along the way. [7]

There are reasons to believe that the opposite of "padding" is
likely to occur. The President naturally enough does not like to
include items in his budget which may be taken out of the budget by
the Congress. Any President of whatever political party hesitates
to accord credit to the Congress for saving funds and reducing his
budget. Instead, the President naturally desires to produce as low
a budget as is possible. An example of this situation was provided
in the Administration's request for fiscal year 1965 discussed during
Congressional hearings in 1964.

The economic aid request was presented as a realistic estimate
designed to stop the cycle of high budgets and sharp cuts. With
respect to military assistance, this phenomenon of basing a budget
request on what the Congress was likely to approve was explicitly
admitted by the Secretary of Defense, who stated:

> We are presenting a request of only $1 billion for fiscal
> year 1965 solely because the Congress has made it
> crystal clear to the Executive Branch that it is unwilling
> to appropriate a larger amount. [8]

This concept of turning an Executive Branch request into a pre-
diction of Congressional action rather than a statement of what
the Executive Branch recommended was criticized sharply in the
Congress. [9]

THE MECHANICS OF CONGRESSIONAL CONSIDERATION

Under present law, military assistance like many other programs of the federal budget must receive both legislative authorization and appropriations from the Congress.

Authorizations are, technically speaking, laws passed by the
Congress permitting the Congress itself to appropriate money. The
language used for authorizations is normally: "There is hereby
authorized to be appropriated $_____ for _____ purpose for
FY _____." The necessity for annually revising such an authorization by changing the year and perhaps the amount is avoided when
a continuing authorization is provided. Such an authorization is
stated in the following terms: "There is hereby authorized to be
appropriated such sums as may be necessary for _____
purpose."

An appropriation is a law passed by the Congress permitting the
obligation (commitment) and expenditure of government funds. The
Constitution requires such legislation before government expenditures
can legally be made. Severe penalties are provided in case any government official ever commits government funds without a valid appropriation.

Because authorizing legislation sets a ceiling on the amount
which can be appropriated, the authorizing process normally pre-
cedes the appropriation process. Consideration of authorizations by
the Congress does not begin until the President's desires for substantive foreign aid legislation have been made known to the Congress.
The President's recommendations are normally transmitted in the
form of a special message on foreign aid delivered to the Congress
sometime after the January budget is submitted. In 1964 the President's foreign aid message was delivered on March 19. In the preceding year it was not delivered until early April. The President's
legislative recommendations are incorporated in a bill which is
normally introduced by the Chairman of the Foreign Affairs Committee in the House and the Foreign Relations Committee in the
Senate.

In the case of foreign aid, like other important legislation,
most of the important decisions are made when the bill is considered
in committee. As Woodrow Wilson pointed out:

> Congress in session is Congress on public exhibition,
> whilst Congress in its committee rooms is Congress
> at work.[10]

In the House, this bill and any other bill on foreign aid that may
have been introduced is referred to the House Committee on Foreign
Affairs. This committee hears testimony in open and executive
session from witnesses in the Executive Branch. It is the practice
of the Committee to hear testimony from the Secretaries of State
and Defense and the Administrator of the economic aid agency in
sessions which are open to the public. Because these witnesses
obviously cannot discuss classified information in open hearings
they may be asked to reappear in executive session where the public
is excluded and classified information can be and is discussed with
members of the Committee. The Committee then hears a variety
of subordinate witnesses from the Executive Branch, including the
Regional Administrators of the Agency for International Development, various Assistant Secretaries of State who head State's
geographic bureaus and the Director of Military Assistance and
an Assistant or Deputy Assistant Secretary from the Pentagon.
The Unified Commanders also testify in support of the military assistance request in their area. This Executive Branch testimony
normally takes several weeks to complete. During consideration
of military and economic aid programs the committees have before
them classified books showing past and proposed programs and other
data.[11] Frank Coffin, who served for many years as Deputy Director of the economic aid agency, said of these books: "Seldom has so
much been written by so many for so few."[12]

After the government witnesses are heard, the Committee
listens to the positions of various interested groups and individuals.
Twenty-seven groups and individuals appeared in person to make
recommendations to the Foreign Affairs Committee in 1964. Eighteen
more groups and individuals provided statements or letters to be inserted in the printed hearings.

Because these groups do not have access to the classified program figures presented by the Executive Branch, their testimony is
necessarily quite generalized. Most groups make general statements
for or against the foreign aid program but do not attempt to present
precise recommendations on which programs should be decreased or
increased. The exceptions to this statement are those organizations
which maintain professional staffs in Washington who analyze proposed

foreign aid legislation in some detail, especially the Chamber of
Commerce, the Citizen's Foreign Aid Committee, the AFL-CIO
and the Farm Bureau.

The following is a listing of the groups and individuals which
took a position on the proposed military assistance program and the
nature of the position which each took. Groups that merely attacked
foreign aid or endorsed foreign aid in general terms are excluded.

Group	Position on Military Aid
Liberty Lobby	Cut to zero as the Department of Defense budget could "take care of any military aid that might be necessary."
National Farmers Union	Separate military from economic assistance, "not only wise in our effort overseas, but it would make for greater understanding at home."
Citizens Foreign Aid Committee	Cut to the amount ($453 million) requested for the Far East, terminate elsewhere as the strategic nuclear power of the U.S. will protect other countries.
National Council of Churches	"Separate development assistance from military assistance."
American Legion	Provide military assistance for national security objectives only.
Methodist Church	Separate military and economic aid, unless the economic aid program would be jeopardized by such action.
AFL-CIO	Support requested amount, would consider supporting more if Secretary of Defense decided more was required.
Farm Bureau	Reduce request about 10% to $900 million because of unexpended balances and "fat in DOD budget."

Group	Position on Military Aid
Farm Bureau (continued)	Separate military and economic assistance.
Chamber of Commerce	Support full amount requested. Recommend separation of military aid from economic at least for purposes of "budget accountability."

As can be seen from this listing most private groups, without access to the classified justification books, did not feel it appropriate to recommend precise appropriation levels.

Because hearings before the Foreign Affairs Committee are normally quite well attended by members of the committee and because of the limited time available, the committee operates under a so-called five minute rule. Under this rule each member of the committee, in decreasing order of seniority, is given the opportunity to ask questions and receive answers for five minutes, at the end of which time the floor is given to the next ranking member. If time permits, the cycle is repeated.

The questions asked by members of Congress in these committee hearings tend to fall in four general categories. First, supporters of the foreign aid program attempt to build a record which will enable them to defend the program with their colleagues on the floor of the House and in informal discussions. This "record" can also be used by members of Congress seeking reelection, who are forced to defend their votes for foreign aid programs. This "record" is created by asking questions that will elicit quotable material from high-ranking officers of the Executive Branch.

The second function of Congressional questioning is to permit opponents of a program to get adverse material on the record, thereby justifying votes against the program. This type of questioning may take the form of "have you stopped beating your wife?" questions or of questions which center on past mistakes or present programs which are considered to be more than normally dubious.

The third function of a hearing is the one most commonly assumed to be the only function of Congressional hearings, that of providing members of the committee with sufficient information to evaluate a program for the purpose of determining what level of funds should be provided and what substantive legislation should be enacted. This is clearly the function performed by the bulk of the questioning of Executive Branch witnesses other than cabinet officers and of some of the lobbyists who have done enough "homework" to be able to present independent opinions about pending legislation.

The fourth and final function of a hearing is that it enables members of Congress who, especially in the case of lower ranking members, may not normally have access to cabinet officers to present special problems of their district or other problems which they consider important to high ranking Executive Branch witnesses. These problems may or may not relate directly to the subject of the hearings. Even for persons who have no difficulty in obtaining access to cabinet members the hearing presents an opportunity to talk to Executive Branch representatives about problems. In the informal atmosphere of a closed hearing a Senator or Congressman may well save a great deal of time and trouble by rapidly solving a few problems not directly related to the subject at hand. In many cases these conversations are obviously quite friendly and informal. For example, the following colloquy took place when the Administrator of the Agency for International Development appeared before the Senate Foreign Relations Committee:

THE CHAIRMAN. Mr. Bell, there has been presented to me a proposal for an amendment. This isn't related to you--you are interested in the overall bill--it is in regard to the Sabbatino case.

Are you familiar with that?

MR. BELL. Sabbatino?

THE CHAIRMAN. It is a case recently in the Supreme Court.

MR. BELL. No; it is not a case I am familiar with; I am sorry, Mr. Chairman.

THE CHAIRMAN. The proposal which has been submitted to other members of the committee--I first heard of it this morning; in fact, just a few minutes before I came over here--involved a rather technical legal problem.

I raise it with you at this time only because you are interested in this bill. It is properly, I think, a matter for the legal authorities of the Department of State, and I have asked you to look into it.

If you haven't been notified of it, will your aide or you request the State Department to prepare their comments

upon this proposed amendment. I am just using you as
a communication center.

    MR. BELL. Yes, sir; I will be glad to.

    THE CHAIRMAN. It has been submitted, and Senator
Hickenlooper mentioned it to me the other day, because it
is related to the Hickenlooper amendment. It is sort of a
modification, we might say, of the Hickenlooper amendment
and they took it to him first. It is my understanding he is
considering at least proposing such an amendment, and all
I am saying this morning is would you see that the State
Department legal authorities prepare their legal position
on this proposal.

    MR. BELL. Yes, sir, we will be glad to do that. [13]

    The authorizing procedure followed in the Senate is similar to
that of the House, although the fact that the Senate is only one-fourth
the size of the House and that the Senators' constituencies are considerably larger than those of the members of the House of Representatives means that Senate consideration of any bill is normally
less extensive than that of the House. Not only do Senators have
less time for committee business than House members, the Foreign
Relations Committee has more responsibility than the House Foreign
Affairs Committee. The Constitution vests responsibility for con-
firmation of Presidential appointments and the ratification of treaties
in the Senate, not the House. These functions are handled by the
Foreign Relations Committee reporting to the full Senate. [14]

    Therefore, the Senate Foreign Relations Committee tends to
concentrate in its hearings on broader issues of strategy and foreign
policy and less on particular program problems and details than the
House. For this reason, the Senate Foreign Relations Committee
does not normally hear testimony from lower level Executive Branch
officials and hears fewer interested private groups.

    Allocation of responsibility among Senate Committees for review
of the military assistance program has varied through the years.
The Greek-Turkish aid legislation in 1947 was reviewed by Foreign
Relations alone. When the Administration requested the military
assistance legislation which became the Mutual Defense Assistance
Act of 1949, both the Chairman of the Foreign Relations Committee
(Connally) and the Chairman of the Armed Services Committee
(Tydings) claimed jurisdiction. [15] The dispute was resolved by
having the bill considered by a combination of the two committees.

This practice was followed in 1950 and in the review of the Mutual
Security Act of 1951. Joint hearings were discontinued in 1952.
That year and in the following two years the Foreign Relations
Committee considered the program first and its recommendations
were referred to the Armed Services Committee for military re-
view. In 1955 the present system of sole review by the Foreign
Relations Committee was established.[16]

Following the hearings the House and Senate committees meet
separately in executive session to formulate the committees' recommendations to the House and Senate, respectively, regarding
the bills pending before them. In the House, due primarily to the
fact that decisions must be made by a very large committee, these
sessions can consume two to three weeks.[17] In the Senate sessions
are normally somewhat shorter.

These sessions are called "mark ups" because their primary
function is the "marking up" (amending) of the bill or bills pending
before the committee. In considering proposed amendments to
pending bills and in analyzing foreign aid generally, both these committees rely upon committee staff members as well as the staffs of
individual senators and congressmen.

Following these deliberations each committee issues a report
and a bill which represents the recommendations of the committee.
Minority reports are common. The bill is then considered on the
floors of the House and Senate. In the case of the House, debate
usually consumes two to three days. Senate debate is often as
extensive. After this debate, authorizing bills are passed by both
the House and the Senate and the differences between the two bills
are resolved by a conference committee composed of senior members
from both parties from both the House and Senate committees. The
deliberations of the conference committee result in a conference
report which is normally accepted with little debate by both houses.

The authorization, which sets a ceiling on the amounts which
may be appropriated, having been passed, the budget for foreign
aid can then be considered by the Appropriations Committees of
both the House and the Senate.[18]

The House Committee on Appropriations is divided into a number
of subcommittees, one of which is the Subcommittee on Foreign
Operations which considers foreign aid requests. The House Appropriations Committee has developed a traditional viewpoint that

Executive Branch bureaucrats will normally request more funds than the minimum required in the national interest. [19]

The function of the Appropriations Committee, unlike that of the Foreign Affairs Committee, is to determine how much money is required to meet recognized needs. The committee does not normally evaluate foreign policy; rather it assumes the validity of policy and attempts to determine what it should cost to carry out the policy. For that reason, the hearings before the subcommittee tend to concentrate more on management matters, pricing and cost reduction than on the foreign policy aspects of the program. This subcommittee normally hears the same cabinet level witnesses as the Foreign Affairs Committee but spends most of its time with lower level witnesses who are more intimately familiar with program details and management problems. The Passman Subcommittee hearings normally last as long as a month. Even with extensive quantities of classified material deleted, 285 pages of printed hearings were consumed by the questioning of Defense witnesses testifying on military aid in 1964.

In accordance with committee practice, the subcommittee, like other subcommittees, studies the pending bill and meets as a subcommittee to develop its recommendation on the appropriation and any language restricting its use which might be put in the appropriation bill. Because this subcommittee is quite small, it normally does not take much time for this process. After the subcommittee has stated its readiness to present its report, the full House Appropriations Committee meets to accept or reject the report. Unless the matter under consideration is being strongly pressed by the President (it is assumed that agency heads will howl over any cuts in their budgets), it is normal for the full Committee to accept the conclusions of its subcommittee. Such a deviation from this tradition of support occurred in 1964 when the full Committee produced a report which the subcommittee chairman concerned with foreign aid did not support.

The full Committee on Appropriations then reports the "marked up" bill to the House of Representatives which normally follows the recommendations of the Appropriations Committee. During the past seven years the House has accepted the recommendations of the Appropriations Committee on military assistance on five occasions and has increased the amount for military assistance twice (in 1960 and 1961).

In the Senate the military assistance program is considered as part of the foreign aid program before the Senate Appropriations Committee. This committee, composed of members who all have additional committee assignments, is forced to pass on each item in a federal administrative budget of some $100 billion per year of which military aid represents only 1%. For this reason the role assumed by the Senate Appropriations Committee in many fields is that of serving as a forum for appeals (in bureaucratese, these are called reclamas) from the decisions of the House. [20] Because House decisions tend to be made late in the year in the case of foreign aid appropriations, the committee from time to time must drop this role and hold hearings before House action is completed. These hearings are normally short and limited to one or two high level witnesses from the agencies requesting appropriations. In 1964 Secretary McNamara testified for one meeting of the committee and other Defense witnesses in a second meeting. The Senate Appropriations Committee then makes its recommendations to the entire Senate, which has accepted the committee's military aid recommendations during each of the past seven years. After the Senate votes, both the Senate and the House appoint conferees who become members of a Conference Committee to compromise House and Senate differences on the foreign aid appropriation. The compromise bill reported out of conference is then normally passed with little or no debate and sent to the President for his signature.

One of the foreign aid difficulties in recent years has been the unwillingness or inability of the Congress to provide an appropriation by the beginning of the fiscal year. The government fiscal year begins in July and it would seem that if appropriations were not made by that time the military aid program would grind to a halt. To avoid this problem the Congress normally passes continuing resolution authority, which is blanket authority for all agencies having appropriation requests pending before the Congress but not acted on by it to spend money until such time as an appropriation is received. This authority usually takes the form of permitting the agency to obligate funds at a rate equal to the prior year rate or the rate requested in the budget being reviewed, whichever is lower. Occasionally, even this step is omitted and military assistance must operate for some days with no authorization whatever. [21]

During the past seven years the foreign aid appropriation has never been made before the new fiscal year began. In fact, during

the seven years the Senate Appropriations Committee--normally
and appropriately the last committee to report--has reported the
foreign aid appropriation bill twice in August, four times in September and once in December.

This phenomenon of late appropriations has a substantial effect
on the efficiency with which the foreign aid program is managed.
The problem is magnified in the case of foreign aid because there
is uncertainty until the last moment as to how large the appropriation will be. Some other appropriations bills--such as the regular
Department of Defense bill--are also frequently passed after the
fiscal year has begun, but in those cases it is normally possible
to proceed with most of the programs because of the relative
certainty that Congress will pass the amount which it is considering.

The effect of late appropriations has been widely recognized.
Secretary McNamara, appearing before a Congressional committee,
stated that the effect of the late appropriation combined with the
substantial reduction in 1963 made in the military assistance program made it necessary to completely realign the entire program.
"You can imagine that this introduced inefficiencies, disorder,
and probable waste into the program." [22]

The Director of Military Assistance told the same committee
that although the Defense Department had been able to continue with
the program under continuing resolution authority, the Pentagon
delayed ordering equipment until the appropriation was passed. [23]
Senator Chavez, after observing military operations in the Far East,
found that delays in funding resulting in cancellation of some training
programs did reduce training to some extent. Senator Chavez also
noted that the Unified Commander was forced to submit his program
recommendations for the following fiscal year before he knew what
his program was to be for the current fiscal year. [24]

Late appropriations for military assistance cannot be solely
attributed to delays in the Congress. Congress cannot begin to consider requests for foreign aid when the budget is submitted by the
President because the authorizing process depends upon a review of
the President's recommended legislation for foreign aid as well as
upon the budget request. For that reason, hearings do not begin
until after the President's foreign aid message, which has frequently
been submitted some two months after the budget. During the past
five years through 1964 that message has been submitted once in

February, three times in mid-March and once in early April.
President Johnson submitted his 1965 message in January.

The foreign aid hearings and the foreign aid debate in the Congress have an importance which transcends the foreign aid program
itself. The foreign aid bill presents the best opportunity that members of the Senate and House have to examine Executive Branch
witnesses about, and themselves comment on, current directions in
United States foreign policy. Particularly in the House, which, unlike the Senate, does not have the power to confirm or deny confirma-
tion to appointees of the President nor the power to ratify or refuse
to ratify treaties, the foreign aid bill is treated as having considerable importance. Without it, many believe a committee like
the House Foreign Affairs Committee would be rendered almost
powerless.

CONGRESSIONAL CONTROL OVER MILITARY AID

The military assistance program is presented to the Congress
in great detail. Executive Branch witnesses can discuss the dollar
value of assistance planned for a country, the number of persons to
be trained with the funds requested, the number of aircraft to be
purchased and the countries to receive them and the planned quantities and prices of practically all other items. However, in a
legal sense, all of this justification and detail is "illustrative" in
that the Congress does not appropriate funds for the projects presented. Instead the Congress appropriates a lump sum for military
assistance which can be spent as the Executive Branch sees fit
within the limits of authorizing legislation.

Specifically, the President can, without Congressional approval,
start new military assistance programs to various countries, terminate assistance to nations receiving assistance, alter the dollar value
of programs for particular countries or the content of these programs
and increase or decrease the number of persons to receive training.
Much the same situation prevails in the case of economic aid except
that economic aid appropriations are made in about five major categories. Within any given category similar flexibility exists in the
economic program, and authority is given to the President to transfer between categories.

The basic reason for permitting this freedom in the administration of the program is a legislative branch recognition that the President under the Constitution is charged with responsibility for foreign policy, and in many cases military assistance is but a tool of foreign policy. In addition to this factor, the Congress recognizes that the world situation is subject to sudden change and that it is in the United States interest to be able to react quickly to these changes. The final reason for this arrangement is the difficulty inherent in any other arrangement. Because military assistance programs presented to the Congress are developed in the summer and fall before they are presented--a full year before the beginning of implementation--they generally need substantial revision at the time of implementation. The Congressional penchant to cut military aid requests is also a factor, as Congress can hardly ask the Executive Branch to adhere to the program presented when the funds to finance the program are not appropriated.

Another factor which may seem relevant to the committees which consider the military aid program is that any system of approving changes in detailed programs would put the committees in a difficult spot. Because the committees, under other arrangements than the present one, would have approved each program change and the basic program itself, the committees could no longer criticize past actions of the administrators of the foreign aid program as they would have approved each action before it was taken.

Although there is frequent criticism of changes made in the military assistance program presented to Congress, the present arrangement has not been changed. The Defense Department would apparently accept such a change. As Secretary McNamara told Congressman Passman in 1964:

> You know and I know that this program is presented to you--and as a matter of fact the Congress has asked that it be so presented--on a preliminary basis, with the recognition that the Department will change it as the world changes in the year in which the funds are appropriated. If the Congress wishes to handle this in any other effective way, we will be happy to do so.[25]

Some illustration of the present flexibility can be found from a table appearing in the record of the House Appropriations Committee hearing on the fiscal year 1965 military assistance request in which

is inserted a comparison of the Executive Branch program presented to the Congress for fiscal year 1963 and the program that
was actually implemented for that year.[26] The following are some
of the larger changes:

Country	Change	Reason
Denmark	Cut by 40%.	Deleted combat aircraft.
Norway	Practically doubled.	Added aircraft, tanks, ar-mored personnel carriers, communications equipment and ammunition.
Spain	Cut $27 million.	Deleted aircraft, vehicle parts and ammunition, etc.
Infrastructure	Cut $20 million.	Reduced estimate.
Cameroon	Reduced from $1,265 thousand to $37 thousand.	Deleted materiel.
India	Established new program of $60 million.	Established after Chinese attack.
Yemen	From 0 to $10 thousand.	Created new training pro-gram.
China (Taiwan)	Reduced by $85 million.	Deleted long list of items.
Vietnam	Increased $123 million.	Deleted long list of items.
Non-regional	Up $50 million.	"Added aircraft for central-ized training and transferred items from 'Country Pro-grams' for accounting pur-poses."

There is, of course, some check on the use of funds by the Executive Branch. The mere fact that Congress will later review the actions taken can be assumed to be influential in the decisions taken in the administration of the program. Ceilings in authorizing legislation prevent sharp increases in military assistance for Latin America and Africa and prescribe the conditions under which aid must be given. At one time in the early years of the Mutual Security Program, authorizations were made on a regional basis, but the regional approach no longer seems feasible as the Defense Department no longer considers the military aid program on a regional basis; instead programs are grouped by purpose or function.

CONCLUSION

Military assistance is considered by Congress as part of the over-all foreign aid program. Although the belief that military assistance enjoys more public and Congressional support than economic aid is widespread, the Congress over the past ten years has cut equal percentages from the requests of each of these programs. The strongest opposition to foreign aid seems to come from Congressmen in the least danger of being defeated at the polls. In the only record vote in recent years, the opponents of military assistance who were supporters of the over-all foreign aid program had similar party and geographic characteristics to the Congressmen traditionally opposed to foreign aid.

Four separate Congressional committees consider military assistance: two in the authorization process and two in the appropriations process. Most of the testimony in Congressional hearings comes from Executive Branch witnesses, partly because it is difficult for private groups and individuals to testify meaningfully about a program when most of the details are "classified."

Congressional control over details of military assistance is very limited, because the Executive Branch can--within the total appropriation--shift programs at will.

NOTES

1. Frank Coffin, Witness for AID (Boston: Houghton Mifflin Company, 1964), pp. v-vi.

2. Taken from a table prepared by Congressman Passman, HAC, CY 64, p. 343. FY 1965 figures added by the author.

3. This does not mean that the preconceived positions are wrong, only that the debate on foreign aid is usually not informative.

4. Table developed by the author from record vote in Congressional Record. Where a Congressman was not recorded or paired on the appropriation for foreign aid, his authorization vote was used.

5. This amount may double-count some funds as, presumably, there is a tendency for the Executive Branch to put into a subsequent program an item deleted from a prior program for lack of funds.

6. However, the padding alternative is widely recognized as a probable result of a consistent habit of Congressional cuts. For example, Secretary McNamara told the House Appropriations Committee: "I think it is wrong, and I do not mean to appear critical of your procedures, to receive budgets time and time and time again and cut them 30 percent. This leads to padding of budgets, or alternatively, in our case, complete recasting of programs late in the process, and without adequate consideration. It is wasteful." (HAC, CY 64, p. 360.)

7. SFRC, CY 64, p. 309.

8. HAC, CY 64, p. 201.

9. See, for example, the hearings before the House Foreign Affairs Committee and the House Appropriations Committee in 1964.

10. Woodrow Wilson, Congressional Government (New York: Meridian Books), p. 69. First published in 1885.

11. Complete descriptions of the two books used for military aid can be found in the prepared statement of General Robert J. Wood, the Director of Military Assistance, in HFAC, CY 64, pp. 485-490.

12. Coffin, op. cit., p. 47.

13. SFRC, CY 64, p. 449.

14. A description of the various functions of the Senate Foreign Relations Committee can be found in David N. Farnsworth, The Senate Committee on Foreign Relations (Urbana, Illinois: University of Illinois Press, 1961).

15. Congressional Record, Vol. 95, 81st Cong., 1st Sess., 1949, pp. 10327-10332.

16. Farnsworth, op. cit., pp. 87-88.

17. See the daily reports of these sessions in 1964, for example, in newspapers like the Washington Post, New York Times or the Wall Street Journal.

18. In some years, as in 1964, one or both Appropriations Committees may hold hearings before an authorization is passed to expedite

consideration of the bill by Congress. In 1964, in fact, an appropriation was actually passed by the House before work on the authorization bill had been completed. This unusual procedure requires waiver of the point of order that could legitimately be raised against it.

19. The "ethos" of this committee is explained in detail in Richard F. Fenno, Jr., "The House Appropriations Committee," American Political Science Review, Vol. 56, June, 1962, pp. 300-324. Although it is frequently assumed that the Subcommittee Chairman, Congressman Passman, is himself personally responsible for the severity of questioning of Executive Branch officials, this study would seem to indicate that any senior member of the Appropriations Committee would pursue a similar course of action if he chaired the Subcommittee considering foreign aid.

20. This appellate role is widely recognized in both statements by members of the committee and academic literature. See, for example, Holbert N. Carroll, The House of Representatives and Foreign Affairs (Pittsburg: University of Pittsburg Press, 1958), pp. 289-292.

21. This happened in the fall of 1964 in the period between the expiration of continuing resolution authority at the end of September and the signature by the President of the Appropriations Bill on the 7th of October.

22. HAC, CY 64, p. 317.

23. Ibid., p. 466.

24. U.S., Congress, Senate, Committee on Appropriations, Report on United States Military Operations and Mutual Security Programs Overseas by Senator Dennis Chavez, 86th Cong., 2d Sess., 1960, p. 176.

25. HAC, CY 64, p. 307.

26. HAC, CY 64, pp. 309-311.

The purpose of this chapter is to provide a reasonably systematic discussion of the criticisms made of military assistance and
the facts which relate to (not necessarily answer) those criticisms.
Such a review, which involves primarily a repetition of facts made
in other portions of the book, is provided to let the reader review
the comments which he has heard about the program in the context
of the facts, which seem, at least to the author, to relate to the
criticisms. This approach also is useful in that it forces to the
surface a number of facts not considered elsewhere in the book.

Military Aid is Furnished to Dictators: As a factual proposition, it is incontrovertible that military aid is furnished to governments headed by men considered to be dictators. Just how many
dictatorships receive military aid depends on one's definition of
dictatorship. However, a fair list of the countries widely considered to be dictatorships can be compared with the unclassified
list of countries receiving military assistance in fiscal year 1964
to produce the conclusion that few of the countries receiving military assistance are democracies in the American sense. This follows from the fact that few of the countries in the world are democracies in the American sense. Omitting military juntas and one-man
rule situations similar to present day France, the following countries
which receive military aid are frequently called dictatorships:
Portugal, Spain, Ghana (which seems to the author to be a doubtful
conclusion), Iran (ruled by a Shah), Jordan (ruled by a King),
Cambodia, the Republic of China and Indonesia. A number of other
countries are or have recently been ruled by a group that was not
elected. This group includes Turkey, Pakistan, Vietnam, Thailand
and many African and Latin American countries.

If it is wrong to provide military assistance to countries governed
by "dictators," the military assistance is wrong indeed. However,
if the purpose of military assistance is to build military strength
against the Communist Bloc on the theory that that strength is required to deter or defeat communist aggression, then the value of
that aid does not depend upon the form of government of the recipient.
For example, the United States is committed by treaty to come to
the defense of Turkey and the Republic of China if either of them is
attacked. These treaties say nothing about the form of government
of Turkey or the Republic of China--the obligation exists no matter
what the form of government. In this circumstance the question is

not whether the United States will aid dictators but what form that
aid will take. Will it take the form of a large commitment of
United States forces if these countries are attacked and not properly equipped through military aid, or will it take the form of
supplementing the defensive efforts of troops well-trained and
well-equipped through military aid? It may, of course, be argued
that the treaties themselves are wrong, but if this is the case, the
cure is to change or revoke the treaty. If military aid is cut, but
if United States troops are to fight alongside the forces whose arms
are inadequate because of lack of military assistance, the United
States has put itself in a situation resembling that of Korea.

    The comments above only make sense, of course, in the case
of countries where overt communist aggression is a real possibility.
In the case of Latin America and Africa, for example, the situation
is different. Here, proponents of military aid must argue that assistance to the regime in power is preferable to a possible communist takeover which the loyalist troops could not prevent unless
they receive United States arms, or that the armed forces and the
dictator are so far apart that aid to one is not aid to the other, or
that United States policy should recognize that the underdeveloped
countries will not all be democratic for some time.

    Military assistance is an endless program: Under the pre-
sently conceived objectives of military assistance and the most
optimistic projections of the economic development of recipient
countries, in the immediate future there appears to be no end
to military assistance. This situation would, of course, change
if there were a general easing of world tensions, or disarmament.
President Kennedy's citizens committee appointed to study the
foreign aid program reported that the Defense Department saw the
need for $1 billion to be appropriated for military assistance in
fiscal 1968. [1] It would seem, from the standpoint of judging the
necessity for military aid, the question is not whether or not it
is endless, but whether or not it is required.

    Military assistance is trying to do too much for too many:
Some 64 different countries were scheduled to receive deliveries
of United States military assistance in fiscal year 1964. Some two-
thirds of the funds allocated to military aid is allocated to eleven
key countries bordering communist countries. The remainder is
spread over 53 other countries. What is trying to do too much and
is too many depends upon one's judgment of what is the right amount

to try to accomplish and what is the right number of places in which
to accomplish it.

European nations should do more to help the United States bear
its world burdens: This criticism is presumably based on the further
assumption that if these countries don't do more, the United States
should compensate by doing less. On the military aid side the European nations have done very little, in part because the United States
has thought it better to encourage these countries to increase their
own defense budgets and economic aid programs as the fields of
primary emphasis. In addition, there are some situations where it
is unrealistic to expect these nations to help. The British, who do
not support our China policy, could hardly be expected to provide
the wherewithal for us to carry it out. If retaliation against Europe
for not helping enough is considered necessary, withdrawal of
United States troops might be more sensible than cutting off aid
halfway around the world in Korea.

Military aid causes a drain in the United States balance of payments: The military assistance program proposed for fiscal year
1965 was estimated to involve some $138.5 million for overseas
spending--composed primarily of contributions to NATO cost-
sharing programs, close-out of old commitments in Europe and
a bit of offshore procurements and construction costs. However,
it was estimated that this amount would be more than offset by
$393 million of procurement in the United States induced by mili-
tary aid programs. [2] If military sales are thrown into the equation,
the net balance would be over a billion dollars per year in favor of
military aid.

Military aid is given to communist countries: Almost $800 mil-
lion worth of military aid has been provided to Yugoslavia. Other
amounts have been spent in countries which some consider to be
communist, such as Indonesia. Logically speaking, opposition to
the former Yugoslavia military aid program is not grounds for opposition to military aid generally. However, unless Congress
tightens the Foreign Assistance Act, occasional instances of aid to
communist nations can be expected.

Military aid is run by incompetents: Under the President's
direction, military aid is "run" at the policy level primarily by the
State Department and the Defense Department. Within the Defense
Department practically all control at the operating level is in the

hands of regular United States military personnel. If there is a problem of incompetence, it should, of course, be corrected, but if such
a problem does exist in the military aid program it permeates the
entire national military and diplomatic establishment.

Military aid encourages large military forces where they are
not needed: There can be no question but that United States military
aid encourages the maintenance of any country's military forces
more than they would be encouraged if the aid were not provided.
In some special cases, such as that of Iran, United States aid was
specifically tied to a reduction in the country's forces. In other
cases, United States aid certainly encourages the country to maintain the forces to which the United States is providing aid. In Latin
America, for example, United States military aid alone probably did
not encourage the maintenance of the large Latin American armies
as much as other facets of United States policy.

It is important to remember that many countries maintain very
large military forces, in terms of the percent of the population
under arms or in terms of the percent of gross national product used
for military expenditures, without the stimulus of foreign aid. The
United States itself is an example. Other countries which do receive
United States aid might well attempt to maintain large forces even
in the absence of United States aid. It seems likely that the Nationalist Chinese, for example, if left to their own devices, would maintain large military forces even if those forces could not be adequately
equipped.

The ultimate question, of course, is whether there is a military
requirement for forces being supported with United States assistance.
This military question is addressed in the next chapter.

Military assistance discourages economic development: Unless
it can be assumed that funds not spent for military aid would be used
for economic aid, it is clearly not true that military aid hinders
economic development. Provision of military equipment on a grant
basis avoids the use of foreign exchange for military procurement,
which would probably take place in most countries if United States
aid were not provided. The local budget expenditures in the countries which receive extensive United States assistance are devoted
to the local currency costs associated with local procurement and the
pay and allowances of local military personnel. Most of the troops in
these countries are paid at a bare subsistence level, and if the armed

forces were disbanded, their economies would have to find ways to support them. In these countries a shortage of manpower caused by large conscription programs is normally not a problem. In many countries, in Latin America and Africa particularly, military units are engaged in projects contributing to economic development.

Military aid provides equipment which recipients cannot utilize: Although equipment has occasionally been delivered before countries had completed the training required to use it, on the whole it seems that military assistance has been adequately related to the capabilities of countries to absorb the equipment provided. It must be remembered that the basic principle of the military assistance programs is to assist countries which need United States help in building effective military establishments. At such time as the recipient countries acquire the sophistication to operate all our equipment perfectly, much of the present program will no longer be necessary. We should in the meantime not be too surprised when the nations we are teaching to maintain vehicles do not perfectly maintain them from the day they are shipped. Even in the United States forces, a period of adjustment is required before new weapons systems are effectively utilized and understood by the troops expected to operate them.

Military assistance causes arms races: A wide variety of factors has caused "arms races" throughout history. Just as those "arms races" existed centuries before military assistance began, they are likely to persist long after the United States no longer conducts a military aid program. One of the hottest arms races in the world today, that of the Middle East, is clearly not related to United States military assistance.

On the other hand in selected cases, such as in Latin America, past United States assistance may have induced expanded requests for assistance from the United States and purchases from third countries. United States assistance to Pakistan has influenced Indian consideration of the nature of its military requirement.

CONCLUSION

This chapter has listed some major criticisms of military assistance along with attempts to assess their truth and relevance.

NOTES

1. Report to the President from the Committee to Strengthen the Security of the Free World (Washington: Department of State, March 20, 1963), pp. 19-20.

2. HAC, CY 64, p. 341.

CHAPTER 15

The previous fourteen chapters of this book have been an attempt to describe the United States military aid program as it has evolved since World War II. Those chapters have included, where appropriate, the criticisms which have been made of military assistance and the reasons which have been used to justify various programs. This chapter drops the format of factual exposition of the arguments and ideas of others and presents the author's own conclusions about the program.

It is somewhat presumptuous of this author or any other author to attempt to present conclusions on the value of the over-all military aid program. These conclusions are presented because, although no one is in a position to give final or perfect answers, decisions involving millions of dollars and millions of people throughout the world are continuously being made and there will never be time to wait for final and definitive solutions to the problems raised by a program of this magnitude.

The persons most familiar with military aid are those employed by the State Department and the Department of Defense (primarily military officers) who are engaged in its administration. Those persons can never present to the public an objective analysis of the programs they administer because government employees are not permitted to write criticisms of programs which they will continue to administer. Because this is true, the only material published by these officials appears in the form of vindication of their own actions, and is normally somewhat discounted by the academic community and the Congress. No such constraints inhibit academic and journalistic writers but, unfortunately, those writers generally have neither the time nor the inclination to master the details of a program of this type.

A few studies of military aid have been conducted over the past ten years and most of these will be referred to in these conclusions. The most significant of these studies were two papers prepared for the Special Committee to Study the Foreign Aid Program in 1957, the Draper Committee Study in 1959 and the Clay Committee Study in 1962.

The classification of country programs adopted by the Executive Branch appears to be the most useful categorization for the purpose of understanding and criticizing the present effort. Instead of dealing

with the importance and impact of military aid on the basis of countries considered in regional groupings, this categorization defines
military aid programs in terms of the purposes which they are intended to serve. The major categories utilized are:

1) Forward Defense Programs--where the purpose of aid
is primarily the development of military strength on the periphery
of Russia and Communist China;

2) Alliance for Progress Security Programs covering military
aid in Latin America;

3) Military Base Programs covering military aid which is in
large part rental for United States overseas bases;

4) Phase Out Programs covering programs soon to be terminated;

5) Free World Orientation Programs where no immediate military purpose is served by military aid which, instead, is intended to
enhance free world orientation or preclude or minimize communist
influence; and

6) United States Force Support and Administrative Costs which
is a potpourri of the administrative costs associated with the above
functions as well as some costs associated with military sales and
certain NATO programs which are considered military aid costs for
historical reasons which have little relevance under modern circumstances.

In suggesting these conclusions the author has assumed the validity of present basic United States policies reflected in present alliances and bilateral treaties and supported by a large portion of
the regular United States defense budget. Major changes in policy
toward particular countries, such as Nationalist China, would require equally major changes in the optimum level and type of military
aid. Likewise, a decision to rely more heavily on the nuclear deterrent, or not to rely on it at all, as a device to prevent or cure communist aggression against countries on the periphery of the Soviet
Union and China would require military aid policies very much different from those recommended in this book.

FORWARD DEFENSE PROGRAMS[1]

The forward defense programs represent about two-thirds of
the military assistance which the United States has extended every
year for the past several years. It includes programs for Greece,
Turkey, Iran, Pakistan, India, the Republic of China, Korea, the
Philippines, Vietnam, Thailand and Laos. In all cases it is generally conceded that a communist military threat to these countries
exists. In the cases of Korea, the Republic of China and India
overt attacks have occurred against the recipients of United States
military aid. In the cases of Greece, Laos, Vietnam and the
Philippines a large communist guerrilla campaign has been or is
being waged. In the case of Thailand, Turkey, Iran and Pakistan
communist diplomatic pressures and communist statements have
indicated clearly to the nationals of these countries and to the
policymakers of the United States that the communists would
shift these countries into the category of neutrals or satellites of
Russia or China if they could get away with it.

The first critical question which United States policymakers
have had to face is whether or not the United States would undertake to assist these countries in resisting communist aggression.
The decision to assist or not assist is extremely important as it
carries with it the possibility that by its support the United States
may commit itself as it did in Korea to a major war. The general
decision to assist these nations, at least with military aid if not the
deployment of military forces, was made in about 1947 and is sometimes called the Truman Doctrine. That decision is rarely seriously
questioned.

The second major decision confronting United States policymakers
is whether or not the United States would be willing to commit its
military forces to the defense of these countries. The answer to
this question has been that under most circumstances of communist
aggression the United States would be prepared to commit and would
commit United States forces to the defense of these nations. In the
case of Greece and Turkey, the NATO membership of these countries and the United States means that the United States is bound by
treaty to defend these countries if they are attacked. In the case of
the Republic of Korea, the United States willingness to commit forces
is evidenced not only by a piece of paper but by the past United States
action in coming to the aid of the Republic of Korea and the presence
of two United States divisions in Korea. In the case of the Republic

of China the United States is committed by treaty to the defense of
Taiwan and the Pescadores and showed its willingness to assist with
United States forces in various Taiwan Straits crises. The United
States, the Philippines, Pakistan and Thailand are allied under the
terms of the SEATO Treaty. The United States deployed troops to
Thailand when this appeared to be necessary for the defense of that
country. United States forces are also deployed in the Philippines.
Although the United States written commitments to Iran, India, Laos
and Vietnam are limited, the importance which the United States
attaches to the continuance of free governments in these nations is
obvious from the actions which have been taken under both Republican
and Democratic administrations. Laos and Vietnam are so-called
protocol states under the SEATO Treaty. This means that the
United States and its SEATO allies have declared that aggression
against either of these states would be considered a threat to the
security of Southeast Asia. The United States commitment to Iran
and to India in terms of economic and military aid and diplomatic
support can leave little doubt that the United States is not prepared
to see these nations plucked by force from the free world and moved
into the communist orbit.

The importance of each one of these commitments is underlined
by the interrelationships among them. Each nation bordering either
Communist China or Russia is aware that either Communist China or
Russia could successfully defeat it if it chose so long as United States
assistance were not made available. If the United States were ever
to fail to assist any one of these nations in the event of communist
aggression, these nations would probably draw the conclusion that
the creditability of United States support of it was also in doubt. The
result would inevitably be a scampering for some type of accommoda-
tion with the communists, perhaps resulting in eventual communist
takeover. These facts and commitments are indications that the
United States is firmly committed to a policy of drawing the line of
United States defense around the periphery of the Communist Bloc
rather than on the East and West Coasts of the United States. That
policy forms a framework in which military aid to these nations
should be considered.

Given the fact that the United States will assist these nations in
their own defense, the problem becomes to determine what form
this defense should take. There are basically two options available.
The first is to meet any communist attack in any form by all-out
strategic retaliation with the tremendous nuclear potential which the

United States possesses. The second is to graduate the United
States response to the seriousness of the threat or the action
taken by the communists. The entire question of whether deterrence alone is enough has been continuously explored in public
debate and academic literature since the mid-1950's.

The problem in relying solely upon a strategic deterrent stems
in large part from the fact that in today's world the use of the strategic deterrent, even in a first strike situation, is not only to risk
but to ensure the virtual annihilation of the United States. Only if
the strategic retaliatory power of the United States can deter nib-
bling actions on the periphery of the Sino-Soviet Bloc can this deterrent be said to be successful. Neither the Russians nor the
Chinese are likely to be deterred by any nuclear capability no matter
how large so long as they believe that it will not be used in retaliation
for the threats they present. For example, communist forces re-
cruited from a variety of places, using a variety of weapons, are
presently threatening the government of Vietnam. It is difficult
in such a circumstance to say that an appropriate United States
response would be an all-out nuclear attack on Communist China.
Likewise, it is difficult to say that the appropriate response to
Chinese Communist fomenting of insurgency and rebellion in
Africa would be to unleash a nuclear holocaust on Communist China.
So long as the use of full nuclear retaliation for less than a total
attack seems unlikely, the strength of the United States nuclear
deterrent will not prevent all guerrilla warfare, communist in-
cursions and minor tours de force. [2]

Regardless of the merits of the arguments as to whether or not
the United States could or should meet every communist aggressive
act with missiles and rockets, it is clear that present United States
defense policy is based on the assumption that strategic retaliatory
forces alone will not do. Of the $50 billion defense budget voted by
the Congress for fiscal year 1965 less than half of the total was provided for the cost of the strategic deterrent, of the air defense of
the United States and civil defense. The remaining expenditures
are for purposes which are closely allied to the utilization of military force in situations not involving an all-out nuclear exchange.
The United States has developed an army force structure and logistics backup designed to permit a modern army to move rapidly
to scenes of crisis and to fight there with or without nuclear weapons. Air transport capabilities have been augmented. Special
forces have been increased and the Army, Navy and Air Force

are spending large quantities of time, effort and money to develop
capabilities to deal with insurgency and less than all-out war.
Whether this approach is correct or not need not be debated in this
book as the President has traditionally presented and the Congress
has almost unanimously adopted a Department of Defense budget
based on this assumption. If the military aid program is not also
based on this assumption, it is clear that something is plainly
amiss. If the military aid program is based on this assumption,
then the debate of deterrence vs. limited response can be carried
out in the context of $25 billion a year worth of United States defense
expenditures and the disposition of military aid programs in the
"forward defense" category can be made in accordance with the
outcome of that debate.

Assuming that the military requirements in these countries
are two-fold--first, to prevent communist takeover from within
and second, to resist communist takeover from without, in conjunction with United States forces--the requirements for United States
military aid seem relatively clear. Korea can be taken as an
example. The successful defense of Korea against communist
attack would unquestionably involve both Korean and United States
forces. The military problem is how to provide the best defense
at the least cost. In the event of external attack the largest
component of ground forces immediately available would be those
of the Republic of Korea. United States forces could rapidly be
deployed, as they were during the Korean War, to supplement
Korean forces. Deficiencies in Korean training, discipline, equipment, air power and sea, air and land supply capabilities would have
to be made up by deployments of appropriate United States units.
Those United States units which could be deployed to Korea could
also be deployed elsewhere. A balance should obviously be struck
between the funds which are utilized to equip two United States divisions presently in Korea and the Korean forces presently manning
the line in Korea. It is obviously silly to equip the United States
units with the finest equipment available anywhere and to deprive the
Korean units of adequate military equipment. Such action would
leave the United States units to face part of a communist attack when
the Koreans who are fighting on their flank would presumably be
crumbling before the communist onslaught. On the other hand, it
is clearly not desirable to equip the Korean forces with arms and
ammunition better than those available to the United States forces
which will fight beside them.

There seems to be no inherent reason why a military judgment as to the allocation of resources between Korea and the United States cannot be made. There may be no simple mathematical formula which will produce the appropriate answers but it is at least clear that such answers are primarily military ones.

Some idea of the extent to which these decisions are military is indicated by the fact that most of the important decisions on allocation of resources to the Korean forces have nothing to do with the Korean economy. If the Korean Air Force is equipped with a squadron of F-84 aircraft which are largely obsolete by modern standards, the substitution of a squadron of more modern aircraft and the appropriate retraining of pilots would have no effect on the Korean economy. The same number of pilots would be flying the same number of airplanes from the same bases and receiving the same pay and allowances. The effect of this type of hardware decision is on the United States military budget, not on the Korean budget. Likewise, such a decision should not have any impact on the domestic political situation in Korea, on the development of social and educational facilities or on any other facet of Korean life.

These types of resource allocation decisions depend upon a variety of assumptions and facts about enemy capabilities and intentions, enemy weapons inventory, terrain, the speed with which additional United States forces can be deployed and the like which are obviously not available for use in a publication of this kind. However, it would seem that any determination made on the basis of these factors by the personnel who plan and budget for the procurement of equipment for United States forces should be given considerable weight in determining the extent of modernization of Korean forces which will be undertaken with United States funds. At the present time this principle is not followed.

As Secretary McNamara advised the Congress on numerous occasions in 1964, he believes there is an imbalance between local forces supported with military aid, such as the Korean forces, and United States forces supported out of the regular Defense Department budget. This imbalance stems, he said, from the fact that inadequate funds have been available through military aid for equipping local forces such as those in Korea. Under present procedures it is impossible to correct such an imbalance by allocating resources between the regular Department of Defense budget and the military aid budget in such a way as to achieve maximum effectiveness of each dollar spent for military security.

A similar situation exists in those countries where there is a significant threat to internal security as well as the possibility of overt communist aggression. Again, the extent of United States involvement-- such as that in Vietnam--must be considered in relation to the efficiency of equivalent expenditures for equipping local forces.

Korea

The military problem in Korea is obvious to anyone who remembers the Korean War. The United States cannot rely upon diplomacy alone to prevent another communist attack. At considerable cost, the United States has deployed two divisions of its own forces in Korea. Korean planning to meet this threat raises two questions: what level of Korean forces is required and what modernization of those forces shall be accomplished.

On the question of modernization, as indicated in the section on Korea in Chapter 2, the level of modernization of Korean forces is considered inadequate by all military observers. This shortfall in modernization is caused by a lack of military assistance resources, not by any failure on the part of the Koreans. Apparently, no plans have been made to remedy this situation. As Admiral Felt stated:

> With the funds available to us in the 1964 bill and what
> we see in the 1965 submission, the Korean Army... will
> not have adequate modernization. There is no question
> about that. [3]

Because one-for-one replacement of existing obsolete equipment will have no economic or political impact in Korea (except to prove the firmness of United States intentions that Korea shall not be taken by force), there seems to be little excuse for failure to modernize these forces to whatever extent military judgment dictates, within the total funds available for national defense.

On the question of the size of Korean forces there has been considerable comment that the present size of the Korean forces exceeds that required and inhibits economic development. Korea, of course, is a sovereign nation and the determination of the manpower to be devoted to defense must ultimately be made by the Koreans themselves. However, because the United States provides equipment and training to these forces and supports the government of Korea with

economic aid, United States recommendations on the matter of force
levels should carry some weight.

One important factor should be noted. Reductions in Korean
forces would not result in proportionate decreases in the requirements for United States military assistance. The greatest military
assistance expenditures are for major items of military equipment
such as replacements of obsolete aircraft and weapons. The deficiencies in this equipment and any actual shortages of equipment
should be filled regardless of whether Korean forces are to be
larger or smaller in the future. It should also be noted that reductions in forces have little economic benefit unless the demobilized
forces can find gainful employment in the civilian economy.

On the basis of unclassified information alone, it would seem
impossible to make a final judgment as to the appropriate level of
forces in Korea. However, it would seem that such a judgment
should be based on the principle that such Korean forces should be
no smaller than required in a military sense to continue the capability to prevent renewed communist aggression. Because the cost
of maintaining a Korean soldier, $263 per man-year, is less than
a tenth of the cost of maintaining a United States soldier, [4] it would
appear to be false economy to curtail sharply support of Korean
forces, thereby leaving a greater burden for United States forces.

The Republic of China

Correctly or incorrectly, the United States has committed itself
to assist Chiang Kai-shek in the defense of Taiwan and the Pescadores,
and, when the offshore islands were being shelled by the communists,
took a variety of steps to assist the Republic of China. So long as
this policy is in effect, it would appear shortsighted to increase the
burdens on United States forces by inadequate support of the forces
of Nationalist China. If Republic of China forces are inadequately
equipped, the Communist Chinese will be able to confront the United
States with the alternatives of watching the loss of the offshore
islands or Taiwan itself or of intervening with United States forces
at any time the Chinese Communists choose to trigger such a situation. On the other hand, if the Republic of China forces are adequately equipped with airpower and sea defense forces, the Chinese Communists would not be able to involve the United States at times of
their own choosing and would face military reversals should they
choose to attack the Republic of China. The value of defeats of

Communist Chinese armed forces in air warfare or in attempted
attack by sea, even in terms of communist "loss of face" in Asia,
is incalculable, as such an event would mean a communist loss to
other Asians and would no doubt convincingly demonstrate to other
Asian nations that the Chinese Communists are not invincible.

As in the case of Korea, the public record makes it clear that
modernization of Nationalist Chinese forces has not proceeded at
the pace which military and civilian officials of the Department of
Defense consider adequate. As in the case of Korea, it would seem
that Republic of China forces should be modernized at the pace which
military planners consider appropriate, within the total resources
available for national security.

For the same reason that the United States should ensure that
the Chinese Nationalists--without the intervention of United States
forces--have the capability to defeat limited Chinese aggression, the
United States should not encourage Chiang's dream of return to the
mainland so long--as presently appears to be the case--as such a
dream would only result in clear military and political defeat of
the Chinese Nationalists. Therefore, United States military assistance programs should not provide weapons which are primarily
useful for a return to the mainland rather than defense of Taiwan
and the offshore islands. Specifically, equipment like parachute
equipment, transport aircraft in large quantities and amphibious
landing craft should be avoided. Should Chiang's dream of return
ever coincide with a United States desire for such action, appropriate vessels and support should be deployed from United States
inventories and kept under United States control.

One of the most significant problems in United States military
assistance policy is sharply evidenced by the present China problem.
The President, under our system of government, controls foreign
policy, with little exception. Yet the President does not control the
amounts which he can use for foreign aid. These must be appropriated by the Congress. Those who advocate a withdrawal or
diminution of present United States support for Chiang may take out
those feelings in the only manner possible, by encouraging the
reduction of military aid to Chiang. Yet by adopting that approach--
without the capability to change the basic United States commitment--
they encourage the United States intervention and involvement which
they fear. The best method to avoid drawing the United States military establishment into every military conflict between Chiang and

the communists is to give Chiang the capability to supply the offshore
islands, control the air in the Taiwan Straits, repel amphibious landings on Taiwan and prevent the limited Chinese Communist Navy from
controlling the Taiwan Straits.

So long as United States policy postulates extensive involvement
in support of the Chinese Nationalists, it is clearly necessary to commit substantial military assistance resources to the support of that
policy.

The Philippines

The Philippines offers a perfect case of a situation in which military assistance programs should be developed by a consideration
of the relative results to be achieved by a given expenditure of military funds for United States forces and local forces. The United
States maintains valuable bases in the Philippines. Protection of
these bases is necessary if the United States is to maintain the capability to operate with military forces in Southeast Asia. To achieve
this, protection of sea lanes of communication against minelaying
and submarines is required and a modicum of land defense against
sabotage and air drops must be provided. Air defense must be
adequate to defend against attacks on the United States bases.

From the Philippine point of view the situation is similar though
not exactly the same. The Philippine people and government realize
from their early experience with the Huks that the communists pose
a significant threat to all that they hold dear. To prevent loss of
their country they maintain military forces designed to protect
their islands against air, naval and ground attack. They will accept
and use practically any modern equipment which the United States
is willing to furnish without cost to them.

A number of military alternatives appear in this situation. Take
the case of air defense. One feasible alternative--assuming that the
Philippine Government would make available the requisite manpower--
would be to turn the entire air defense of the islands over to the
Filipinos, providing them with fighter aircraft, radar, ground control, airfields and air defense missiles. Such action would free
United States air forces for deployment elsewhere or permit a
reduction in United States air forces. A significant savings for
the United States would result even if the United States paid all the
costs of equipping and maintaining this force. Even if the United

States were to provide, directly or indirectly, for pay of the air force personnel, the costs would be less than one-fifth of that of maintaining a comparable number of United States airmen.

On the other hand, it might be determined that because air units can be quickly redeployed, it would be more economical and efficient to spend no money at all on Philippine air forces. Instead additional funds could be spent to equip United States air units-- some of which could be stationed in the Philippines--which could defend the Philippines or be deployed to Japan, or Korea or Europe or wherever the need required.

The most probable conclusion is that some "mix" of Philippine and United States air units would provide the air defense capabilities required. Just what air defense is required and what the proper mix might be are unknown to the author and most readers of this book. For this reason, it is impossible to say whether the United States is providing exactly the right amount of military assistance in the Philippines. However, it can be concluded that if the United States is providing the proper amount of assistance, the result is more a matter of luck and the dedicated efforts of a few individuals than any systematic planning. For reasons discussed in the final chapter of this book, the present methods for determining military aid programs are not conducive to the development of a balanced combination of United States and Philippine forces for the defense of the Philippine Islands.

If such a military review of the Philippine situation should produce the conclusion that military assistance being provided to the Philippines is too large in relation to the United States defense effort for the defense of the islands, additional assistance which might seem politically required in light of the long existing close relationships between the United States and the Philippines, the existence of United States bases and the importance of the Philippines as one of the staunchest anti-communist powers in the Far East should not be provided in the form of military goods. If such assistance is necessary, but is not required for military purposes, it should be provided in forms that will contribute to economic development. Should the Philippine Government wish to maintain larger forces than seem necessary from the point of view of United States military planning, the costs of those forces should be borne by the Philippine Government. The United States, however, should in such cases stand ready to sell military equipment on as favorable terms as are offered by competing suppliers.

Laos, Vietnam and Thailand

These key countries of Southeast Asia face both threats of communist subversion from within and communist attack from without. In a case such as Vietnam, the political, economic, social and military capabilities of the country are not sufficient to permit the building of military capabilities to maintain internal security and protect against external attack. In such a case, United States assistance should be concentrated on helping the countries do what the United States cannot do for them--maintain internal security. United States units cannot effectively perform police and internal security tasks in these countries without the real risk of aggravating the problem. [5] The United States, on the other hand, can contribute effectively to external defense. For this reason, United States assistance policies should be designed to deal with internal threats first, and assist in developing military potential against external attack only when the internal situation is secure. To make such a policy palatable to the countries concerned, United States determination to apply whatever force is required to assist in the event of an external attack must be clear beyond doubt. In some cases, to make that resolution clear byond doubt it may be necessary to deploy United States forces or to respond affirmatively to requests for military assistance designed to meet an external threat. However, such assistance should be limited as much as possible, so as not to detract attention from the main task of internal security.

Because the Southeast Asia problem has been accorded a first priority in United States resource allocation, any problems in the area are not the result of a lack of military assistance funds. So long as the United States remains committed to its present course of action in assisting these countries to resist subversion, the military assistance bill will continue to be quite large.

India

Overt aggression by either Russia or China against India would seem to offer little advantage to either power due to India's size, the logistical difficulties of supporting a penetration deep into India and the clear setback that such aggression would presumably produce in communist African and Latin American policy. Nonetheless, the fact remains that the Chinese Communists did attack India in the fall of 1962 and demonstrated a clear military superiority over the then existing Indian military forces. The border problems which

served as the excuse or reason for that attack still exist and the
Indian people and government have committed themselves to a
military buildup to prevent a recurrence of communist successes.

Into this situation the Soviet Union, the British Commonwealth
and the United States moved as strange bedfellows to respond to
India's requests for assistance. The Soviet Union is confronted
with one of its most difficult dilemmas in India because a failure
to assist India can ruin what is left of the communist party in India
and end a decade of cordial Soviet-Indian relations. On the other
hand, Russian military aid is bound to exacerbate tensions between
Russia and China. No such difficulties are presented by United States
military aid to India, although Pakistan continues to fear that equipment furnished to India for use against China will ultimately be
used against Pakistan.

In these circumstances continued United States military aid to
India appears highly desirable to (a) increase the possibility that
further communist aggression against India can be stopped in its
tracks, (b) continue to demonstrate that the United States is at
least as concerned with preventing renewed Chinese aggression as
the Soviet Union is and (c) expose the Indian forces to United States
training and doctrine so that the Indian armed forces, although
remaining non-political, can serve as a bastion of strength against
the possibility that internal Indian communist strength might increase.

Ultimate United States objectives in India must continue to
center around helping India to prove that a large underdeveloped
country can develop into a modern state without resorting to the
totalitarian system and methods used by Communist China. One of
the limiting factors in Indian economic growth is a shortage of
foreign exchange. If United States military aid provides items
which the Indians would otherwise buy on the world market, military
aid is as good as economic assistance in helping India to maintain
adequate foreign exchange.

Although these factors make the continuation of a substantial
level of assistance to India desirable, such assistance must be
limited in light of the over-all military requirements of those nations
which have traditionally been closely allied to the United States
which also depend upon limited military aid funds. India, although
now aware of the communist threat to its security, is still neutral

and probably cannot be expected to enter a conflict initiated by a
communist attack on the United States or one of its allies. Also,
too much assistance to India is bound to exacerbate United States
relations with Pakistan, which as a loyal and long standing ally
feels it should receive better treatment in the hands of the United
States than that afforded India.

United States military assistance to India should be provided
only on the basis of Indian agreement not to use the equipment
against Pakistan no matter what the circumstances. Such agreements will not satisfy the Paks, who will understand that United States
assistance to Indian units deployed against the Chinese Communists
will free Indian resources to purchase equipment to be used against
them. However, to at least some extent there will be a less than
one to one ratio between funds freed by United States aid and funds
applied to forces which could be used against Pakistan. In the event
of any actual shooting war between India and Pakistan, the temptation
by India and Pakistan to use equipment furnished by the United States
will no doubt be irresistible unless the United States is willing to
take quite strong steps to prevent such uses of United States-provided assistance.

Pakistan

Pakistan, as a member of SEATO, represents one of the countries which could be expected to fight along with the United States
in the event of serious aggression anywhere in Asia, and is a country which the United States is committed to help in the event of
attack against it. These facts, coupled with Pakistan's limited
economic capabilities, make continued military aid imperative. As
in the case of India, such assistance should only be furnished under
conditions which spell out Pakistan's obligation not to utilize United
States-provided equipment against India. As in the case of other
allies, the optimum level of United States military assistance should
be determined by a military analysis of the value of each increment
of possible aid to Pakistan as compared with similar expenditures
for United States forces. If such an analysis produces the conclusion
that the level of military assistance required for military purposes
is politically insufficient to convince Pakistan to maintain the international backbone which it has shown in the past, then additional
assistance might be considered. However, in the determination of
whether to provide such assistance, the alternative of deployment of
United States forces--for example, an air force squadron or two--
should be considered.

Iran

Iran has been seriously threatened by communist aggression in
the past and there is no guarantee that such a circumstance might
not recur. The most important problem in Iran is to ensure the
economic and social development of the country free from threats to
internal security. The Shah is presently taking a variety of steps to
accelerate economic growth. Strong but necessary economic measures have proceeded satisfactorily in part because of the presence
of the gendarmerie and armed forces equipped through United States
aid. These forces are capable of suppressing the kind of armed
anti-governmental actions which might be taken by dispossessed
large landlords and similar groups.

So long as the internal security mission can be accomplished
with comparatively little effort, it appears desirable that the alternative of easy military victory by overt attack be closed to the communists as well. Assisting Iran to develop the capability to meet
the initial thrust of communist aggression for a sufficient time to
permit free world forces to arrive is clearly desirable. Where
feasible, such assistance should also be used to build airfields,
petroleum facilities and other military infrastructure which could be
used by United States forces should deployment of those forces to
Iran ever be necessary.

Turkey

Turkey has been threatened by Russia for hundreds of years.
The Turks have never faltered in their willingness to maintain large
military forces poised to participate in the defense of all NATO
countries (including the United States). The development of large
able forces in Turkey costs the United States only a fraction of the
cost of developing similar United States forces. In these circumstances, so long as there remains a possibility of a ground war in
Europe (the United States presently maintains six divisions in Europe
on this assumption), adequate support of Turkish forces is clearly
in the national interest. Turkey, with a per capita gross national
product of about $200.00 per year as compared to over $3,000.00 in
the United States, is in no position to pay for modern equipment for its
forces.

In addition to their military importance, Turkish armed forces
represent a major modernizing force, contributing literacy training,

technically trained individuals, and work on projects conducive to economic development. So long as military requirements call for Turkish forces of substantial magnitude, it will be necessary for the United States to provide major assistance to equip them; however, the fact that these forces do perform other valuable functions in economic development is an important bonus.

As indicated in the section on Turkey in Chapter 6, there appears to be a consensus of military opinion that serious deficiencies presently exist in the military capabilities of Turkish forces and that these deficiencies are caused by inadequate United States assistance, not by inability or unwillingness on the part of the Turks. It would seem that either a general increase in the level of military assistance for Turkey or a one-time large expenditure for modernization of these forces should be undertaken as rapidly as possible. Assistance to Turkey should then continue at whatever level military authorities consider necessary within over-all ceilings imposed by the President and Congress on the resources which the United States can devote to national defense.

Greece

Economic assistance programs of the United States are being reduced in Greece which has a gross national product twice that of Turkey. The military importance of Greece, however, continues and the deficiencies which military authorities have found in the military posture of Turkey have also appeared in Greece. For reasons similar to those expressed in the case of Turkey, it seems clear that substantial military assistance should continue in Greece. However, as Greek economic development continues it should be possible to negotiate agreements under which Greece shares with the United States some of the costs of United States military assistance. This could be accomplished by a Greek payment for United States assistance which would initially be substantially less than the value of the assistance provided, but which would be increased as Greek economic circumstances permit.

Greek and Turkish quarrels over Cyprus do not in any way decrease the importance of either country to NATO defense. Decreases in or termination of United States military assistance will not suddenly make the existing capabilities of these two countries to fight wars disappear. These two countries were involved in long and bloody wars--though not with each other--long before the United States was even discovered. Because changing the nature of United States military aid would only reduce the capabilities of NATO against the Soviet Union and the East European satellites, but would not terminate hostility over the Cyprus situation, the wisest policy appears to be to use every means possible to prevent such hostilities, but at the same time not to abandon Greek and Turkish forces committed to NATO defense.

Summary - Forward Defense

The purpose of the programs discussed in this section is to extend the defense of the United States to the very borders of Russia and Communist China. So long as this forward defense continues to be the strategy of the United States and so long as the regular Defense Department budget continues to be devoted in large part to defending countries on the periphery of China and the USSR, military assistance must be continued at a substantial level.

Just what level is required should be a military determination[6] made on the basis of the comparative effectiveness of United States forces and local forces in contributing to the defense of the free world. Any other method is bound to produce an imbalance in the nation's military posture. No one knows just what the result of such a review would be until it is undertaken. Some inkling, however, is probably given by the statements which Unified Commanders, the Chairman of the Joint Chiefs of Staff and the Secretary of Defense have made before Congressional committees.

The President presented to Congress in 1963 a program of $1.4 billion for military aid, which the Congress cut to an even $1 billion. The following year the President presented a program of an even $1 billion, later raised by $55 million to handle special problems in Vietnam. The Chairman of the Joint Chiefs of Staff called this 1965 program "a holding action of borderline adequacy." General Taylor also stated that:

> A continuation of military aid at this level indefinitely will offer us but three options: A gradual reduction of indigenous military capability in strategically important areas of the free world; a buildup of U.S. forces at a far greater cost to compensate for the loss in indigenous strength; or the acceptance of inadequate military strength to support our national interests in some quarters of the world.[7]

   Apparently the Joint Chiefs of Staff considered a much larger
amount than the $1 billion requested to be necessary. The Secretary
of Defense told a Congressional committee that:

> To even approximate the recommendations of the Chiefs
> would require a 40% increase in the level we propose
> without taking into account possible future emergencies
> in Vietnam or elsewhere. [8]

The testimony of Unified Commanders, who are responsible for both
military assistance and United States forces in their areas of
responsibility, before the House Foreign Affairs Committee during
the same year indicated that they, without exception, felt that more
was required for military assistance than provided for by the $1
billion request. The Army General serving as Director of Military
Assistance suggested that he preferred a program of $1.4 billion. [9]

   The views of the nation's highest military officers are accepted
by the Secretary of Defense who said in a speech in May of 1964 that the
Chairman of the Joint Chiefs of Staff:

> Believes that we cannot operate with that level ($1 billion)
> in the next few years "without a serious loss of military
> effectiveness in many countries which it is our interest
> to support."

McNamara told his audience that he agreed with this statement but:

> In light of public attitudes toward this program reflected
> in the reductions made each recent year by the Congress,
> I was unwilling to recommend that the President request
> a higher figure. [10]

   Some idea of the figure which military authorities feel is required
was given by Secretary McNamara in testimony before Congressman
Passman. McNamara stated that more was needed than $1 billion
to meet equipment requirements. Congressman Passman asked how
much more and Secretary McNamara responded: "We need at least
$400 million more."[11] Addition of $400 million to one billion yields
an estimate of $1.4 billion, an amount considerably below the $2
billion per year which the Draper Committee told President Eisenhower was required when it reported in 1959. Thomas Gates, the
Republican Secretary of Defense who preceded McNamara in the

Pentagon, said in 1960 that military aid should remain at about the
$2 billion level for five years.[12]

Whatever the amount for military assistance should be within
the total which the United States spends for its military security, it
seems clear that as a result of a combination of causes the United
States does not now operate a military assistance program which is
the result of careful military budgeting in which various alternative
solutions to a given military problem are carefully weighed against
each other. It likewise seems clear that a combination of historical
accident and extraneous consideration have so shaped public and
Congressional consideration of military aid and the regular Department of Defense budget that the Congress trusts the recommendations of the nation's military authorities on the one hand, and almost
totally rejects the advice of those same authorities on the other. As
will be indicated in the following chapter, it would seem that most of
the faults which plague the present system are curable.

Before that point is considered, however, it is necessary to
examine the other uses to which funds appropriated to military aid
are put, besides the two-thirds of the total devoted to major forward
defense programs.

ALLIANCE FOR PROGRESS
SECURITY PROGRAMS

The growth of the military assistance program in Latin America
is striking. In fiscal year 1951 there were no military assistance
deliveries to Latin America. Five years later in fiscal year 1956
deliveries of $23.5 million were charged to the military aid appro-
priation. Largely as a result of a commitment made to Brazil and
resulting increased deliveries, military assistance from fiscal 1958
through fiscal 1960 averaged $36.5 million per year. In fiscal 1961
deliveries were increased to $45.0 million; in fiscal year 1962 to
$54.3 million. In fiscal year 1963 there was a decrease of over
$9 million in deliveries to Brazil, but increases in other programs
resulted in total deliveries valued at $51.8 million. In fiscal year
1964, the last year for which delivery figures are available, the $60
million mark had been reached and passed by deliveries of $62.9
million.[13]

Even more striking is the extent to which Latin American military programs have consumed an ever-increasing percentage of all military aid funds. Figures provided by the Department of Defense indicate that in fiscal year 1961 Latin American programs accounted for 3% of the total; in 1962, 4%; in 1963, 5%; and in 1964, 6%.

This sharp increase in military aid to Latin America has occurred in circumstances which would seem to call for a reduction rather than an increase in these programs. First, most of the increase occurred after the United States policy shifted to the view that Latin American forces would not be supported for the purpose of defending the hemisphere from external attack. This decision alone should presumably have lowered, not increased, the costs of military aid. Second, this increase occurred at a time when United States interest in Latin America supposedly shifted from an alliance for defense to an Alliance for Progress with stress on economic assistance. Third, this increase in programs for Latin America came at a time when all military authorities were complaining of shortages of funds available for key forward defense programs in Greece, Turkey, the Republic of China and Korea.

This increase is by no means accounted for by programs of civic action to use military forces to contribute to economic development as these programs represented only 15% of the program presented for fiscal 1965. [14] It should also be noted that these increases occurred at a time when Congressional and academic criticism of military aid to Latin America was probably greater than similar criticisms of military aid to all other areas of the world combined. These attitudes are reflected in a legislative ceiling on the assistance which can be furnished to Latin America. But for this ceiling, such assistance might even have been higher than it has been.

The most recent Presidential study of United States foreign aid--the Clay Committee study--recommended:

> With regard to U.S. military assistance programs in Latin America, training, civic action programs, internal security assistance where necessary, and military equipment of a small arms or communications nature should be continued and the remaining activity eliminated. Latin American military forces are not required for hemispheric defense in the event of external attack, and U.S. supply of modern, sophisticated equipment in response to the pressures

of local military prestige contributes to dangers which
outweigh whatever temporary value they may be designed
to serve.15

There seems little or no reason for the recent increases in military aid to Latin America. While some assistance in grant form for
internal security and civic action may be required, the costs of these
programs tend to be small in relation to the costs of more sophisticated weapons. Training programs are unquestionably valuable, but
such programs must be carefully conducted. It seems unlikely that
the training programs which are used to whet the appetites of European officers for United States equipment also serve to convince
Latin American officers to reduce their forces and purchase less
equipment. However, practically all academic writers and Congressional study groups have cited the value of these programs, and, on
the whole, continuation of training at about the present levels appears
appropriate.

To cite the near unanimous conclusions of members of Congress
and academic observers and agree with them is not enough. There
should remain in the minds of every reader the question: if these
programs are so bad why do so many intelligent, well-informed
people in the Executive Branch support them and spend increasing
amounts on them year after year? A review of the justifications of
these programs which have been presented by their supporters
seems to indicate that this support is based upon a confusion between
giving things away and selling them.

The United States has an interest in avoiding European influence
in Latin America, especially in Latin American military establishments, which long predates any communist threat. In fact, this
interest is as old as the Monroe Doctrine. The United States also
has a clear interest in avoiding communist influence in Latin America. For this reason there is widespread recognition of the necessity
of maintaining close relationships with Latin American military
forces. In recent years, however, the thought has apparently developed that the only way in which the United States can maintain close
military relations with an underdeveloped country is to initiate and
increase a program for giving military equipment and training away.
This is an assumption which is historically demonstrably wrong and
which appears to be a costly mistake.

Yet this assumption finds its way into justifications of the military aid program in terms of maintaining historically close relations with Latin American naval forces or of the traditionally close relations between these countries and the United States. These historical relationships, however, were developed by the use of military missions, which the Latin Americans largely paid for themselves, and by sales--not grants--of military equipment, albeit on reasonably favorable terms. The reducto ad absurdum of this kind of thinking is found in what is otherwise an outstanding book on military policies in Latin America. Edwin Liewen in Arms and Politics in Latin America, 16 a scholarly study prepared for the Council on Foreign Relations, spends some two hundred pages proving that United States military assistance to Latin America has, on the whole, been a mistake and should be reduced. Yet when the author reaches his conclusions, he suggests that military assistance should be continued only at the level necessary to preclude significant acceptance of equipment from countries other than the United States. Adoption of such a policy in grant aid would probably immediately double the costs of United States assistance to Latin America.

The simple fact is that neither the communists--except in the case of Cuba--nor the nations of Europe are offering any grant aid to the nations of Latin America. 17 In the area of grants the United States seems to be competing for influence against no other country at a cost of almost $70 million a year. These grants carry obvious disadvantages. When the United States grants a new aircraft, it encourages the recipient to accept it--after all it is free--and raise and maintain the forces to use and maintain it. Thus, the United States becomes identified with the maintenance of military establishments in Latin America which are drains on scarce money and manpower and which in many cases are disliked by the people. In recognition of these problems recent United States policy has attempted to confine grants to equipment designed to maintain internal security and promote civic action. Such a policy if seriously pursued would probably result in a military assistance grant program about half the size of the present one. While the Latin American nations might not be happy about such a policy, one doubts that any Latin Americans believe that they have a "right" to receive grants and, if any do, the sooner they understand that no such "right" exists, the better for all concerned.

In its military sales policy in Latin America the United States may take one of two approaches. First, it can treat Latin American

nations as sovereign states governed by intelligent beings and sell
military equipment to Latin American nations on the same basis
that such equipment is sold to other nations of the world. As a
practical matter any other policy can only lead these nations to
purchase their military equipment in Europe, which has ample production capabilities to supply Latin American needs. The second
alternative is to refuse to sell equipment to these countries unless
the United States determines that such equipment will be used to fill
what the United States considers to be a legitimate military require-
ment--in other words, to apply the criteria for grant military aid
to the sales program.

This latter policy is the one which has been adopted. For
example, the Director of the Military Export Sales Program told
a Congressional committee in 1964 that:

We are not promoting sales in Latin America or in other
areas where we do not want large military establishments.[18]

In explaining the new credit guarantee proposals as part of the sales
program, the Secretary of Defense told another Congressional committee:

We would not use credit guarantees to foster procurement
of equipment from us when it meant that a developing nation,
such as most of those in Africa and Latin America, would
be diverting needed funds from economic development to
military procurement.[19]

The result of this policy is that when Latin American nations
decide that they wish to procure military equipment which the United
States believes they do not need, they are forced to purchase this
equipment from European sources, thereby frustrating the traditional United States objective of keeping European nations out of a position of military influence in Latin America. At the same time such
a restrictive policy on sales can only evoke feelings of hostility from
nations who are told "no" on sales requests. In addition to these
factors, the effect of this policy on economic development is the reverse of what is intended. By denying United States military equipment to these countries, the purchasing countries may lose the opportunity to buy at a price lower than the European price for a given
item--thereby increasing the effect of military procurement on
foreign exchange holdings and economic development.

The present complex of United States military policies in Latin America thus forms a collection of contradictions involving the expenditures of large sums of money to produce results largely the reverse of those intended. The United States wishes to discourage the development and maintenance of large military establishments in Latin America and encourage economic development. To implement this policy large quantities of military equipment are given away, but economic development assistance is furnished on a loan basis. The United States wants to encourage Latin American nations to realize that they are in fact sovereign and independent but pursues a sales policy that refuses to recognize that the nations of Latin America may see their security problems in a different light from the way which the United States sees those problems. The inevitable irritation which this policy produces is to no avail as the military equipment desired can always be purchased in Europe, with resulting loss of sales to United States manufacturers. To calm the troubled waters of relations between the Latin American and the United States military, the only available expedient is more grants from the United States.

The problem of checking this type of "runaway" grant aid is more difficult than might be imagined. A single United States Ambassador or State Department country desk officer may believe that the country for which he is responsible could do without increased grant aid, but is not in a position to recommend such reductions because he has no assurance that grants will be proportionately reduced in the neighboring countries of Latin America. Rather than risk the inevitable frictions when grants are reduced and rather than place "his country" in a poorer position vis-a-vis United States largesse than its neighbors, individual Ambassadors have little choice but to continue to endorse grant programs as large as the total resources available for military assistance will permit.

It would seem that a reduction in the levels of grant military aid to the levels of deliveries of the late 1950's or lower and a United States willingness to compete with European suppliers for military procurement--in the event that attempts to discourage the procurement fail--would better serve United States and Latin American interests and result in a significant savings of military assistance funds.

MILITARY BASE PROGRAMS

The fiscal year 1965 program for military assistance presented to the Congress by the Defense Department contemplated assistance of $24.4 million connected with continued access to United States bases in Portugal, Spain and Libya. In addition, certain economic assistance programs were justified as partial payment for the use of bases in foreign countries.

These programs have on occasion been criticized as being too large for the purposes which they serve. The Senate Foreign Relations Committee in its report in 1963 on the foreign aid bill suggested that programs for Spain and Portugal were too large. The Clay Committee stated:

Moreover, every effort should be made to reduce assistance to foreign countries in return for these rights, especially Spain and Portugal, which are already more than adequately compensated.[20]

On the whole, it seems difficult to criticize these programs, so long as the necessity of the bases involved is assumed. The guideline for negotiation of any right is undoubtedly to ensure the greatest United States return for the least diplomatic, military and financial cost. On the basis of the available facts, grounds for extensive second guessing of the results of negotiations do not readily appear.

GRANT AID PHASE OUT

As indicated in the chapter concerning Europe, the United States has become committed to certain programs, in Norway and Denmark particularly, which would not be undertaken if the decisions were being made today. These commitments will continue to require a part of the new appropriations for military aid for several years to come. However, in the words of Robert Service, "a promise made is a debt unpaid,"[21] and the time for tactful repudiation of that debt has long since passed.

FREE WORLD ORIENTATION PROGRAMS

The United States maintains a number of small military assistance programs in countries which are unlikely to become significant military factors in the world strategic equation. Most of these nations are the newly developed nations of Africa. The purposes of these programs include the preclusion or limitation of communist influence in the armed forces of these nations, the expression of United States interest in the countries concerned and the development of internal security.

The most striking aspect of these programs is that no application of military judgment will produce answers as to when and where they should be started or ended and what form they should take. The determination of what grants will preclude communist influence or express United States interest in a country's continued independence is very much a foreign policy decision and not a military decision. Even the question of internal security is essentially political in an area like Africa. While military judgment is valuable in determining what mix of weapons should be supplied, the basic question is whether the United States should commit itself to a particular government, thereby alienating any future government which might come to power by forcible means.

For these reasons the limited military assistance programs in Africa should be under the very close control of the State Department. If the United States is to pursue a policy of indicating friendship for new nations by giving things away, the State Department is in the best position to determine whether that assistance should take the form of loans for economic development, agricultural commodities, Peace Corps activities, technical assistance or military aid. It would seem that military assistance should be considered as the least desirable of these alternatives, lest the United States image become that of one vast arsenal across the sea. As the Clay Committee put it:

We believe the problems created by military assistance programs in the African countries generally would be greater than those they would forestall or resolve. [22]

If military assistance in the new states becomes necessary for political reasons, such assistance can most appropriately take the form of training in the United States and development of civic action capabilities.

UNITED STATES FORCE SUPPORT
AND MAP ADMINISTRATION

The other military assistance expenditures are a miscellany of items, most of which should not be considered as being military assistance. They include:

1. NATO Infrastructure and Military Headquarters. The costs of United States participation in NATO construction projects and command headquarters amount to some $50-80 million per year as the United States share of NATO costs. These costs are in support of United States forces deployed in Europe and are not related to military aid; indeed, most of the major participants in NATO no longer receive significant military aid. Congressional leaders have suggested that the United States should attempt to reduce the share of these costs which it pays and State and Defense Department representatives have agreed, and have indicated that they are attempting to negotiate a lower share. Similar determinations have probably been made in every other NATO country.

2. Credit Assistance. To the extent that credit assistance requirements under the military sales program exceed funds available in the credit sales revolving funds, money must be taken from the grant aid account for this purpose. Funds for financing sales seem out of place in a program of grant aid, and the situation in which grant requirements compete for funds with sales financing requirements seems to create a "trade-off" of resources where none should exist. The credit assistance fund should be adequately capitalized and separated from the grant aid account.

3. Program Administration. The administration of military assistance has cost less than $25 million and more than $23 million for years and can be expected to continue to cost about that amount.

CONCLUSION

Roughly half of the United States $50 billion defense budget is based on the premise that the United States should stand ready to help countries on the periphery of the Soviet Union and Communist China to defend themselves against communist aggression. If this premise is wrong, it should be corrected in the context of the defense budget as well as the military aid budget as the two are

complementary. The appropriate level of military assistance expenditures in countries threatened with communist aggression should
be determined by weighing military aid costs and advantages against
those of increased deployments of United States forces and against
those of improving the equipment and transportability of United States
forces. Such a careful weighing of military costs and advantages is
not now undertaken, with the result that many civilian and military
officials have indicated that there is an imbalance between regular
Defense Department expenditures and military aid expenditures.

Military assistance to Latin America costs about twice what it
should, mainly because there is a general preference for grant programs over sales programs. Military assistance to the new nations
of Africa may serve a useful purpose but such programs should be
developed under the control of the State Department and should generally be considered inferior to economic aid.

NOTES

1. This section does not consider the possible results of a
military review of the cost effectiveness of various combinations of
United States deployments, or possible deployments and the development of greater indigenous capabilities. It is the author's view
that intelligent recommendations on such subjects can be made only
on the basis of facts on United States, enemy, and allied capabilities
which are properly classified. The purpose of the comments in this
section is to suggest that this type of review needs to be made by
persons with the power to decide or at least recommend both the
levels of military aid and our own defense budget. Readers who
wish to explore the military questions are referred to Colonel Amos
Jordan's Foreign Aid and the Defense of Southeast Asia (New York:
Praeger, 1962) and Charles Wolf's Foreign Aid: Theory and Practice
in Southern Asia (Princeton: Princeton University Press, 1960).
Both these books cover considerably more than their titles imply.
Both are written by persons who have had the opportunity to consider
the problems involved on the basis of data available within the government, Colonel Jordan through the Draper Committee and Mr. Wolf
through the RAND Corporation.
2. This is obviously a simplified exposition of a complex problem. The books, articles and speeches of Henry Kissinger and
General Maxwell Taylor explore the problem in detail.
3. HFAC, CY 64, p. 698.

4. Cost of maintaining soldier data taken from HAC, CY 64, p. 462.

5. For this reason, the United States forces deployed to Vietnam in a combat, as distinguished from a support or advisory role, have been used to defend fixed positions from external attack, not as roving security forces.

6. "Military determination" is not intended to indicate that the decisions of this type should or should not be made by "military" men. The problem is to make sure that military assistance requirements decisions and requirements decisions for the costs of United States forces are made by the same men in the same time frame on the same strategic and tactical assumptions. The formulation of those assumptions, especially in terms of the circumstances in which United States and local forces can be used in less than all-out war, should be accomplished by the same groups which will make the decisions when the actual situation arises. This means that the President and the State Department have an important role to play in "military determinations." Once these determinations are made, military judgment should be applied through whatever combination of civilian and military personnel the President and the Congress determine is appropriate for the nation's defense effort as a whole. Such military determinations are and should be subjected to the same type of political review by the Department of State which occurs when significant deployments of United States forces or establishment of new bases abroad are under consideration.

7. Testimony of General Taylor, then Chairman of the Joint Chiefs of Staff, HAC, CY 64, p. 325.

8. HAC, CY 64, p. 329.

9. Testimony of General Robert Wood, HFAC, CY 64, p. 544.

10. Address by Secretary McNamara before the National Industrial Conference Board, May 21, 1964 reported in various newspapers the following day and issued as a Department of Defense press release.

11. HAC, CY 64, p. 359.

12. HFAC, CY 60, p. 75.

13. All figures from Military Assistance Facts, 1964 ed., published by the Department of Defense, p. 21.

14. HAC, CY 64, p. 322.

15. Report to the President from the Committee to Strengthen the Security of the Free World (Washington: Department of State, March 20, 1963), p. 14.

16. New York: Praeger, 1961.

17. Communist satellites did once ship equipment to Guatemala, but the problem there was not solved with United States military aid.

18. Testimony of Deputy Assistant Secretary of Defense, Mr. Henry Kuss, HFAC, CY 64, p. 509.

19. SAC, CY 64, p. 226.

20. Report of Committee to Strengthen the Security of the Free World, op. cit., p. 18.

21. The Cremation of Sam McGee, various editions have been published.

22. Report of Committee to Strengthen the Security of the Free World, op. cit., p. 10.

CHAPTER **16** ON ENDING THE
FOREIGN AID PROGRAM

The "foreign aid" program as it is known today can be said to have begun when economic and military assistance were combined into a single piece of legislation as the Mutual Security Act of 1951. This act was passed at the height of the United States series of military and economic responses to the communist threat as manifested particularly by the communist aggression in Korea. That program was an integrated series of economic and military steps designed primarily to restore the military strength of the members of NATO. Economic aid was used to build military production facilities and military aid was used for essentially the same purposes. Hundreds of millions of dollars were transferred from military to economic programs.

These mutual security programs were, with a few exceptions, considered together by the committees of the House and Senate handling foreign relations. During the 1950's the mutual security bill continued to be a package of economic and military proposals with most of the economic proposals consisting of assistance for defense production or indirectly to provide for pay and other costs of foreign forces being supported with military aid.

During the 1950's the primary motivation of United States assistance was clearly military and most programs of assistance, economic and military, were closely related to meeting immediate military threats. Little consideration was given to the longer run security interests of the United States, and the programs of economic development which those interests seemed to require if defense against communism was to be more than a mere transitory military holding action. As the decade of the 1950's began to draw to a close, the difference between the short run military purposes of "mutual security" or 'foreign aid" and the longer run economic purposes began to be recognized.

This recognition brought in its wake criticism of the fact that narrow security interests seemed to dominate United States aid. To many, the United States objectives seemed to be hazy as programs moved away from immediate defense needs. National understanding, or at least national support, of the programs began to wane and many observers began to call for increased recognition of the economic assistance effort by separating it from the military effort. Concurrently economic programs, especially those not related directly to immediate defense needs, were increasing in relation to military

assistance. Separation of military and economic assistance began to
be increasingly seriously considered.

The pressures for separation of economic and military assist-
ance--and thus the elimination of the foreign aid program as presently conceived--were augmented by the recognition of the interrelationships between military assistance and the regular Department of Defense budget. In the latter half of the decade, for example,
military assistance funds relieved the regular defense budget of the
costs of supporting the forces of the Republic of Korea. From Japan
to Western Europe military aid funds were equipping units the existence of which permitted United States forces to perform different
missions and make different deployments than would otherwise have
been the case.

In 1956, James P. Richards, a former chairman of the House
Foreign Affairs Committee, conducted a study of foreign aid for the
committee. Richard's report cited the close relationships between
Department of Defense programs and military aid and the limited
public understanding of "foreign aid" as then being administered.
The Report included the recommendation that military assistance
should be completely separated legislatively and administratively
from assistance for other purposes. Part of the reason for this
recommendation was stated to be:

> From the standpoint of the people of the United States
> and the Congress it is not clearly understood that foreign
> aid for military purposes is part and parcel of our own
> defense. Such aid is always confused with economic aid.
> If military aid is placed in our own defense budget, it
> will soon be understood by all that our military leaders
> consider that foreign aid is essential to our own defense
> and is a necessary part of our own defense program.[1]

In 1957 a similar recommendation for separation of economic
and military programs came from a Presidential Committee concerned with the economic aid program. A group of highly placed
business, labor and educational leaders appointed by President
Eisenhower reported to him that the economic aid program should
be established, considered and budgeted on its own merits as an
instrument of foreign policy. The group noted that:

The present intermingling of military and economic assist-
ance--both budget-wise and in the public mind--has created
misunderstanding at home and suspicions abroad. 2

In a study prepared in 1957 for the Senate Special Committee to
Study the Foreign Aid Program, the Brookings Institution considered
at length the existing interrelationships between economic and
military aid and the administrative arrangements applicable to both
programs. This study concluded that the military and economic
programs should continue to be considered legislatively, financially
and administratively as parts of an over-all foreign aid program. 3

In 1957 the Special Senate Committee for which the Brookings
Report was prepared noted the support for separation of economic
and military assistance, including the fact that the State Department
had interposed no objection and concluded:

With particular reference to the proposal which has been
made to place funds for military aid in the Department of
Defense Appropriation the committee believes that, if
the President so desires, this change should be carefully
considered. If the change is made, however, the committee
believes that such funds should continue to be clearly earmarked for foreign military aid and that Congress should
continue to authorize such appropriations annually, pending
a clear determination of the role of military aid in the total
strategy of national defense. 4

The Committee also recommended that whether or not military aid
and regular Department of Defense programs were put in the same
budget they should be reviewed competitively so that the needs for
one were weighed against the needs of the other.

In considering this problem the Special Committee had been confronted with an impressive array of witnesses supporting separation
of economic and military assistance. Some indication of the problems
involved in the combination of economic and military assistance were
supplied by these witnesses. 5 Max Millikan, the Director for International Studies of the Massachusetts Institute of Technology, indicated that:

The purposes of development assistance are likely to be
more effectively served if it is separated out from assistance

designed for these other ends more clearly than it has been
in the past. There is a large measure of agreement among
all the reports made to the Government on the desirability
of a clearer separation, at least as between military and
development assistance. [6]

The Chairman of the Board of Trustees of the National Planning Association, which had prepared a study on economic aid
programs for the Special Committee, suggested that mixing economic and military aid had confused the public. He stated that he would:

Put whatever is military under our defense expenditures
because then the country knows exactly what we are really
sacrificing, what we are really giving abroad and what we
get back for it. [7]

The President of the Systems Analysis Corporation, which prepared a study on military aid for the Committee, argued for removing
military assistance from foreign aid and putting it in the Defense
budget so that all expenditures in the defense area could be put under
one manager. [8]

Mr. Benjamin F. Fairless, the coordinator of the President's
Citizens Advisors on the Mutual Security Program (Fairless Committee), presented a summary of the Committee's recommendation
to the President in March, 1957. He explained that the Committee
has unanimously agreed that military assistance should be a part
of the regular defense budget. [9]

Secretary of State Dulles suggested that both military assistance
and a redefined category of defense support should be authorized on a
continuing basis and appropriated annually to the President in appropriations for the Department of Defense. In support of this recommendation he stated:

We believe that this way of treating military assistance,
which also is recommended by many of the recent studies on
the subject, would avoid a wide degree of misunderstanding
abroad and at home by making apparent the degree in which
we wish our aid to serve military defense. [10]

The Department of Defense took a similar position, recommending
that military assistance be included in the Department of Defense

appropriation act rather than in the foreign aid appropriation act.
To make this possible it was considered necessary to recommend
continuing authorization for these appropriations as part of the
Mutual Security Act. [11] The Defense Department refused to take
a position on whether the Senate Armed Services Committee or the
Foreign Relations Committee should consider such a request for
continuing authorization. [12]

Such diverse groups as the Cooperative League of the United
States, the American Association of University Women, the United
Automobile Workers, and the Chamber of Commerce supported
separation of military and economic aid in statements presented
to the Special Committee.

Active consideration of separation of military and economic aid
continued in 1958. In its report on the mutual security authorization
bill in that year the House Foreign Affairs Committee stated:

> Although the bill reported includes authorizations for
> both military and economic assistance, the committee
> questions whether the practice of including the provision
> of military aid in the same legislation as that providing eco-
> nomic assistance and technical cooperation should be con-
> tinued in the future. The supplying of arms and military equip-
> ment to our allies is based on considerations and involves
> decisions which differ in important respects from those
> relating to providing aid to underdeveloped nations. The
> separation of the program into its two major components
> should facilitate an informed evaluation by the public and
> the Congress of the different elements of the program. It
> is argued that the linking of economic and technical coopera-
> tion with a military program detracts from the effectiveness
> of our nonmilitary operations in certain areas. [13]

The Committee Report recommended that the Executive Branch initiate a new study of the question of bringing in separate bills for
military and economic aid.

The co-mingling of economic and military aid and the military
security "cast" which this gave to the entire foreign aid program was
also criticized in the Senate. In 1958 after the Senate had completed
action on the mutual security appropriations, a number of Democratic
Senators--including then Senators John F. Kennedy and Hubert

Humphrey--wrote to President Eisenhower to inform him of their
deep concern over the present concept and administration of the
mutual security program. The Senators concluded that:

> There is a serious distortion in the present relative importance
> which is attached to military and related aid on the one hand
> and technical assistance and self-liquidating economic develop-
> ment assistance on the other.

The letter was critical of the extent of military assistance--for
which $2.4 billion was being spent during the fiscal year in which the
letter was sent. It stated:

> Overemphasis on military assistance has tended un-
> avoidably to involve the United States in situations in which
> our aid may have contributed to the maintenance in power of
> regimes which have lacked broad support within the countries
> we have assisted. It has helped to create abroad a militaristic
> image of the United States which is a distortion of our national
> character. It has distracted attention, energy and perhaps
> economic aid, from more pressing problems. And, finally,
> we believe military assistance by its very nature tends to
> create and then to perpetuate military hierarchies which
> even in the most well-developed countries may endanger the
> very values of individual freedom which we seek to safeguard.[14]

As a solution to these difficulties the group recommended less emphasis on military aid in the foreign aid package rather than separation
of economic and military assistance.

Partly in response to the criticisms made by the Democratic
Senators, President Eisenhower created a special committee to study
the United States Military Assistance Program (the Draper Committee). Part of the charter which the President gave the committee
was to study the relative emphasis of economic and military aid.[15]

The preliminary report of the Draper Committee, made in
March, 1959, did not address whether military and economic assistance should be separated. However, the sentiment in the Congress
for a closer relationship between military aid and the regular Department of Defense budget was strong. To ensure this relationship the
Senate Foreign Relations Committee inserted into the pending foreign
aid bill a paragraph which stated that:

In order to make sure that a dollar spent on military assistance to foreign countries is as necessary as a dollar spent for the United States military establishment, the President shall establish procedures for programming and budgeting so that the programs of the military assistance come into direct competition for financial support with other activities and programs of the Department of Defense.[16]

The explanation of the purpose of this provision was contained in the Foreign Relations Committee Report which stated:

This is designed to insure that the budget process itself will approach military assistance and domestic defense funds as parts of a single program. The last dollar spent on either military assistance or domestic defense should buy as much as the last dollar spent on the other.

Under present procedures within the Executive Branch, the Department of Defense budget is made up against one target figure and the military assistance budget is made up against a second target figure. In the future both budgets should be made up against a single figure. (Emphasis added.)[17]

The provision was accepted by representatives of the House in Conference Committee and enacted into law in 1959.

The development of this competitive budgeting provision is largely the result of the dilemma which the Democratic majority of the Senate Foreign Relations Committee found itself in 1959. These Senators had indicated to the President in 1958 that there was an overemphasis on military aid. Despite the Draper Study with its recommendations for continued military assistance at a high level, these members were still probably in a mood to cut military assistance. However, testimony presented in support of the program by Defense Department witnesses indicated that dollar for dollar military assistance programs were as important as those of the regular defense budget. This military testimony was hard to ignore at a time when the Congress was appropriating over $40 billion for the regular Department of Defense budget. The Committee concluded its deliberations by recommending a military aid program at the level the President requested but indicated that a minimum of $1.1 of the $1.6 billion total could only be spent for NATO countries.

Although the statements of the military value of military aid could
not be ignored, the Committee realized that those statements were
not really based upon a detailed analysis, but rather upon a general
feeling on the part of military and civilian authorities in the Defense
Department. To put this general assertion to the test of hard budget
review, the Committee added the competitive budgeting provision
which became Section 504(b) of the Foreign Assistance Act of 1961,
as amended.

The Draper Committee, although recommending a level of military assistance of about $2 billion per year, also recognized the
competitive budgeting problem in its report released to the public
on June 24, 1959. The Committee recommended that the military
assistance appropriation request be made a part of the regular
Defense Department budget. In support of this recommendation
the Committee Report stated:

> Inclusion of the Military Assistance Program in the
> Defense Department budget should permit more precise
> evaluation of the relationships and priorities between
> this program and the other United States military pro-
> grams and should lead to more effective planning for
> all United States military programs resulting in greater
> economy. [18]

To comply with the recommendations of the Draper Committee
the President included military assistance as part of the regular
Department of Defense budget in his budget request for fiscal year
1961. However, military assistance was still made a part of the
foreign aid program by inclusion of military assistance in the
President's Foreign Aid Message. The proposed program was
considered by the traditional committees on the traditional
schedule for foreign aid. Review of the program in the Congress
was not meshed with review of the regular Department of Defense
program and the appropriations for the two programs were not
made at the same time. However, the Administration told Congressional committees that the Draper Committee recommendations had been complied with by the mere shifting of the item in
the budget document presented to the Congress. [19] Mr. Draper
in 1961 said that the program was then being properly directed,
budgeted and administered by the Department of Defense. [20]

Shortly after he took office, President Kennedy sent his first foreign aid message to the Congress. In that message he indicated that:

> If our foreign aid funds are to be prudently and effectively used, we need a whole new set of basic concepts and principles.[21]

The eighth of these new concepts was:

> Separation from military assistance: Our program of aid to social and economic development must be seen on its own merits, and judged in the light of its vital and distinctive contribution to our basic security needs.

Accordingly, President Kennedy stated:

> I shall propose a separate authorization for military assistance with appropriations as part of the Defense budget.

The draft legislation presented by the Executive Branch to the Congress, however, included military assistance as part of the overall foreign assistance bill. This bill, however, separated the legislation applicable to military assistance in a separate title with a name of its own--The International Peace and Security Act. The military assistance program continued therefore to be considered as a part of the foreign aid program on the same schedule and by the same committees as the economic program. Some indication of what happened to the proposal made in the foreign aid message is shown by an explanation given by the Deputy Assistant Secretary of Defense then responsible for military aid who gave the following explanation to the House Foreign Affairs Committee of why he was appearing before them:

> The whole question of how to present this entire foreign aid program was discussed within the administration. The suggestion was aired and rather quickly rejected, that it be put within the Defense Department budget in the full sense and presented to the Armed Services Committees. We didn't feel that was the proper thing to do because it is intimately related to our foreign policy. When you poke at almost any one of these decisions and programs, you end up

with a political aspect and for that reason we felt it appropriate to continue to go before this committee.[22]

The separate legislation contemplated by President Kennedy's
foreign aid message thus died a quiet and slow death as the fiscal
year 1962 military assistance program was considered, though with
a new label, exactly as it had been in the past. In the following year
the military aid program was again presented as part of an over-all
foreign aid request and considered in the traditional fashion. Finally,
in presenting the fiscal year 1964 program in the spring of 1963, the
Executive Branch recommended that even the separate title of the
military assistance portion of the foreign aid bill be dropped. The
Congress accepted this recommendation.[23]

The scope and structure of the entire "foreign aid program" including military assistance was again reviewed in the fall of 1963 by
a high level Presidential task force headed by George Ball, then an
Under Secretary of State. The press at the time reported that some
of the members of this group were considering an approach that would
involve separation of the "foreign aid" package into its various components including separation of military aid from the remaining programs.
This concept caused a substantial public debate.[24]

In his first appearance in 1964 before a Congressional committee
to discuss the foreign aid program, Secretary of State Rusk explained
that during the period leading to the Administration's legislative proposals a "hard look" was taken at the structure of the aid program.
"After full consideration," he said, "the President decided to continue
the organization developed in 1961."[25] AID Administrator Bell reported that the President had "conflicting advice" from various members of the Senate and the House, but recommended a "combined program."[26]

Although members of the House Foreign Affairs Committee
were apparently quite pleased by the outcome of this review,[27] many
leading Senators opposed it. The Chairman of the Senate Foreign
Relations Committee, Senator Fulbright, introduced separate bills
for military assistance, development loans and various other parts
of the foreign aid package presented by the Administration.[28] The
Senate Majority Leader, Senator Mansfield, was quoted by a Washington newspaper as stating that military assistance should be considered as part of the regular Department of Defense budget.[29]

Senator Fulbright's opposition to including military assistance
in the foreign aid bill was particularly strong. As he put it:

> It (military aid) has nothing to do with foreign aid. It
> is just an aspect of our military budget.
>
> ... The military spend more in the foreign field
> directly out of their own budget than is carried here. It is
> an anachronism to call this thing military aid. It is just
> a special item. But the payment of our troops, for example,
> in Germany and in Korea is not in this. How do you dis-
> tinguish in its purpose and functions, between, we will say,
> the billion dollars they spend on the payment of troops in
> Germany and the $1 billion that is carried here and was
> carried in this year's foreign aid bill for the purchase of
> hardware?
>
> I cannot see any distinction.... It would seem to me
> it is essentially military. 30

Despite the Senate opposition, military assistance and economic assistance continued to be combined in the foreign aid authorization and appropriations passed by the Congress in 1964.

In connection with the Administration 1965 request, the events
of 1964 were repeated. The Administration considered separation,
but finally dropped the proposal. Senator Fulbright pressed separation but failed to achieve it.

THE EFFECT OF CO-MINGLING
MILITARY AND ECONOMIC PROGRAMS

The major results of co-mingling economic and military aid
have been (a) to cause Congressional, public and foreign misunderstanding of both programs, (b) to cause even those who administer
the programs to be confused over their proper scope and objectives,
a confusion which has resulted in major "studies" of foreign aid
practically every year with no solutions in sight, (c) to cause a
serious imbalance between military aid and other Defense programs,
and (d) to prevent the businesslike management tools of the Department of Defense from being applied to military aid.

So long as military and economic aid are presented as part of a total foreign aid program it seems inevitable that the public and Congress will continue to be confused over exactly what foreign aid is and what it is intended to accomplish. The temptation for administration officials, with one eye on the near unanimous public and Congressional approval of military budgets in excess of $50 billion, to attempt to justify the entire foreign aid program as part of national defense needs is normally too great to be resisted. Congressmen likewise tend to rely upon a military rationale in justifying votes for foreign aid. These justifications, however, have failed to convince either the public or the Congress that foreign aid is just like the defense budget--as the extent of public opposition and Congressional cuts in programs so eloquently testify. One of the major reasons for this public and Congressional reaction is that the argument that economic programs, in Africa for example, make contributions to national security similar to those made by the defense budget is so false that Congressmen and the public not only see through the rationale but also distrust the other recommendations of those who use it. One result of this phenomenon is that "foreign aid" has fared much worse with the Congress than economic assistance programs which are presented with straightforward economic justifications. The Peace Corps and the Marshall Plan provide excellent examples of the legislative success of "pure" economic aid programs.

Over-reliance on the security rationale for the foreign aid program has not only helped make economic aid acceptable, it has made military aid less acceptable than it might otherwise be. No matter how strongly the President and other officials may stress the point that military assistance is an essential part of free world defense, the fact remains that those officials have not included that program as a part of the Department of Defense budget. Who can blame the public and Congress from concluding that no matter what may be said, the actions of the past three Administrations have proved that in the minds of those who administer the program, military assistance is more "foreign aid" than "defense"?

The competitive budgeting provisions of the Foreign Assistance Act are designed to give Congress assurance that the programs of the regular Department of Defense and military aid programs are reviewed in competition with each other. However, a review of the testimony presented in 1964 indicates that these provisions have not been implemented. The Secretary of Defense in testifying on the Department of Defense budget was quick to point out that no

arbitrary ceiling had been used in developing the regular defense
budget, but stated that such an arbitrary ceiling had been applied
in the case of the military assistance budget. It will be recalled
that the Senate Foreign Relations Committee in passing the competitive budgeting provision had indicated that both military assistance
and the Department of Defense budget should compete for resources
within the same ceiling. The military assistance budget for fiscal
year 1965 was held to $1 billion, according to Secretary McNamara,
"solely because the Congress has made it crystal clear to the
Executive Branch that it is unwilling to appropriate a larger
amount." [31] No such criterion was mentioned in connection with the
regular Department of Defense budget for the same fiscal year.
These reasons, coupled with the fact that military assistance budgets and regular Department of Defense budgets are obviously
developed on different cycles, reviewed by different persons and
agencies in the Administration, transmitted to Congress on different
schedules, reviewed in Congress by different committees and appropriated at different times, have denied the public and the Congress
the assurance that military assistance and regular Department of
Defense funds are considered competitively. [32] Thus, the Congress
and the public are never quite sure that foreign aid is an integral
part of national security.

Another difficulty caused by mixing military and economic programs has been to punish one program for the sins of the other and
visa versa. Some examples of the wide public recognition that the
"sins" of the military program are often attributed to "foreign aid"
as a whole (and thus economic aid) are indicated by testimony of
representatives of interest groups before Congressional committees.
For example, a representative of the National Farmers Union told
the House Foreign Affairs Committee in 1964:

> We have found, Mr. Chairman, that there are groups
> that point a finger at a few of the failures that we have had
> in our assistance program, by pointing at the fact that we
> provided developing countries military assistance, technical
> assistance, built a strong military and consequently the
> military rose up and put down the democratically elected
> government... (Separation of economic and military aid)
> would eliminate a stigma which has been falsely attached
> to the program and would consequently enhance its chances
> of maintaining a strong and expanding program. [33]

A representative of the Methodist Church told the same committee:

> That portion of the program (military aid), for example,
> which has seemed to encourage military coups in Latin
> America has undermined seriously the public support for
> the aid program. There may well have been military
> reasons for the assistance, but I think that the military
> proposals should stand on their own feet and not impair
> the economic. [34]

The domestic political difficulties and the misunderstanding of
and confusion about the purposes of the foreign aid program are
serious. More serious is the impact which the co-mingling has on
the programs themselves. So long as a security rationale is used
for the economic aid program, in order to sell it at home, administrators of that program abroad are likely to confuse the long run
necessity for economic development with our immediate security
interests. As a result economic aid may in some cases be misunderstood by the giver and is probably more often misunderstood by
recipients. As a representative of the National Council of Churches
put it:

> We of the churches are concerned that official arguments
> in support of assistance programs often lack a solid ethical
> basis, and consequently are psychologically unacceptable
> to other countries...We of the churches are especially
> disturbed by some official arguments which defend the pro-
> gram almost exclusively on the basis of narrow self interest,
> stressing its value in counteracting communism and other
> threats to our security without genuine concern for the
> welfare of people as people. [35]

Overemphasis on the security rationale for economic aid has
undoubtedly resulted in overlooking the major importance of economic
aid. Military assistance, and indeed the entire defense budget, is
based upon a defensive strategy. The mission of military forces
and the budgets which support them is to prevent things from hap-
pening, not to make them happen, so long as the United States does
not plan military aggression. If military aid to Greece and Turkey,
coupled with the United States forces which could be brought to bear,
are sufficient to convince the communists that they cannot seriously
consider attacking these countries, these military expenditures have
served their purpose. Military forces are developed in response to

a military threat developed by a potential enemy. As the threat
increases more forces are required; when the threat decreases
military expenditures can decrease. In other words, military
expenditures accomplish nothing but defense, and the level of
required military expenditures is largely controlled by the enemy
through his determination of what forces to maintain.

Economic assistance, on the other hand, has positive objectives.
Such assistance can create viable countries and thereby assist
people as people, improve living standards, demonstrate that free
economies and free people can succeed as well or better than the
communists, and create the strong economies that ensure that the
countries assisted will want to remain free. These are positive
objectives, not mere reaction to the day to day moves of the communists. So long as the economic program is considered by the
people who administer it as merely military expenditures in another
form, the long range objectives are likely to be ignored. By ac-
centuating the negative aspect of "security" and de-emphasizing
the many positive aspects of economic assistance, "foreign aid"
has been turned into a program which will probably never gain the
enthusiastic support of the American people and their elected representatives.

In addition, the administrators of the economic aid program,
by relying on a security rationale, are leaving a legacy of misunderstanding which some day will do great disservice to their successors.
The American public and the Congress are being conditioned to
believe that the only legitimate purpose of an economic aid program
is to stop communist aggression. Should the communist threat ever
disappear, who will be able to argue with those who demand an immediate termination of all economic aid? If the communist threat
should ever diminish, who will be able to argue with those who will
demand a proportionate reduction in programs of economic aid?

In addition to ending much of the confusion which surrounds present economic and military aid programs and policies, abolishing
"foreign aid" by making military assistance a part of the Defense
Department budget would end the serious imbalance which has developed in military assistance and the expenditures made for regular United
States forces.

The present "foreign aid" bill is considered by the public and
the Congress as a total package, not in particular parts which add

together to make a total. As a result the Congress in considering a
program considers how much the total foreign aid bill can be reduced, not whether military assistance or development loans or the
Alliance for Progress programs should be reduced. As the Chairman
of the Senate Foreign Relations Committee--who should know--
describes the process:

> The publicity that usually accompanies the foreign aid
> bill has the headline "$4,500 billion for foreign aid,"
> and the response is 'This is a big giveaway of the tax-
> payers' money down a rathole." ...We have only
> bought enemies, they say, we cannot buy friends.
> Everybody hates us, they say. These are the usual
> rejoinders you have with this target of $4.5 billion to
> shoot at. In my experience the usual way to cut this amount
> is not to say, 'Well, we don't like this particular activity,
> let us take it out," but to say, "We just want to cut it 10
> percent, just cut off $500 million or $1 billion."[36]

The fact that consideration of various alternative levels for particular parts of the foreign aid bill--such as military aid--is subor-
dinated to considerations of the over-all total for foreign aid means
that in general the economic and military aid programs are reduced
proportionately to the total reduction. There are several reasons
for this phenomenon. First is the fact that increases in one program
cannot be considered because as long as the total foreign aid figure
is considered fixed, an increase in one program would have to be
accompanied by a corresponding decrease in another. This point is
not lost on the highest levels of any Administration. For example,
when asked in 1964 to comment on an amendment to increase military aid, David Bell, the Administrator of the Agency for International Development, stated:

> I take it that if there were serious consideration given to
> increasing military assistance, there would be strong
> moves simultaneously to reduce the economic assistance.[37]

Because no Administration wants to encourage cuts in any of the
pieces of the foreign aid package beyond those which would normally
occur, it is extremely unlikely that a larger amount than the President's request will ever be appropriated for military or economic
assistance.

There is also an assumption that all of the estimates presented
by the President are equally sound, in other words, that no one
program has a higher percentage of "fat" than the others. For this
reason there is a tendency to cut all the components of foreign aid
proportionately to preserve "balance."

Whatever the reasons may be, the historical record is clear
that over the past ten years the Congressional percentage cuts in
economic aid have almost exactly equalled the percentage cuts
in military aid.

Unless the President and the Secretary of Defense are willing to
"pad" the military aid request presented to the Congress (which,
given the attitudes of the present incumbents toward budgeting,
appears to be out of the question) or the Congress is willing to dis-
continue cutting "foreign aid" (which seems equally out of the
question), the funds made available for military aid will continue
to be substantially below what authorities in the Defense Department, in the State Department and in the White House consider to
be necessary. However, the Defense budget will continue to reflect, more or less, what these groups consider to be the correct
level of effort. As a result an imbalance of programs is built into
the present situation. So long as a "foreign aid" program exists in
its present form, the United States resources applied to providing
military assistance to countries on the periphery of the Soviet Bloc
will be less than the appropriate resources in relation to amounts
spent in the regular defense budget for forces deployable to those
areas to assist in the defense of any country which comes under
attack.

This situation can never be corrected by the Congress so long as
neither the committees of the Congress nor Congress as a whole consider the defense budget and the military aid budget together. The
Congressional attempt to correct the problem by the requirement for
competitive budgeting has been a failure.

In addition to other advantages, inclusion of military aid in the
defense budget and review of that program as part of the regular Department of Defense program will improve management and save
funds in a variety of significant ways. The regular budget of the
Defense Department for any year is developed by taking the costs of
what will be required and deducting reimbursements from military
aid purchases to derive the amount of new funds which the Congress

will be asked to appropriate. Because military aid appropriations are not usually known until well after the beginning of the Department of Defense fiscal year is underway, it is difficult to plan these reimbursements accurately and such planning as is possible is usually made meaningless by cuts in the request for military aid. Combined Congressional reviews of military aid and the military budget would end this problem.

Such a combined review would also result in the savings which competitive budgeting can produce, and permit the other valuable fiscal and management controls of the Department of Defense to be applied to military aid.

WHY HASN'T IT BEEN DONE?

Despite the weight of evidence furnished by impartial Congressional and Presidential study groups, despite the obvious fact that an end of "foreign aid" as a collection of various slightly related programs would undoubtedly please the American people, despite the fact that competitive budgeting can only be accomplished if military aid and the Department of Defense budget are considered together, despite the fact that the security rationale limits the understanding of economic aid at home and confuses objectives abroad, the fact remains that military and economic aid have not been separated.

The major reason why this step has not been taken is the obvious attachment of those responsible for economic aid to the "security rationale" and the assumption that economic aid can only be sold if it is made to appear as an adjunct to the defense budget. The presumed value of this strategic rationale can be seen by the frequency with which the economic aid agencies invoke it. For example, after the request for "foreign assistance" was sharply cut by the Congress in 1963, the entire foreign aid program was presented in 1964 with the label "Mutual Defense and Development." Economic aid officials were quick to point out to Congressman Passman that nearly half of the economic aid request was for countries around the Sino-Soviet Bloc and that "development funds help defense by enabling the recipient to bear a greater share of the cost of that defense." [38]

A similar attachment is found in the attitude of most of the members of the House Foreign Affairs Committee. The pages of the House Foreign Affairs Committee hearings in 1964 are filled with explanations by members of the committee for their opposition to separation. [39] Many of these explanations were triggered by the near unanimous support of groups testifying before the committee for separation of economic and military aid. [40] The most striking of these statements was made by the committee's chairman who said:

> I think it is possible that they (economic and military aid, if separated) might be more effective overseas, but they wouldn't be more effective here on the floor of the Congress because it has always been my strong contention unless you had all of this in one package, you wouldn't get any economic aid bill at all through the Congress. Many of us are able to vote for foreign aid because military assistance is part of the package and is part and parcel of the security of the United States.

> I realize that there are special problems in Latin America where we have a small military program and in Africa where military aid is limited to internal security. Let me say, that as floor manager of this bill, it is important to have military assistance included with economic assistance. [41]

The logic of this statement is difficult to understand. It first of all assumes that it is proper for a Congressman, who is chairman of one of the most important committees in the House of Representatives, to mingle one program with another simply because he believes that one of the programs couldn't stand on its own political feet. If a majority of the Congress does not want economic aid, it would seem inappropriate for a committee chairman to use a gimmick so that they will vote for it.

Even if the assumption that such a gimmick is appropriate is accepted, it must be assumed that members of Congress who otherwise would not vote for economic aid are being fooled by the gimmick, a dubious assumption. Or it may be assumed that Congressmen are not fooled by the gimmick but think that they are fooling their constituents, another dubious assumption. Such an assumption must be based on the idea that some Congressmen have difficulty voting for economic aid for fear that they will not be reelected, yet as shown in Chapter 13 most of the opposition to foreign aid comes from Southern Democrats and Midwestern Republicans whose seats are as safe as any in the Congress.

The final assumption underlying a statement of this kind is that economic aid cannot, in President Kennedy's words, "be seen on its own merits, and judged in the light of its vital and distinctive contribution to our security needs" without being rejected by Congress and the public. It would seem that the supporters of this view have much to learn from the Marshall Plan and Peace Corps experience.

Another potential source of opposition to inclusion of military assistance as part of the Defense Department budget stems from fear that competitive budgeting will cause a decrease in either the military assistance program or in the programs of the Army, Navy and Air Force for United States forces.

The suggestion frequently appears in hearings that if the Defense Department control of military assistance were increased, the result would be to cut the level of military assistance programs below the level necessary because military departments would cut military assistance programs to free funds for their own uses. A related criticism is that "foreign aid" could become so intertwined with other military expenditures that it would be impossible to isolate and analyze the expenditures for equipment and supplies being provided to other countries. To avoid problems like these practically all of the studies recommending inclusion of military assistance in the Defense budget have recommended that military assistance be a separately identifiable portion of that budget.

Just as some supporters of military assistance have feared that it might be cut as a result of a serious review of its value in relation to expenditures on United States forces, so supporters of the regular budget have feared that it might be cut as a result of being reviewed in competition with military aid. For example, Admiral Carney, a former Chief of Naval Operations, was asked whether including military assistance in the Defense budget would handicap the operation of the military departments. He replied:

> I cannot speak for their feelings on the subject now...
> but I would imagine that there would be some apprehension
> on their part that if these funds were included within the
> defense ceiling, that there would be the tendency, which is

sometimes encountered, to expect them to absorb these
responsibilities within their ceilings to the detriment
of their own operating forces. [42]

These fears have probably been aggravated because of the
method which has been used for some years to justify the military
assistance program to the public and Congress. Many Defense
witnesses and Presidential committees, including both the Draper
Committee and the Clay Committee, have stated in substance that
dollar for dollar military assistance contributes more to national
defense than equivalent expenditures for United States forces. If
these statements are taken at face value, it logically follows that
it would be in the interest of national security and the "optimum
balance" of the two types of expenditure to increase military assistance expenditures at the expense of Army, Navy and Air Force
expenditures if the two were considered under a fixed ceiling. [43]

Such problems, however, do not arise so long as the regular
Defense budget continues--as it has been since 1961--to be considered
without regard to arbitrary dollar ceilings. Even if an arbitrary
ceiling were established for major national security expenditures, it
does not necessarily mean that the "dollar for dollar" type of analysis
will result in more rather than less expenditures for military assistance. Most important is the fact that no matter what the outcome of
such a competitive review, that outcome--if the review is fairly con-
ducted--results in the best free world military posture at the least
cost.

The final suggestion made in connection with the proposal to
abolish foreign aid as presently constituted and place military assistance in the Defense Department budget is that the control of the State
Department over foreign policy would be reduced by such action. As
a legal matter, of course, this is not a problem. The present language of the Foreign Assistance Act of 1961, which gives the State
Department considerable control over military aid, could be put intact into any bill authorizing military assistance. As a practical
matter it would also seem that the State Department could exercise
its present forms of control more effectively with separation than
under the present system.

At the present time the State Department has not seen fit to take
upon itself the function of exercising the powers of the Secretary of
State to review military assistance. Instead, those powers are vested

in the Administrator of the economic aid agency.[44] If military assistance were included in the Department of Defense budget, the State Department would probably return to the position of control which it
held in the last years of the Eisenhower Administration.   The State
Department coordinating function would probably be vested in the
State Department office which handled other military problems like
deployment of United States forces, criminal jurisdiction arrangements where forces are deployed, base rights negotiations and the
like.   This change in State Department review would increase the
possibilities of optimum use of military resources for foreign policy
purposes.

For example, as a case where military assistance can serve
foreign policy objectives, take the hypothetical state of Protonia, an
unaligned nation to which the United States has been furnishing a
small amount of training but no equipment.   Assume further that,
from the point of view of the Joint Chiefs of Staff, Protonian forces
are not required for the defense of the free world.

One day without advance warning a major communist power begins an intensive propaganda campaign against the present Protonian
leadership and that leadership discovers that the underground communist party in the country is plotting a revolution.   The Protonian
police forces begin to round up the local communists and seem to
have the situation under control.   However, the neighboring communist power begins to move forces toward the Protonian border.
Meanwhile the communist power protests "fascism" in Protonia.
The socialists in Protonia, who did not object to the action in
weeding out the communist leaders, now begin to fear that the
government has gone too far and should attempt to mollify the outside communists.   The Protonian Government explains the situation
to the United States and requests that the United States indicate in
some tangible manner that it will stand by Protonia in the event of
communist attack.

At this point the United States has a number of diplomatic and
military options.   After the appropriate warnings to the communists
are issued indicating that the United States would consider an attack
on Protonia as requiring serious consideration of United States security interests in the area and that such attack would cause grave
alarm, etc., etc., it presumably then becomes necessary for the
United States to make a few tangible indications of its support for
Protonia.   These indications, to meet the political requirement,

should be sufficient to impress both the outside communists and the socialists within Protonia.

The State Department, at this point, in both its regional bureau and in the office of politico-military affairs should have before it the alternative ways of expressing United States military interest. One of these methods is the announcement of a United States military assistance program of a large scale with planeloads of equipment to be furnished within a week or so. However, as the Protonian forces would not be trained to use the equipment at the time it arrived, this approach might not make sense in terms of the best use of military resources. On the other hand, if the equipment were scheduled to arrive several months later when the Protonians had been taught to use it and maintain it, the political impact might be lost. Other alternatives would include sending a United States Air Force fighter squadron to perform joint exercises with the Protonian forces. Such an alternative--especially if the squadron were due for some type of exercise in any case--costs considerably less than military aid and familiarizes United States forces with the environment in which they might someday have to fight. United States jets zooming over the skies of Protonia, dashing toward the nearby communist borders but stopping before reaching them and flying low over most villages can have considerably more reassurance value to the population than a mere announcement and planeloads of equipment, which the population never sees when it is offloaded at the airport in the capital. Other alternatives to military assistance include having a United States destroyer or carrier group call in the harbor of the capital and a joint exercise of United States Army forces and local forces.

In ways such as these and in numerous other ways our national military establishment can be a tool of foreign policy. In each case the greatest economy can be achieved when, in the State Department as in the Defense Department, those concerned with military aid can weigh the costs and advantages of that aid against other actions, and those concerned with other actions can weigh them against provision of military aid. So long as military aid and the rest of our national military expenditures are considered separately by the State Department and the economic aid agency, it is difficult to make such decisions involving choice among resources intelligently. Thus, foreign policy control of military assistance might well be made more rather than less effective by putting military aid and other costs together in the Defense budget and returning military assistance responsibilities to the State Department.

CONCLUSION

Much of the opposition to "foreign aid" has been caused by the fact that Administration after Administration has presented a "foreign aid package" composed of heterogeneous components. This package has understandably been rejected by the American people and the Congress in part because its heterogeneity makes its objectives unclear and its size alarming. Military aid should be included as part of the Defense Department budget and reviewed as a part of that budget, so that it does not include programs less effective than expenditures of equivalent amount for our own forces. Such an action would involve abolition of the "foreign aid program" as now conceived. That abolition, in addition to providing a great psychological lift for the American people and their representatives, would lead to better definition of objectives, better administration at lower cost and wider acceptance of both economic and military aid as important and necessary United States programs.

NOTES

1. U.S., Congress, House, Committee on Foreign Affairs, Report of the Committee to Study the Foreign Aid Program, 84th Cong., 2d Sess., 1956, p. 83R.

2. U.S. International Development Advisory Board, A New Emphasis on Economic Development Abroad: A Report to the President on Ways, Means and Reasons for U.S. Assistance to International Economic Development (Washington: U.S. Government Printing Office, 1957), p. 13.

3. Brookings Institution, "Administrative Aspects of United States Foreign Assistance Programs," Study No. 6 in U.S., Congress, Senate, Special Committee to Study the Foreign Aid Program, Foreign Aid Program: Compilation of Studies and Surveys, 85th Cong., 1st Sess., 1957.

4. Report of the Special Committee, p. 30.

5. The following material is summarized from U.S., Congress, Senate, Special Committee to Study the Foreign Aid Program, Hearings, 85th Cong., 1st Sess., 1957.

6. Ibid., p. 3.

7. Ibid., p. 58.

8. Ibid., p. 93.

9. Ibid., pp. 345-382.

10. Ibid., p. 397.

11. The practice of requiring annual authorizations for major parts of the Defense budget had not yet developed.

12. Testimony of the Deputy Secretary of Defense (Reuben Robertson), Special Committee Hearings, op. cit., pp. 427-455.

13. U.S., Congress, House, Committee on Foreign Affairs, Report on Mutual Security Authorization, 85th Cong., 2d Sess., 1958, p. 14.

14. The Senators' letter of August 25, 1958 was widely publicized at the time. It appears, among other places, as an attachment to the Composite Report of the Draper Committee.

15. The President's instructions are printed in the front of the Composite Report of the Draper Committee.

16. This is Section 504(b) of the present Foreign Assistance Act of 1961, as amended.

17. U.S., Congress, Senate, Committee on Foreign Relations, Report on S. 1451, Senate Report No. 412, 86th Cong., 1st Sess., 1959, p. 10.

18. Report of the President's Committee to Study the Military Assistance Program (Draper Committee) (Washington: U.S. Government Printing Office, 1959), pp. 37-38.

19. Testimony of then Secretary of Defense Thomas Gates, HFAC, CY 60, p. 85 and of Assistant Secretary of Defense Irwin, HFAC, CY 60, p. 107.

20. In a foreword dated April, 1961, in Amos A. Jordan, Foreign Aid and the Defense of Southeast Asia (New York: Praeger, 1962). However, in the book itself Colonel Jordan concludes that the competitive budgeting requirement was ignored in the 1960 and 1961 appropriations process, p. 201.

21. The message appears, among other places, in 107 Cong. Rec. 4276.

22. Testimony of Deputy Assistant Secretary of Defense W. P. Bundy, HFAC, CY 61, pp. 121-122.

23. Section 201(a) of the Foreign Assistance Act of 1963 amended the Foreign Assistance Act of 1961 by deleting the title of the separate military assistance section of the law.

24. Typical of the many postmortems of this exercise is Helen Miller, "AID-Diagnosed to Death," New Republic, January 18, 1964.

25. HFAC, CY 64, p. 13.

26. SFRC, CY 64, p. 161.

27. This is clear from various statements made during hearings before the committee. These statements are sprinkled throughout the 1093 pages of printed hearings, HFAC, CY 64. Some of these statements are quoted later in this chapter.

28. Senator Fulbright's reasons for this approach are explained in a discussion which he had with Harlan Cleveland included as pages 120-124 of SFRC, CY 64.

29. Washington Star, January 12, 1964, p. 14.

30. SFRC, CY 64, pp. 123-124.

31. HAC, CY 64, p. 301.

32. The point of this section is not to criticize any Administration for failure to implement the competitive budgeting provision of the Foreign Assistance Act, but to point out that competitive budgeting is impossible so long as military aid is included in the foreign aid bill.

33. HFAC, CY 64, p. 797.

34. Ibid., p. 966.

35. Ibid., p. 905.

36. SFRC, CY 64, p. 123.

37. HFAC, CY 64, p. 1050.

38. HAC, CY 64, p. 270.

39. Because motive is so difficult to assess, the author has not considered the argument that members of this committee are merely reflecting a narrow jealousy over the importance of their committee. Holbert Carroll, in The House of Representatives and Foreign Affairs (Pittsburg: University of Pittsburg Press, 1958), see especially pp. 92-93, has pointed out that before foreign aid the House Foreign Affairs Committee was one of the most unimportant in the House and that opposition to long term foreign aid authority was caused by a desire to avoid a reduction in the committee's prestige, not by substantive objections to the proposal. It is clear that a shift of jurisdiction over military assistance to the Armed Services Committee would reduce the importance of the Foreign Affairs Committee; however, separation of economic and military aid does not inevitably mean that the House Armed Services Committee would then consider military aid, although the logic of viewing military aid and military requirements in competition with one another applies to the Congress as well as the Executive Branch.

40. See the list of the positions taken by these groups in Chapter 13.

41. HFAC, CY 64, p. 966.

42. Special Committee Hearings, op. cit., p. 115.

43. In technical terms this type of testimony states that the marginal utility of the last dollar spent on military assistance is greater by an unspecified margin than the marginal utility of the last dollar spent on the regular defense budget. By definition, the optimum allocation of resources among various forms of programs is that

which makes the marginal utility of the last unit of resources
(dollars, for example) the same in each of the programs. Assuming that the total resources available for national security in
any given time period is fixed, it would follow that dollars should
be taken from the regular Department of Defense expenditures with
the least marginal utility and applied to military assistance projects in order of decreasing marginal utility until the marginal
utility of the last dollar (the least important dollar) in each program would be equal.

    44. See Chapter 9.

APPENDIX A

UNITED STATES TREATY OBLIGATIONS

United States military assistance and a substantial part of the United States defense budget are based on the premise that the United States will provide military support to many non-communist nations should they come under attack by the communists. For this reason the formal commitments which the United States has made are relevant to any consideration of the scope and distribution of military assistance. Accordingly, the following is a listing of the major United States military commitments. The fact that a country does not appear on this list does not mean that the United States would not come to its assistance in the event of attack, only that the United States is not committed to do so.

NATO: Article 5 of the NATO treaty states, in part:

> The Parties agree that an armed attack against one or more of them in Europe or North America shall be considered an attack against them all; and consequently they agree that, if such an armed attack occurs, each of them, in exercise of the right of individual or collective self-defense recognized by Article 51 of the Charter of the United Nations, will assist the Party or Parties so attacked by taking forthwith, individually and in concert with the other Parties, such action as it deems necessary, including the use of armed force, to restore and maintain the security of the North Atlantic area. [1]

The parties to the treaty include the United States, the United Kingdom, France, Germany, Norway, Italy, Denmark, Greece, Turkey, Belgium, the Netherlands, Luxembourg, Iceland, Portugal and Canada.

SEATO: Article 4 of the Southeast Asia Collective Defense Treaty states:

> Each Party recognizes that aggression by means of armed attack in the treaty area against any of the Parties or against any State or territory which the Parties by unanimous agreement may hereafter designate, would endanger its own peace and safety, and agrees that it will in that event act to meet the common danger in accordance with its constitutional processes. [2]

The parties to this treaty are the United States, the United Kingdom, France, New Zealand, Australia, the Philippines, Thailand and Pakistan.

As the above quotation indicates, the treaty members contemplated designating territory of non-members to which the basic declaration would apply. The designation--of Cambodia, Laos and South Vietnam--was made by a protocol to the SEATO treaty.

ANZUS: Article 4 of the ANZUS pact states:

Each Party recognizes that an armed attack in the Pacific Area on any of the Parties would be dangerous to its own peace and safety and declares that it would act to meet the common danger in accordance with its constitutional processes. [3]

Australia, New Zealand and the United States are the parties to this pact.

Rio Pact: Article 3 of the treaty includes the following:

The High Contracting Parties agree that an armed attack by any State against an American State shall be considered as an attack against all the American States and, consequently, each one of the said Contracting Parties undertakes to assist in meeting the attack in the exercise of the inherent right of individual or collective self-defense recognized by Article 51 of the Charter of the United Nations. [4]

The parties to the treaty are Argentina, Bolivia, Brazil, Chile, Colombia, Costa Rica, the Dominican Republic, El Salvador, Ecuador, Guatemala, Haiti, Honduras, Mexico, Nicaragua, Panama, Paraguay, Peru, Uruguay and Venezuela. Cuba also signed when the pact was adopted shortly after World War II.

In addition to these four multilateral treaties to which the United States is a party, the United States has indicated the importance it attaches to the territorial integrity of the members of the Central Treaty Organization by a declaration made in 1958. Paragraph four of this declaration stated in part:

... The United States in the interest of world peace,
and pursuant to existing Congressional authorization,
agrees to cooperate with the nations making this Declaration for their security and defense, and will promptly
enter into agreements designed to give effect to this
cooperation. [5]

Acting under this declaration the United States signed bilateral
agreements with Iran, Pakistan and Turkey which became effective
in March, 1959. The operative clause of these agreements was:

The Government of_____is determined to resist
aggression. In case of aggression against_____, the
Government of the United States of America, in accordance
with the Constitution of the United States of America, will
take such appropriate action, including the use of armed
forces, as may be mutually agreed upon and as is envisaged
in the Joint Resolution to promote Peace and Stability in the
Middle East, in order to assist the Government of_____
at its request. [6]

Bilateral Agreements: The United States has negotiated bilateral defense agreements with Nationalist China, the Philippines,
the Republic of Korea and Japan. The operative provision of these
agreements follows the pattern of that with the Philippines which
states:

Each Party recognizes that an armed attack in the
Pacific Area on either of the Parties would be dangerous
to its own peace and safety and declares that it would act
to meet the common dangers in accordance with its
constitutional processes. [7]

Other: The development of fairly elaborate treaty structures is
a method of diplomacy which fell from favor after the Democrats
took office in 1961. It has been replaced primarily by a medley of
assurances to various nations issued at times when they are being
threatened or believe that they are being threatened. An example is
the reassurance of the Secretary of State to the Thailand government
in 1962. [8] A declaration of United States intention to assist in defense
of a country or area may also be made by the Congress as in the case
of the Formosa Resolution of 1955[9] and the Eisenhower Doctrine on
the Middle East. [10]

Although, as the quotations indicate, some of these treaty obligations have "loopholes" in a legal sense, they are part of a policy--and the best evidence of a policy--that is predicated upon a forward defense of the United States. Of course, formal treaties do not limit the possible commitments of United States forces. As the Korean War indicated, when a threat to a non-communist government arises, the United States may provide assistance, even though such assistance is not required by a treaty of any kind.

NOTES

1. TIAS 1964.
2. TIAS 3170.
3. TIAS 2493.
4. TIAS 1838.
5. TIAS 4084.
6. Iran is TIAS 4189; Pakistan is TIAS 4190; and Turkey is 4191.
7. TIAS 2529. The Korea agreement is TIAS 3097; the China one, TIAS 3178; and the Japan treaty, TIAS 4509.
8. Department of State Bulletin, March 26, 1962, pp. 498-499.
9. PL 4, 84th Cong., 1st Sess.
10. PL 7, 85th Cong., 1st Sess.

APPENDIX B

HOW TO FIND OUT
ABOUT MILITARY ASSISTANCE

There is no shortage of general statements for and against military assistance, but there is a marked shortage of material available to the public which provides facts about military assistance such as the costs of programs, the distribution of funds among country programs, the type of assistance provided, and the objectives, achievements and failures of assistance to particular countries. In part this paucity of information has been caused by the fact that many facts about military assistance are considered "classified." Although some progress has been made in recent years, much valuable data is unavailable to the public. For example, until 1960 the quantity of United States assistance to various countries was classified. Even today the value of programs to a few countries--such as India and Pakistan--is classified and the very existence of military assistance programs to a few countries is classified. Public and academic consideration of the program has also been hindered because the administrators of the program have been reluctant to volunteer information about it for fear of running afoul of restrictions against using government funds for propaganda purposes.

The most valuable source of information about military assistance is the documentation resulting from Congressional consideration of the President's requests for authorizations and appropriations. As the pattern followed each year is about the same, specific citations are omitted. This pattern creates the following sources:

The Federal Budget includes a military assistance portion dealing with the program in general terms and providing some data on the proposed program by types of equipment to be procured on a worldwide basis. The "budget" is available in most good libraries and is sold by the U.S. Government Printing Office.

The President's Foreign Aid Message contains the President's recommendations for foreign aid for the coming year. These messages are generally available as (1) House or Senate Documents, (2) White House Press releases, and (3) in the Congressional Record for the day of delivery. The New York Times normally carries either the text of Presidential statements or rather complete stories about such messages.

Bills and Amendments: Consideration of the foreign aid request is usually based on the legislation recommended by the President and introduced (by request) by the Chairman of the Foreign Affairs Committee in the House and the Foreign Relations Committee in the Senate. The number of the bill is normally that appearing on the cover page of hearings in each house. For example, the 1964 House Foreign Affairs Committee hearings were on H.R. 10502. The nature of pending amendments is usually apparent from the debates reported in the Congressional Record.

Committee Hearings: The Senate Foreign Relations Committee, the House Foreign Affairs Committee, the Senate Appropriations Committee and the Foreign Operations Subcommittee of the House Appropriations Committee hold hearings on foreign aid--including military assistance--each year. The House Foreign Affairs Committee hearings are published in pamphlet form as rapidly after actual hearings as possible. Each of these pamphlets is from one to several hundred pages in length. After all hearings are completed the committee publishes all these pamphlets as a single bound volume with a good index. The House Appropriations Committee usually publishes hearings on foreign aid in several books, one of which contains the military assistance testimony. Senate Foreign Relations and Appropriations hearings are each published in a single volume.

Committee Reports: Following the hearings each of these committees reports a recommended bill. These reports, including minority views, if any, and the description of the bill being reported are printed as House or Senate documents. Following passage of bills in the House and Senate, conferees from each house are appointed to iron out differences between the two houses. The report of these conferees is also printed as a House or Senate document.

House and Senate Debate: After the committee reports, debate is scheduled on the authorization or appropriation bills in each house. Thus, the foreign assistance program is debated four times in each year. These debates are reported in the Congressional Record and can be found by consulting the indexes of that document. The indexes also identify those speeches given on foreign aid generally, or on military aid, at times when those subjects are not pending business. For example, Senators Morse and Gruening in the spring of 1964 gave a series of detailed statements on foreign aid.

Legislation: New legislation is separately printed in the form of
Public Laws (called "slip laws") and slowly finds its way into a variety
of sources familiar to any legal librarian such as the United States
Code, the United States Statutes at Large and a variety of privately
published legal references. Especially for persons not familiar with
legal research, the best source of Foreign Assistance Legislation is
a document of some 600 pages published annually by the Foreign Affairs Committee of the House entitled Legislation on Foreign Relations,
which contains all relevant legislation as well as executive orders and
other documents.

In addition to the documentation produced in the cycle of review
of authorization and appropriation requests the Congress frequently
generates other sources of information about military assistance.
Many Congressional trips--too often dismissed as junkets--generate
serious and carefully researched reports, dealing directly or tan-
gentially with military assistance. These reports can be discovered
by a review of the Government Printing Office's Monthly Catalogue of
Government Publications. The annual Staff Survey Team reports of
the House Foreign Affairs Committee and the periodic reports of
trips by Senator Mansfield are usually particularly well done.

PUBLICATIONS OF THE EXECUTIVE BRANCH

Unclassified presentation of new programs: Each year the economic aid agency prepares for public distribution (on request to the
economic aid agency or through the Government Printing Office) a
summary of the economic and military assistance programs being
presented to the Congress. This document normally is about 200
pages long. The title varies with the catch words being used to sell
the program.

Reports on old programs: Present law requires an annual report to the Congress on activities under the foreign aid program.
The coverage of military assistance in these reports has been limited
in recent years. These reports are listed in the Monthly Catalogue
of Government Publications under various titles. Similar reports
were issued for the Greek-Turkish Aid Program and other predeces-
sors of the foreign assistance program.

Statistical data: Annually in the spring the Department of Defense
publishes a short pamphlet entitled Military Assistance Facts which

is the best source of data about military assistance. The document
is available on request from the Department of Defense, but is not
sold by the Government Printing Office. Some, but not all, of the
same data is contained in a more comprehensive publication
(covering economic and military assistance) published by the
Agency for International Development. The most recent title of this
document is U.S. Overseas Loans and Grants and Assistance from
International Organizations: Obligations and Loan Authorizations.
This document contains some estimates for military assistance
expenses which are not actually costs paid for from military aid
appropriations--such as the cost of ships loaned to foreign govern-
ments--and, therefore, should only be used after a careful reading
of the notes which generally appear in the first few pages of the
volume. This document is available from the Agency for International
Development.

Certain information from these documents finds its way into
other sources such as books and articles on foreign aid. The military assistance program figures for the most recent year available
also appear in the Statistical Abstract of the United States.

The Department of the Air Force periodically publishes a document entitled Information and Guidance on Military Assistance.
This handbook is primarily concerned with organizational and management questions, rather than with policy. It contains listings of
the Department of Defense Directives and Army, Navy, and Air
Force regulations applicable to the administration of military assistance. The document is available on request to the Air Force.

SPECIAL STUDIES

From time to time the President or the Congress initiates
special studies of the military assistance or the total foreign assistance program. The more significant of these studies are listed in
the Bibliography.

INFORMATION ON FOREIGN FORCES

The United States Government is reluctant to release information on the military forces of other countries, but such information
is generally available from other sources, or from the countries

themselves. Many countries release to their citizens a great deal
of information about their own forces, similar to the information
which the United States itself publishes about its forces. Defense
budgets, number of combat units and plans for the purchase of
major weapons are frequently available through the records of
foreign parliaments, the foreign press and the English language
public information services published by most embassies in Washington. In addition, there are a number of private intelligence services
such as the Institute of Strategic Studies and the Aviation Studies
(International) Limited of London which provide information on a
subscription basis. Publications like Jane's Fighting Ships (various
editions) and the Stateman's Yearbook (annual) have extensive information on foreign military forces.

APPENDIX C

GLOSSARY

Inevitably any program--governmental or private--develops over the years a set of terms composed of acronyms (words formed out of the letters of other words such as radar, Pert, and USCINCEUR) and words in general use given a specialized meaning. While these terms are handy to those who use them frequently, they are normally confusing to those first exposed to a subject. In the text of this book some attempt has been made to avoid "jargon" and "Pentagonese" but some of each has crept into the text and much of it appears in quotations. This glossary is furnished to make the materials on military assistance somewhat more intelligible to those not familiar with this jargon.

AID - The Agency for International Development, which since 1961 has been the agency administering economic assistance. Its immediate predecessor was the International Cooperation Agency (ICA). ICA in turn was preceded by a variety of other agencies. AID is also used as a symbol for economic aid.

Appropriation - An amount made available by law for obligation and expenditure for a given governmental purpose. For all practical purposes appropriations for military assistance can be considered as (a) new obligational authority and (b) reappropriation of balances remaining unobligated which, unless appropriated again, would "lapse" and revert to the Treasury.

Authorization - A law required as a basis for appropriations. More broadly, permission to do something--as the President is authorized to give assistance to friendly nations.

Carry-over - See unexpended balance.

CENTO - The Central Treaty Organization, which is the Baghdad Pact renamed after Iraq (in which Baghdad is located) dropped its alliance with the West.

CINCEUR - Commander in Chief European Command and, loosely, the Command itself.

CINCMEAFSA - Commander in Chief, Middle East, Africa and South Asia, who is also the Commander of the United States Strike Command and, loosely, the Command itself.

CINCPAC - Commander in Chief, Pacific Command and, loosely, the Command itself.

CINCSO - Commander in Chief, Southern Command, and, loosely, the Command itself.

Civic Action - The use of military forces on projects useful to the local population at all levels in such fields as education, training, public works, agriculture, transportation, communications, health, sanitation and others contributing to economic and social development.

Commercial consumable - A consumable generally available commercially as food and fuel.

Commitment - As used by witnesses and in the Foreign Assistance Act, a statement made by a United States official to a foreign government or an agreement made with a foreign government, indicating the intention of the United States to provide certain assistance in the future. Such commitments are not necessarily either treaties or executive agreements.

Consumable - Any item which is consumed by its use, such as ammunition, gasoline, grease and food.

Contingency Fund - Under the present structure of foreign aid appropriations, an amount appropriated to the President for contingencies.

Cost Sharing Programs - (a) International multilateral agreements such as NATO infrastructure under which participating nations share the cost of a military activity, or (b) bilateral agreements under which military assistance provides part and the recipient country part of the costs of a military project.

CY - Calendar year, the symbol is used to distinguish from fiscal years.

DOD - The Department of Defense.

Draw down - The authority given in Section 510 of the Foreign Assistance Act to use existing military department stocks for military aid without paying for them until the following year.

Excess - In military assistance legislation, the equipment which is not required as a part of the United States mobilization reserve.

Expenditure - In general, the governmental payment for a good or service (payroll, purchase, etc.) as distinguished from the promise to pay (an obligation). Because most military assistance expenses involve transactions within the Department of Defense, expenditure of military aid funds occurs when a military department makes constructive delivery of an item by putting it aboard a carrier bound for the foreign destination. Under present accounting procedures "deliveries" and "expenditures" occur simultaneously for record-keeping purposes. As a result an item which has been held up or diverted or lost in shipment may appear as delivered on the records published by the Department of Defense.

Foreign Aid - An imprecise term generally applied either to the programs authorized by the Foreign Assistance Act or the programs for which appropriations are made in the Foreign Assistance Appropriations Act.

FY - Fiscal year. The government fiscal year begins on July 1.

HAC - House Appropriations Committee.

HFAC - House Foreign Affairs Committee.

MAAG - Military Assistance Advisory Group.

MAP - Military Assistance Program.

Military Assistance Advisory Group - The United States organization in most countries receiving military assistance charged with providing training and with administering other military assistance. Such groups occasionally have slightly different names, and in the case of some countries in Latin America and Africa their functions are performed by military missions or military attaches.

Obligation - In the case of most government expenditures obligations are commitments to pay, such as acceptance of a load of coal creating an obligation to pay for it later. In the case of military assistance, funds are considered obligated when the military departments are asked to begin supply action. New obligational authority is simply additional (new) authority to obligate (appropriations) granted by the Congress.

Program - A military assistance program is the schedule of goods and services which has been provided, is being provided or is planned to be provided in any given year. Thus, the "FY 1964 military assistance program for Portugal includes 2 tanks." More loosely, the program is the value of the goods and services. Thus, "the FY 1956 program for France was $1 billion."

Reappropriation - The act of appropriating again an amount which lapsed because it was not obligated in the fiscal year in which appropriated. Congress generally reappropriates such amounts partly on the theory that if they did not, there would be a frantic and wasteful rush to obligate such amounts the day before the end of the fiscal year.

Recoupment - An amount which has been obligated in a fiscal year preceding the one in which the recoupment is made which is "deobligated" because of a decision not to complete the transaction or a reduced price permitting a reduction in the obligated amount.

SAC - Senate Appropriations Committee.

SFRC - Senate Foreign Relations Committee.

SHAPE - Supreme Headquarters of Allied Powers, Europe (NATO military headquarters).

TIAS - Treaties and Other International Acts Series published by the State Department.

Total Obligational Authority (TOA) - The amount available for obligations in any fiscal year composed of (a) appropriations, (b) reappropriations, (c) recoupments and (d) transfers.

Transfers - Shifts of funds to or from the military assistance appropriation. Such shifts are permitted by the Foreign Assistance Act of 1961.

Unexpended balance - At any given date, funds obligated but not expended.

Unified Commander - An officer designated commander of a "unified" command which includes forces from more than one military department. Four of these commanders have major military assistance responsibilities. See CINCEUR, CINCMEAFSA, CINCPAC and CINCSO in this glossary.

Unobligated balance - That amount of appropriations which has not been obligated.

ANNOTATED BIBLIOGRAPHY

GENERAL

Almond, Gabriel A. and Coleman, James S. (eds.). The Politics of Developing Areas. Princeton: Princeton University Press, 1960.

Baker, Marshall E. "The Case for Military Assistance," Armed Forces Management, V (June, 1959).

Banfield, Edward C. American Foreign Aid Doctrines. American Enterprise Institute, January, 1963.

Bissell, R. M., "Foreign Aid: What Sort? How Much? How Long?" Foreign Affairs, Vol. 31 (October, 1952), 15-38.

Brown, W. A. and Opie, R. American Foreign Assistance. Washington: The Brookings Institution, 1953.
> Definitive work on foreign aid through 1952. See especially pp. 439-539 on military assistance. Bibliography lists all hearings on foreign aid and predecessor programs through 1952.

Castle, Eugene. The Great Giveaway. Chicago: Henry Regnery, 1957.
> Highly critical of American foreign aid programs.

Cleveland, Harlan, et. al. The Overseas Americans. New York: McGraw-Hill, 1960.
> Includes material on military assistance advisory groups.

_____. The Theory and Practice of Foreign Aid. Syracuse: Syracuse University Press, 1956.

Coffin, Frank. Witness for AID. Boston: Houghton Mifflin, 1964.
> Coffin is a former Maine Congressman and member of the House Foreign Affairs Committee who also served as Deputy Administrator of the Agency for International Development. His book is an attempt to make the case for AID, primarily economic. His discussion of the review of foreign aid by Congress (the annual minuet) is particularly interesting.

Connery, R. H. and D. P. "The Mutual Defense Assistance Program," American Political Science Review, Vol. 45, No. 2 (June, 1951).

Council on Foreign Relations, The United States in World Affairs, published annually.

_____. Documents on American Foreign Relations, published annually.

Daaldev, Hans. The Role of the Military in Emerging Countries. The Hague: 1962.

Feis, Herbert. Foreign Aid and Foreign Policy. New York: St. Martins Press, 1964.
    Concerned primarily with economic aid and general "foreign aid philosophy."

Finer, S. E. The Man on Horseback: The Role of the Military in Politics. London: Pall Mall Press, 1962.
    Not easy reading, but a fine analysis of the circumstances under which the military controls politics in both developing and developed countries.

Fox, W. T. R., "Military Representation Abroad," The Representation of the United States Abroad. Final Report of the Ninth American Assembly. New York: Columbia University Press, 1956.

Green, William and Fricker, John. The Air Forces of the World. New York: Hanover House, 1958.

Haviland, W. Field. Foreign Aid and the Policy Process: 1957. Washington: The Brookings Institution, 1958.
    See article under the same title in the American Political Science Review (September, 1958).

Hoag, M. S. "Economic Problems of Alliance," Journal of Political Economy (December, 1957).

Hoffman, Paul. One Hundred Countries, One and One Quarter Billion People. Albert D. and Mary Lasker Foundation, 1960.

Holcombe, John L. and Alan Berg. MAP for Security. Columbia, South Carolina: University of South Carolina Press, 1957.

Institute of International Education. Military Assistance Training Programs of the U.S. Government. New York: Institute of International Education, 1964.
    A pamphlet about military assistance training.

Janowitz, Morris. The Military in the Political Development of New Nations. Chicago: The University of Chicago Press, 1964.

Johnson, John J. The Role of the Military in Underdeveloped Countries. Princeton: Princeton University Press, 1962.

Jones, Joseph M. The Fifteen Weeks. New York: 1955.

Jordan, Amos A., Jr. Foreign Aid and the Defense of Southeast Asia. New York: Praeger, 1962.
    Although focus is on South Asia, the book considers worldwide problems. The author (Colonel, U.S. Army) was on the Draper Committee staff.

_____. "Military Assistance & National Policy," Orbis, Summer, 1958.

Kennan, George. "Foreign Aid in the Framework of National Policy," Proceedings of the Academy of Political Science, Vol. 23, No. 4 (January, 1950).

Kennedy, John. An Examination of MAP (ORO-SP-52, CAMG Paper
    No. 1). Bethesda, Maryland: Operations Research Office,
    April, 1958.

Kintner, W. "The Role of Military Assistance," U.S. Naval In-
    stitute Proceedings, Vol. 87 (March, 1961).

Kissinger, Henry A. "Military Policy and Defense of the 'Gray
    Areas'," Foreign Affairs, Vol. 33, No. 3 (April, 1955).

Kotz, Arnold. "Planning for International Security," Public Ad-
    ministration Review, Vol. 22 (December, 1962).

Lansdale, Edward G. "Civic Action Helps Counter the Guerrilla
    Threat," Army Information Digest, Vol. 17 (June, 1962).

Lemnitzer, Lyman L. "The Foreign Military Aid Program,"
    Proceedings of the Academy of Political Science, Vol. 23
    (1948-1950).

Lincoln, George A. "Factors Determining Arms Aid," Proce-
    edings of the Academy of Political Science, Vol. 25
    (May, 1953).

Liska, George. The New Statecraft: Foreign Aid in American
    Foreign Policy. Chicago: University of Chicago Press,
    1960.

        Excellent theoretical analysis of foreign aid (in the
    Morganthau "school"). Chapter 2 contains the only good
    history of foreign aid since the Greeks which this author
    has discovered.

Loeber, Thomas. Foreign Aid: Our Tragic Experiment. New
    York: Norton, 1961.

        Written by a former ICA employee. Highly critical of
    foreign aid (especially economic aid) as presently admin-
    istered.

Marvel, William W. "Foreign Aid and United States Security." Un-
    published Ph.D. dissertation, Princeton University, 1951.

Mason, Edward S. "Equitable Sharing of Military and Economic Aid
    Burdens," Proceedings of the American Academy, Vol. 27
    (May, 1963).

_____. Foreign Aid and Foreign Policy. New York:
    Harper and Row for the Council on Foreign Relations, 1964.

McClellan, Grant S. (ed.). U.S. Foreign Aid. New York: H.W.
    Wilson Co., 1957.

Millikan, M. F. and Rostow, W. W. "Foreign Aid: Next Phase,"
    Foreign Affairs (April, 1958).

_____. A Proposal: Key to Effective Foreign Policy. New
    York: Harper, 1957.

        Primarily economic aid.

Montgomery, John D. The Politics of Foreign Aid. New York:
    Frederick A. Praeger, 1962.

Morgenthau, Hans. "Preface to a Political Theory of Foreign Aid," American Political Science Review (June, 1962).

Netherland, Robert. "A Challenge in Training the Foreign Military Student," U.S. Naval Institute Proceedings (March, 1960).

Nulsen, C. "Military Aid: An Appraisal." Unpublished Master's dissertation, Tulane University, 1958.

Olmsted, G. H. "Security for the Free World," Armor (May-June, 1952).

Palmer, Norman D. "The Impact of Foreign Aid," Current History (September, 1957).

Pasley, R. S. and TeSelle, J. "Patent Rights and Technical Information in the Military Assistance Program," Law and Contemporary Problems, Vol. 29 (Spring, 1964).

Passman, Otto. "Why I Am Opposed to Foreign Aid," New York Times Magazine, July 7, 1963.

> A typical Passman attack on the program.

_____. "Foreign Aid Program Biggest Flop," article prepared for Advance News Service and printed in several papers (presumably with varying titles). Reprinted in Congressional Record, June 20, 1963.

> States Passman's general position on foreign aid.

_____. "Foreign Aid, Success or Failure," National Review, May 21, 1963, reprinted in the Congressional Record, May 15, 1963.

> The most complete single statement of Passman's objections to the foreign aid program. Includes some of the criticisms most frequently made of military assistance.

_____. "Foreign Aid: Too Much for Too Many," Political Science Quarterly (September, 1963), reprinted in Congressional Record, September 17, 1963.

> Passman's commentary on the Clay Committee Report.

Pye, Lucian. "Soviet and American Styles in Foreign Aid," Orbis, Vol. IV, No. 2 (Summer, 1960).

Ramazani, R. K. "Soviet Military Assistance to the Uncommitted Countries," Midwest Journal of Political Science (November, 1959).

Ransom, Harry Howe (ed.). "Foreign Military Assistance and National Policy: Some Background Materials," Harvard Defense Policy, No. 114 (April, 1957).

Raymond, Daniel A. "Reflections on Mutual Defense Assistance Program," Military Review, Vol. 35, No. 5. (August, 1955).

Roy, Elizabeth C. U.S. Military Commitments. Washington: IDA Research Paper, 1963.

Ruff, Lieutenant Doyle C., USAF. "Win Friends - Defeat Communism," Instructors Journal, Vol. 11, No. 1 (July, 1964).
    A vivid discussion of training of foreign officers at Randolph Air Force Base. Includes description of course content and programs to expose trainees to "democracy."

Schelling, Thomas G. "American Foreign Assistance," World Politics, Vol. 7, No. 4 (July, 1955).

Scott, General S. L. "The Military Aid Program," The Annals of the American Academy of Political and Social Science, Vol. 273.

Shils, E. A. Political Development in the New States. The Hague: Mouton & Company, 1962.
    Includes discussion of the role of the military.

Siddigi. "U.S. Military Aid to Pakistan," Pakistan Horizon, Vol. XII, No. 1 (March, 1959).

Smith, Alphonso. "Military Assistance in the Far East," U.S. Naval Institute Proceedings, Vol. 86 (December, 1960).

Somers, H. M. "Civil-Military Relations in Mutual Security," The Annals of the American Academy of Political and Social Science, Vol. 288 (July, 1953).

Spain, James W. "Military Assistance for Pakistan," American Political Science Review (September, 1954).

Statesman's Yearbook, Annual Edition, includes description of forces in every country in the world.

Stettinius, E. R. Lend-Lease: Weapon for Victory. New York: The Macmillan Company, 1944.

Tansill. America Goes to War. Boston: Little, Brown and Company, 1938.
    Includes a discussion of early United States military aid.

Taylor, General Maxwell D. The Uncertain Trumpet. New York: Harper and Bros.

United States Air Force, Education and Training of Foreign Military Personnel, February 1, 1962.

Vagts, Alfred. A History of Militarism. New York: 1959.
    _____. Defense and Diplomacy: The Soldier and the Conduct of Foreign Relations. New York: King's Crown Press, 1956.

Vernon, Raymond. "Foreign Aid," World Politics (July, 1957).

von der Mehren, Fred and Anderson, Charles. "Political Action by the Military in the Developing Areas," Social Research, Vol. 28 (Winter, 1961).

Wiggins, J. W. and Schoeck. Foreign Aid Reexamined. Washington: Public Affairs Press, 1958.

Windle, C. and Vallance, T. "Optimizing Military Assistance Training," World Politics, Vol. 15 (October, 1962).

Wolf, Charles. Foreign Aid: Theory and Practice in Southern Asia. Princeton: Princeton University Press, 1960.
  Includes an attempt to "quantify" the value of military aid.

_____. Economic Development and Mutual Security: Some Problems of U.S. Foreign Assistance Programs in Southeast Asia. Santa Monica: RAND, 1959.

Wood, General Robert J., USA. "Military Assistance Program," Armed Forces Management (November, 1964).

Yeuell, D. "United States Military Aid as an Instrument of National Policy (1945-55)." Unpublished Master's dissertation Georgetown University, 1955.

FAR EAST

Fall, Bernard B. Street Without Joy. Harrisburg, Pa.: The Stockpole Company, 1961.

Hammer, E. J. The Struggle for Indochina. Stanford: Stanford University Press, 1954.

Howze, Major General, USA. "KMAG," Army-Navy-Air Force Journal (January 8, 1955).

Pye, Lucien. Politics, Personality and National Building. New Haven: Yale University Press, 1962.

Reischauer, Edwin O. Wanted: An Asian Policy. New York: Knopf, 1955.

Romulo, Carlos P. Crusade in Asia. New York: The John Day Company, 1955.
  Story of victory over the Huks.

Wurfel, David. "Foreign Aid and Social Reform in Political Development: A Philippine Case Study," The American Political Science Review (June, 1959).

EUROPE

(Most books on NATO written prior to 1962 contain considerable discussion of United States military assistance programs.)

Ismay, Lord. NATO, The First Five Years, 1949-54. Paris: no date.
  Includes a discussion of early force goals and efforts to meet them.

AFRICA, MIDDLE EAST AND SOUTH ASIA

Gutteridge, William F. The Education of the Military Leadership of
    Emergent States - Its Organization, Content and Political
    Implications. Lake Arrowhead, California: Conference on
    Education and Political Development, June, 1962.
    _____. Armed Forces in New States with a foreword by Sir
    John Slessor. London: Oxford University Press, 1962.
Fisher, Sydney (ed.). The Military in Middle Eastern Society and
    Politics. Columbus: Ohio State University Press, 1963.
    _____. Social Forces in the Middle East. Ithaca, New York:
    Cornell University Press, 1955.
Khadduri, Majod. "The Role of the Military in Middle East Politics,"
    American Political Science Review (June, 1953). Reprinted
    as "The Army Officer: His Role in Middle Eastern Politics,"
    in Social Forces in the Middle East. Ithaca, New York:
    Cornell University Press, 1955.
Lerner, Daniel and Robinson, R. "Swords into Plowshares - The
    Turkish Army as a Modernizing Force," World Politics
    (October, 1960).
Lewis, Bernard. The Emergence of Modern Turkey. London:
    Oxford University Press, 1961.
McNeil, William H. Greece: American Aid in Action, 1947-56.
    New York: The Twentieth Century Fund, 1957.
Rustow, Dankwart A. The Military in Middle Eastern Society and
    Politics. Washington: The Brookings Institution, 1963.
    _____. "The Army and the Founding of the Turkish Republic,"
    World Politics (July, 1959).

LATIN AMERICA

Alexander, Robert J. Communism in Latin America. New Bruns-
    wick: Rutgers University Press, 1957.
    Author believes that United States support of Latin
    American military drives the non-communist left into the
    hands of the communists.
Gailer, Colonel Frank, Jr. "Air Force Missions in Latin America,"
    Air University Quarterly Review, Vol. 13, No. 2 (Fall, 1961).
Gallup, Captain E. L. "Civic Action in Action," Army, Vol. 15,
    No. 2 (September, 1964).
    A discussion of civic action in Peru, including some in-
    dication of items financed by MAP and AID. Primarily con-
    cerned with Army Engineer civic action type projects.

Gruening, Ernest. "Exporting Trouble," The Nation, October 6,
    1962.
        Critical of military aid to Latin America.
Johnson, John J. The Military and Society in Latin America.
    Stanford: Stanford University Press, 1964.
        Outstanding on the social structure of the Latin American
    military. Recommends more emphasis on civic action.
    Little comment on United States aid.
Lieuwen, Edwin. Arms and Politics in Latin America. New York:
    Frederick A. Praeger, 1961.
_____. "Neo-Militarism in Latin America: The Kennedy
    Administration's Inadequate Response," Inter-American
    Economic Affairs, Vol. 16 (Spring, 1963).
Santos, Eduardo. "The Defense of Freedom in Latin America," in
    del Rio, A. (ed.). Responsible Freedom in the Americas.
    Garden City, New York: Doubleday, 1955.
        Critical of military assistance in Latin America.
Stokes, William S. Latin American Politics. New York: Crowell,
    1959.
        Chapter 7, pp. 103-138, deals with the role of the military
    in politics. There is a bibliography at the end of this chapter
    with numerous Spanish language sources.
_____. "Violence as a Power Factor in Latin American
    Politics," Western Political Quarterly, Vol. 5 (September,
    1952).
Taylor, Philip B., Jr. Hemispheric Security Reconsidered. New
    Orleans, 1957.
        Critical of hemispheric security concept.
Wyckoff, Theodore. "The Role of the Military in Latin American
    Politics," Western Political Quarterly, Vol. 13 (September,
    1960).
Zook, Captain David, Jr., USAF. "United States Military Assistance
    to Latin America," Air University Review, Vol. 14, No. 4
    (September-October, 1963).
        A pro-Administration article supporting civic action and
    internal security assistance and arguing that MAP does not
    create coups.

CONGRESSIONAL CONTROL OF MILITARY AID

Annals of the American Academy of Political and Social Science,
        Vol. 289, September, 1953.
        See particularly "Congress and Foreign Relations."

Carroll, Holbert N. The House of Representatives and Foreign Af-
  fairs. Pittsburg: University of Pittsburg Press, 1958.
Dahl, Robert A. Congress and Foreign Policy. New York: Har-
  court, Brace, 1950.
Duke, Paul. "The Foreign Aid Fiasco," The Reporter, January 16,
  1964.
      Includes a description of the Clay and Ball Committees.
Farnsworth, David N. The Senate Committee on Foreign Relations.
  Urbana, Illinois: University of Illinois Press, 1961.
      A study of the committee and its work from 1947 to
  1956.
Freeman, J. Leiper. The Political Process: Executive Bureau-
  Legislative Committee Relations. Garden City, New York:
  Doubleday, 1955.
      This book, which deals with (American) Indian affairs,
  is highly recommended for anyone wishing to understand how
  a government agency and Congressional committees interact.
Humphrey, Hubert H. "The Senate in Foreign Policy," Foreign
  Affairs, Vol. 37 (July, 1959).
Jewell, Malcolm E. "Evaluating the Decline of Southern Inter-
  nationalism through Senatorial Roll Call Votes," Journal
  of Politics, Vol. 21 (1959).
Kesselman, Mark. "Presidential Leadership in Congress on
  Foreign Policy," Midwest Journal of Political Science,
  Vol. 5 (1961).
Riesselbach, Leroy N. "The Demography of the Congressional
  Vote on Foreign Aid, 1939-1958," American Political
  Science Review, Vol. 58, No. 3 (September, 1964).
Westphal, A. C. F. The House Committee on Foreign Affairs.
  New York: 1942.
      Good, but obsolete.

GOVERNMENT DOCUMENTS

Clay Committee. Report to the President from the Committee to
  Strengthen the Security of the Free World. Washington:
  Department of State, March 20, 1963.
Draper Committee. Report of the President's Committee to Study
  the Military Assistance Program. Washington: U. S.
  Government Printing Office, 1959.
U.S. House of Representatives, Committee on Foreign Affairs,
  Report of the Committee to Study the Foreign Aid Program.
  84th Cong., 2d Sess., 1956.

U.S. House of Representatives. U.S. Foreign Aid: Its Purposes,
Scope, Administration and Related Information. House
Document No. 116, 86th Cong., 1st Sess., 1959.

U.S. Senate, Committees on Appropriations, Foreign Relations,
Interior and Insular Affairs. Study Mission to Southeast
Asia November-December 1962. Report of Senators Gale
W. McGee, Frank Church, and Frank E. Moss, 88th Cong.,
1st Sess., 1963.

U.S. Senate, Committee on Appropriations. Report on United
States Military Operations and Mutual Security Programs
Overseas. Report of Senator Dennis Chavez, 86th Cong.,
2d Sess., 1960.

U.S. Senate, Committee on Appropriations. Special Report on
Latin America: United States Activities in Mexico, Panama,
Peru, Chile, Argentina, Brazil and Venezuela. 87th Cong.,
2d Sess., 1962.

U.S. Senate, Committee on Foreign Relations. Latin America:
Venezuela, Brazil, Peru, Bolivia and Panama. Report of
Senator George D. Aiken, 86th Cong., 2d Sess., 1959.

U.S. Senate, Committee on Foreign Relations. United States
Foreign Policy. Document No. 24, 87th Cong., 1st Sess.,
1961.

U.S. Senate, Committees on Foreign Relations, Appropriations,
and Interior and Insular Affairs. Study Mission to Africa
November-December 1960. Report of Senators Frank
Church, Gale W. McGee, and Frank E. Moss, 87th Cong.,
1st Sess., 1961.

U.S. Senate, Committee on Government Operations. The Ambassador and the Problem of Coordination. 88th Cong., 1st
Sess., 1963.

U.S. Senate, Special Committee to Study the Foreign Aid Program.
Foreign Aid Program: Compilation of Studies and Surveys.
85th Cong., 1st Sess., 1957.

U.S. Senate, Subcommittee on National Policy Machinery, Committee on Government Operations. Organizing for National
Security: A Bibliography. 86th Cong., 1st Sess., 1959.